The Ultimate Reward: Eschatology in the Qur'ān

The Ultimate Reward: Eschatology in the Qur'ān

Ahmed Affi

Copyright © 2016 Ahmed Affi
All rights reserved.

ISBN-13: 9780954567224
ISBN-10: 0954567226

Contents

Acknowledgments · ix
Introduction · xi

Chapter 1	The Conception of God ·	1
	The One True God ·	3
	God and Creation ·	6
	God in His Infinity ·	12
	God's Knowledge ·	13
	God as our Guide and Judge ·	15
	Change and Constancy, Space and Time · · · · · · · · · · · ·	18
Chapter 2	The Creation of the Heavens and the Earth · · · · · · · · · ·	20
	Of God, but not in God ·	21
	What is Creation for? ·	23
	The Special Place of Humanity in Creation · · · · · · · · · · ·	25
	Time in Creation ·	26
	God's Power Revealed in Creation · · · · · · · · · · · · · · · · ·	31
Chapter 3	The Creation of Human Beings · · · · · · · · · · · · · · · · · · ·	33
	Why Did God Create Human Beings? · · · · · · · · · · · · · ·	35
	The Nature of Humanity ·	36
	The "Fall" of Humankind ·	38
	Our Place on Earth ·	42
	Death, the Great Leveller ·	44
	Death and the Afterlife ·	45
Chapter 4	Satan and Evil ·	48
	The Jinn and the Origins of Evil · · · · · · · · · · · · · · · · · ·	49
	Iblis, Satan, the Fallen Angel ·	52

	The Nature of Evil · · · · · · · · · · · · · · · · · · ·59
	Avoiding Evil ·62
Chapter 5	The Signs of the Hour · · · · · · · · · · · · · · · · · 64
	The End of the World · · · · · · · · · · · · · · · · · · 64
	Signs and Portents ·67
	Eschatology and Modern Understanding · · · · · · · · · ·70
Chapter 6	The Ultimate Abode · · · · · · · · · · · · · · · · · · ·71
	News of Heaven Received by Muhammad · · · · · · · · · ·73
	Heaven as a Reward for the Just · · · · · · · · · · · · · ·75
	Material versus Eternal Reward · · · · · · · · · · · · · ·76
	All are Truly Equal · · · · · · · · · · · · · · · · · · · 80
Chapter 7	Resurrection ·85
	Understanding Resurrection · · · · · · · · · · · · · · · ·87
	Human Consciousness in this Life and the Next · · · · · · ·93
	Refuting Doubters · · · · · · · · · · · · · · · · · · · 94
	God's Promise · 97
Chapter 8	The Day of Judgement · · · · · · · · · · · · · · · · · 99
	The Nature of Judgement · · · · · · · · · · · · · · · ·101
	Our Essential Judgement · · · · · · · · · · · · · · · ·103
	Transformation on the Day of Judgement · · · · · · · · ·107
	The Judgement of Non-believers · · · · · · · · · · · · ·108
	Puzzling Descriptions of the Day of Judgement · · · · · · ·110
	Punishment and Reward · · · · · · · · · · · · · · · · ·112
	The Absolute Justice of God · · · · · · · · · · · · · · ·114
Chapter 9	Miracles and the Miraculous Night Journey (Miʾrāj) · · · · ·124
	Miracles, the Prophets, and the Everyday · · · · · · · · ·125
	The Context of the Journey · · · · · · · · · · · · · · ·129
	The Reality of the Journey · · · · · · · · · · · · · · ·130
	The Importance of the Night Journey · · · · · · · · · · ·133
Chapter 10	Intercession ·134
	Repentance ·135

	Intercession in the Qur'ān	136
	God's Singular Judgement	140
	Forewarning	143
Chapter 11	Heaven	145
	The People of Heaven	146
	The Sinners' Plea	151
	The Nature of Heaven	152
Chapter 12	Hell	158
	The People of the Fire	160
	The Nature of Hell	168
	The Keepers of Hell	175
	The Truth about Women and Hell	177
	Will Hell Last Forever?	180
Chapter 13	Mutual Wrangling	184
	Discussions of the People of Heaven	184
	Discussions of the People of the Fire	186
	Discussions Between the People of the Fire and the People of Heaven	194
Chapter 14	Scholars' Views of the Redemption of Humanity	196
Chapter 15	The Roads to Heaven and Hell	217
	The Road to Heaven	217
	The Road to Hell	224
	Listening to the Word of God	235
Chapter 16	The Eternity of Afterlife	237
	The Nature and Purpose of the Afterlife	237
	The Promise of More	239
	The True Nature of Islam	239
	Above all, God is Merciful	240
	Index	245
	Bibliography and Further Reading	251

Acknowledgments

ALL PRAISES ARE due to God for His mercy and blessings and for making the completion of this book possible.

I am indebted to Hassan Affi for his kind suggestions and for assisting with the research and typing the complete draft of this book. My heartfelt gratitude also goes to Hussein Affi for his invaluable contribution to this book.

As always, I am thankful to my family for their enduing patience during the completion of this book. A special thank you goes to my dearest wife, Fadumo Farah, for her invariably unwavering support, patience, guidance, and encouragement.

Introduction

WHAT WILL BECOME of us when we are dead and gone? Is this life all there is, or is there more yet to come? If there is an afterlife, will we all be treated equally, or will the inequalities we see on earth persist after our bodily deaths? What can we do to ensure that we are heaven- rather than hell-bound?

These are all questions that most of us ask, often starting in early childhood, when we first begin to understand our own mortality. They are questions asked all around the world, in every sort of cultural context. Clearly, there is something fundamentally human about this need to know what will become of us at the time of death and in the hereafter. Could it be the quiet voice of God, encouraging us to engage in self-reflection now, when every decision we take matters?

It is perfectly normal for anyone who has accepted the reality of God to wonder what will become of him or her in the next life, and certainly the Qur'ān and other revelations sent by God to His people prompt many questions, even while they provide the answers to those who are truly prepared to listen. For example, if we accept that we are all weak and prone to sin, how can we reconcile this with our hope to enter heaven one day? If we accept that Islam is the Word of God, what does this mean for the people we know and love who do not consider themselves Muslims? Does God love them less, even if they have never had the chance to hear His word? Even if we do our best to follow the Word of God and do His will, how can we ever be sure that we are doing enough? Will heaven and hell last forever, or is there yet another world beyond them? Are all sinners to be punished equally, or according to the gravity of their transgressions? Is there any hope that sinners will one day have "served their time" for the dreadful deeds that they have carried out and will be allowed to enter heaven to live with God? If so, does everyone, even the most heinous murderer, have the capacity to be redeemed some day?

Today, more than ever, these questions have acquired a new sense of urgency. Whereas once most people lived in societies that were culturally relatively homogeneous, now a growing number of us dwell in very diverse societies, working and living alongside people whose views are very different to our own. In many ways, this is a wonderful and enriching experience, as we can all benefit from hearing the views of others whose life experiences have been very different to ours, and from learning how to live side by side with others whose views may also seem to be contrary to ours. However, it also represents a challenge to us, insofar as hearing about these diverse experiences, and their associated views, can cause us to doubt what we have been taught. It is our responsibility to ensure that these challenges provide us with the opportunity to expand our horizons and broaden our minds, rather than clinging to old certainties.

While Islamic scholars have not always been in perfect agreement about the answers to all of these compelling questions – to say the least – the observant reader nonetheless will find answers to all their questions in the Qur'ān, which provides us with vivid, compelling information about the Day of Judgement, heaven and hell, and the fate of sinners and the virtuous alike. Today, as ever, this information is profoundly relevant to the way in which we live our lives and the decisions that we make, every day. Above all, it sheds light on God's most central quality; the mercy that He brings to us in more ways than we can count. We learn not only about how we personally can live so as to ensure our eventual entry into heaven, but also how to apply love and tolerance to our interactions with others, and how to recognise that God, and God alone, is qualified to cast judgement on others. With this realisation comes humility, and with humility the capacity to accept that we still have much to learn, and many opportunities to improve.

In Chapter One, we explore the singularity of God, Who is unique, and all powerful. The understanding that God is the sole Creator of the universe, and the One to Whom we owe everything, is at the heart of Islam. God, Who

Introduction

knows and sees all, and Who has given us everything we need in this life, is there for us always; all we have to do is accept Him, and we will see His hand at work. Islam, along with its sister faiths of Christianity and Judaism, considers monotheism to be a fundamental cornerstone of belief. Accepting the uniqueness of God is a necessary element of true faith.

In Chapter Two, we look at what we can learn from God's creation in all its glory, from the desert lands where Islam originally emerged, to the lush jungles of the tropics, to the icy splendours of the polar caps. While diverse cultures around the world have all devised their own theories about the world and all that they can see in it – in each case influenced by the peculiarities of their natural environment – devout Muslims everywhere see creation itself as a daily, living miracle that testifies constantly to God's majesty and His love. In this way, even the smallest, most apparently insignificant creature is a witness to God.

In Chapter Three, we examine the incredible matter of God's creation of humankind. While all of creation is both wondrous and miraculous, we humans are unique among God's handiwork for the special gifts and responsibilities that He has given us. Other creatures react within their environments on the basis of instinct alone, but we have been gifted the capacity for rational thought, wonder, and some comprehension of God. While some faiths have seen humankind's acquisition of knowledge as the consequence of sin, true believers understand that nothing in the universe happens without God's reasoning behind it, and embrace His plan for us.

In Chapter Four, we look at the complex and distressing matter of sin, which is a simple fact of life that we are all obliged to confront. Many have asked themselves why God allows Satan to exist, and why He even made human beings capable of sinning in the first place. The simple truth is that, without sin, there is no good, and that if we were unable to actively choose good over evil, our lives would be effectively without meaning. By giving us the capacity to choose to do good or ill as we go about our daily lives, God has simply granted us the free will that is a fundamental aspect of our very humanity. It is incumbent on each of us to do our best to make wise decisions, every single day.

In Chapter Five, we discuss the signs and portents that will indicate to God's people that the Day of Judgement is on the way, and look at both the folklore and the false ideologies that have grown up around this concept, and the startling parallels we find between the teachings of the Qur'ān and what we have learned from modern scientific breakthroughs. The reality is that, until the last days approach, none of us can ever know when the Day of Judgement (belief in which is a fundamental tenet of Islam) will take place. For this reason, we need to ensure that we are *always* in a good position to meet the One Who has created us.

In Chapter Six, we talk of the prophecies brought to humankind not just by Muhammad, who brought us the ultimate form of revelation, known to us as the Qur'ān, but also by all the prophets who came before him. While life on earth is often characterised by inequality, causing some people to feel more blessed than others, we are all equal in the afterlife. Muhammad's message was one of hope: even those who are unfortunate and dispossessed have the opportunity, through the way they live and the choices they make, to ensure that they will abide forever in heaven with God.

In Chapter Seven, we explore the doctrine of resurrection, and how it can be that generations of humans will return to life on the Day of Judgement to be judged by the One Who made them. It has often been difficult for people to understand how they can expect to return to life after death. The physical reality of decomposition and decay are known to us all. How, then, can we expect to be returned to life when our bodies have returned to the dust from which they were formed? The reality is too complex for us to understand with our current levels of knowledge, but we can rest assured that God can do whatever He wants, and that He is certainly more than capable of creating new bodies for us that will serve our purposes in the afterlife – whether we are heaven- or hell-bound!

In Chapter Eight, we look at what will happen on the Day of Judgement, belief in which is a central tenet of Islam, and examine the awesome reality that each of us will be called upon to account for his or her life, after which God will make a decision about whether we are destined to join Him in heaven, or to experience the torments of hell. On this day, each

Introduction

individual – woman or man, rich or poor – will stand before God in all their humility, forced to confront their misdeeds directly, and to account for every single decision that they have taken in the course of their lives. Just as every new born child enters this world naked, alone, and no better or worse than any other infant, we will each be alone and profoundly equal to all others on this most important of days.

In Chapter Nine, we consider one of the most intriguing and mysterious of the narratives of Islam; the story of Muhammad's "night journey," when he travelled great distances in the course of a single night, and even visited heaven, where he met the prophets who had gone before him and received important messages about God. We look at why this story is so important to Islam, and why it continues to matter greatly – indeed, fundamentally – to the present day.

In Chapter Ten, we look at the idea of intercession. On a popular level, many Muslims hold certain beliefs about intercession that are not backed up by reliable Qur'ānic sources and that are more folkloric than fact-based. Here, we go back to the Qur'ān for its teaching on this matter. The Qur'ān is clear that God, and God alone, will make the final judgement about who will enter heaven, and who hell. It is not for anyone else, even a prophet, to "intercede" and beg for special treatment. Indeed, this would be contrary to the fundamental equality that is a cornerstone of Islam.

In Chapter Eleven, we examine the Qur'ān's teaching on the reality of heaven, looking at what the experience of dwelling in heaven will be like, the physicality of heaven and its inhabitants, and the extraordinary sense of peace and joy that will be experienced by anyone who has earned the right to enter there. While none of us can truly understand what it will be like to experience heaven, the Qur'ān provides us with a glimpse of its extraordinary joys and delights, by using rich, allegorical language, and comparisons with some of the more banal earthly pleasures that we enjoy today.

In Chapter Twelve, we examine the nature of hell, and the experience of the people who will be sent there after the Day of Judgement, as well as the controversial issue as to whether or not hell will be eternal. Islamic scholars have often grappled with the latter. As always, the Qur'ān leads the way by showing us God's truth. It conveys some of the horrors of hell to us with evocative language, and highlights the fact that the sinners who will enter hell will do so purely on the basis of their own misdeeds – for we are all equal in the eyes of God. Finally, it offers hope. God is merciful, and He will not punish anyone as much as they deserve, while everyone in hell will eventually have been punished sufficiently to be considered redeemed, and will be finally allowed to enter heaven to dwell forever with God, the Creator of all, who loves and cherishes each of us.

In Chapter Thirteen, we discuss the conversations that the Qur'ān describes as taking place between and among the residents of hell and heaven. These discussions cast fresh light on the experiences of both, and provide guidance to those of us still living. We see how both the inhabitants of heaven and the inhabitants of hell understand that their destiny was always in their own hands, and that each choice they made as they journeyed through life led them towards their eventual destination.

In Chapter Fourteen, we summarise the views of major scholars of Islam on the topics of redemption, heaven and hell. Different scholars have reached a range of conclusions on topics that include whether or not hell is eternal, who is bound to heaven and who to hell, and whether God will tend more towards mercy than condemnation. While opinions have often been wildly divergent on these matters, as Islamic scholarship has become more sophisticated with the passage of time, we gain a greater insight into the true implications of the Qur'ān, the original and ultimate source of knowledge about God and His plans for us all. Above all, important scholars agree that the Qur'ān is, first and foremost, a lesson in love and hope, in the fundamental equality of all human beings, and an invitation to draw near, listen and learn from the purest of sources of information about God and His intentions for all of us.

In Chapter Fifteen, we explore in some detail the things that we should do, and not do, in order to make sure that we are heaven- rather than hell-bound. Above all, we should try to emulate God Himself in favouring mercy and love over anger and hatred, for God is, above and beyond all other things, endlessly merciful and loving. In each and every interaction with the others

Introduction

in our lives, we are called to prioritise God's teachings. When we do, we will make all of our decisions from a place of kindness, peace and charity.

In Chapter Sixteen, we consider the nature of eternity, the nature of the afterlife, and the issue of whether or not the afterlife will be eternal, in the sense in which we humans currently understand the word. Is it possible that, beyond heaven and hell, there is yet more? While we cannot yet understand, on the basis of the extremely limited knowledge that we have acquired during our lifetimes on earth, we can rest assured that there is much more yet to come.

No mere human, even a prophet, can ever claim to know the totality of the mind of God – or indeed more than a small portion of it. However, in His infinite wisdom, God has provided us with His teaching in the form of the Qur'ān, and with ample evidence of His love and mercy in the world all around us. It is my fervent hope that this book, which has been written to be easily read by the Muslim and the non-Muslim alike, will provide guidance, hope and inspiration to read and learn more about the Qur'ān and the true nature of Islam, which is love.

CHAPTER 1

❖ ❖ ❖

The Conception of God

BEFORE ADDRESSING THE complex matter of Qur'ānic eschatology, we need to clarify how the Qur'ān, and therefore Muslims, conceive of God the Creator, from Whom all beings come, and to Whom all will return one day. After all, everything starts and finishes with Him, and it is to Him that we will ultimately return.

The Qur'ān references and describes God on multiple occasions, using a wide range of names that make reference to His many attributes, such as "the Merciful, the Compassionate, the Creator, the Omnipotent, the Dispenser of Rewards, the Reckoner and the Wise." Above all, however, it refers to God as "Allah," a term that encompasses all His manifold qualities,[1] and that is mentioned over 2500 times.[2]

All Muslims agree that belief in God, and His angels, scriptures and messengers is fundamental to their faith, and encapsulated in the profession of faith that maintains that "There is no god but God, and Muhammad is God's messenger."[3] Without God, there is nothing, because absolutely everything comes from Him, and men and women find their true vocation in worshipping God and living according to His holy law. Thus, a firm understanding of God is absolutely fundamental to this monotheistic faith.

How are we to understand God and His relevance to our lives today? This question has long been at the heart of debate, as each generation has grappled with the problems of its day. The nature and being of God have been a subject

---

1 Saeed, 2008, 62.
2 Rahman, 1989, 1.
3 Chittick, 2013, 66; 68.

of much discussion among Islamic scholars throughout history. As Islam developed and spread, Muslim jurisprudence emerged in four distinct schools of thought: the relatively liberal schools of Abu Hanifa and Shafi'i, and the more conservative schools of Malik bin Anas and Ahmad bin Hanbal. The latter two tended to reject anything other than strictly literal interpretations of the Qur'ān. For example, of the Qur'ānic reference to God "sitting upon the throne,"[4] Malik maintained that the sitting was a given, that God was "sitting" in the literal sense in which we usually understand the word, and that Muslims were obliged to believe in this, and that not doing so was heretic and therefore a serious sin.

As Islamic scholarship developed and became more sophisticated, it became increasingly apparent that the hyper-conservative approach to interpreting the Qur'ān was not adequate to a full understanding of it and the application of its teachings to the lives of the faithful, and did not address the complexity of the Qur'ān, with its abundant use of metaphor, allegory, and rich, poetical language. As Islam spread, it became essential to arrive at a common understanding that would provide Muslims with the clear guidance that they needed, which meant detailed scholarly examination of the Qur'ān and other Islamic texts in order to develop an understanding of the implications of these to which all Muslims could subscribe. This was especially important as Islam was a rapidly growing religion, both attracting converts from and experiencing tensions with pagan and Christian communities.

The need to arrive at this common understanding gave rise to a more sophisticated school of Islamic theology, with much learning emerging from theological debate with the pagans, Christians, and Jews with whom the growing Islamic community was in frequent contact. Among the most diligent of these scholars were the early Mu'tazilite doctors, who defended Islam against the Materialists' attacks.[5]

Thanks to the work of these early scholars, Islam has displayed a remarkable degree of consistency in its core understandings of God, which lie at the

---

4 Q. 7:54; 20:5.
5 Fakhry, 2004, xix-xx.

root of any exploration of Islam and its implications for both the individual and society.

The One True God

The Qur'ān is unequivocal in stating that God is the one true God, "the Most gracious, the Dispenser of Grace"[6] and that He is omnipotent and all-knowing.[7] Moreover, God is an eternal deity. "Eternal" is a small, often-used word, but the concept is an enormous one that is often very difficult for the inherently limited human mind to grasp in its entirety. Quite simply, there was nothing before God, and nothing will ever outlast Him. Even the notion of "time," which continues to elude our understanding even to this day, with our increasingly complex knowledge of scientific matters, is a Creation of God. While these concepts are difficult to fully comprehend, both emotionally and intellectually, they lie at the heart of our understanding of God as unique, all-knowing, and all-powerful.

The Qur'ān uses the name "Allah" to refer to God, affirming in many passages that God is unique, incomparable, eternal, and the creator of everything around us. It is important to recognise that God is the subject of the Qur'ān in more than one sense: He is both the voice in which the Qur'ān is written, and frequently the main subject matter of its text[8] which, after all, is all about revealing the reality and mystery of God to humanity, His greatest Creation.

The Qur'ān explicitly refers to God as being the one true God no fewer than thirty times, repeating the phrase "there is no deity but Him,"[9] lest there be any doubt on the matter. It also makes many references to God's extraordinary qualities, all of which outline His utter uniqueness, pointing out His

---

6 Q. 2:163.
7 Q. 57:3.
8 Madigan, 2006, 79.
9 Madigan, 2006, 80.

"power, majesty, omniscience and beneficence" in many different passages.[10] The Qur'ān states that, even if the polytheists had been correct in asserting that there were also other gods, these would have been bound to worship Him in his almightiness,[11] or they would have striven to take away some or all of God's power, leading to chaos. To put it simply, a belief in the utter oneness of God is fundamental to the true observance of Islam, and anyone who even doubts it cannot be accepted as a good Muslim, or indeed as a Muslim at all.

Because God has no limitations and cannot be understood as a "person" in the human sense of the term, as He transcends the capabilities of human language, when God speaks to Himself in the Qur'ān, He vacillates between the first person singular, the first person plural, and the third person singular, often within the context of a single verse, while similarly varying between the present, past and future tense.[12] Everything except God Himself relies upon God, because everything is part of God's Creation. As humankind is an aspect of God's Creation, and the only being with the intellectual capacity to understand this, as well as the ability to make moral judgements, the relationship between God and the women and men of His Creation is properly that of master and servant.[13] God has clearly created men and women with the intellectual and emotional capacity to create and use knowledge to serve Him.[14]

Drawing on the beliefs and practice of the pagan Arabs of Muhammad's day, the Qur'ān makes reference to the multiple false gods and idols they worshipped, as much to highlight God's uniqueness and supremacy as to point out the redundancy of praying to so-called deities that are merely of man's own making. Unlike God, these false deities cannot make any difference to the world of men and women.[15] The Qur'ān roundly dismisses them as

---

10 Zebiri, 2006, 270.
11 Q. 17:42.
12 Asad, 1987, 146.
13 Rahman, 1989, 2-3.
14 Rahman, 1989, 9.
15 Zebiri, 2006, 270-1.

"names you have invented, you and your forefathers, and for which God has sent down no authority."[16]

How can we, who are so small compared to God, perceive and understand Him? We can never see Him directly in this life, and our limited human minds can only begin to comprehend His majesty, but evidence of Him and all His works is all around us, so long as we are prepared to open our eyes and see it. God created each and every one of us with the innate capacity to perceive Him and His Creation in the world around us.

As God is unique, and everything comes from Him, He alone is the truest and most real being in the universe. From God spring all of His divine qualities: mercy, creativity, justice, truth and reality. Everything comes from God, is cared for by Him and, eventually, returns to Him.[17] Moreover, the Qur'ān underlines the uniqueness of many of the qualities of God. He alone is eternal, glorious, utterly self-sufficient and the first and the last.[18] In its exhortations that we should do good, and vivid descriptions of an afterlife in which wrong-doers are viciously punished, the Qur'ān helps us to focus our minds on the here and now, and to query every day if the way we are living, and the things we do, are pleasing God or doing the opposite. Because God is merciful, and wants above all for us to return to Him at the end of time, He prompts us each and every day to strive to do our best according to the instructions He has provided to us in the form of divine revelation.

Whereas the Qur'ān frequently acknowledges the prophets who came before Muhammad, including Jesus, clearly the understanding of God as utterly unique cannot be reconciled with the Christian idea of Jesus as God and as the son of God. The Qur'ān references this tension explicitly, stating, "God is only one god. He is exalted far above having a son,"[19] and also dismisses the idea in bald, concrete terms, stating that God simply cannot have a son as

---

16 Q. 7:71; 12:40; 53:23.
17 Chittick, 2013, 67-8.
18 Madigan, 2006, 81.
19 Q. 4:171.

He has no spouse,"[20] while Muhammad is quoted as saying that if the "Most Merciful" had a son, he would be the first to worship him.[21] However, as God is unique and all-powerful, He alone is worthy of our praise and worship and it is abhorrent to Him when misled or foolish humans worship false deities or ideas rather that listening to the word of God as sent down to them by their creator. The Qur'ān suggests that most of those who mistakenly believe in multiple gods, or in the possibility of God being "incarnated" as a human being, do so without thinking about it properly, often under the weight of traditions and practices that they have inherited from their cultural background, and from a place of profound irrationality.[22] Each of the prophets has been given the same basic, underlying message, which is stated in the Qur'ān as, "There is no God but I, so worship me."[23]

God and Creation

According to Islamic thought, God has absolute authority over everything, including each entity's beginning, duration, end and afterlife.[24] God created everything, and is present in every aspect of His Creation, providing us not only with the wonderfully rich world that we have been gifted to live in, but also with bountiful examples of His hand and will in action, all of which are abundant proof of His majesty and supremacy. While the intricacies of nature have many interlocking parts, which depend upon one another to survive, there is nothing in nature to explain its own beginning. To understand this, we have to comprehend the role of God in not just creating, but also sustaining, everything around us.[25] What does this mean? Simply that He is embodied in each aspect of the universe, no matter how small or great, and no matter

---

20 Q. 6:101.
21 Q. 43:81.
22 Asad, 1984, 585, note 62.
23 Q. 21:25.
24 Idleman Smith and Yazbeck Haddad, 2002, 2.
25 Rahman, 1989, 10.

how difficult to see or find, for everything ultimately comes from Him.[26] In night and day, the orbits of the sun and the planets, and the movements of even the most apparently inconsequential of creatures, we can clearly see God's hand in action. The act of Creation itself sets God apart from all other beings insofar as there cannot be a relationship of "equality" when, without Him, there would be nothing, and without the constantly active hand of God, the functioning of nature and of humankind would be meaningless and without purpose.[27] Instead, everything that happens in nature and among women and men happens in the presence of God, and everything created by Him, no matter how small, is peerless evidence of His work.

How does God enact Creation? When God wishes to create something, He need only say "Be!" and the thing in question simply comes into being, fully formed and perfect.[28] It is God who creates all things, and the act of Creation is continuous, rather than restricted to an initial moment or action;[29] Creation is a continuous, ongoing process that is part of the essence and meaning of God in and of itself. There is no Creation and no power but God, whose actions have led to the universe and all the things it contains.[30] We can see the hand of God in the reality of Creation, even though, in our smallness, we cannot perceive God Himself.[31] The Qur'ān makes frequent references to our need to recognise God's hand at work in the world around us, imploring us to consider how He has caused beautiful gardens to grow, life-giving water to fall from the sky as rain, majestic mountains, the continents that we call home, and everything around us. A failure to recognise the majesty of God in this natural abundance is irrational, and comes from a place of emotion rather than the human intellect that we have been gifted.[32]

---

26 Q. 57:5.
27 Rahman, 1989, 4.
28 Q. 36:82.
29 Madigan, 2006, 83.
30 Chittick, 2013, 70.
31 Asad, 1984, 836.
32 Q. 27:60-1.

We also see the hand at work in the cyclical nature of life. For all living beings, life has a rhythm that starts with birth, proceeds through growth and adult life, and ends in decay and death and the return to the dust from which all life is ultimately made. All living matter must one day die, and in its turn, nourish and contribute to a new generation. In this natural cycle, effortlessly – from sea to steam to clouds to rain to rivers, and back to sea again, we see God's plan for all living beings and further proof of His existence.[33] God, who created all of this specifically for humankind, the only species capable of acknowledging and worshipping Him, is truly the only deity in existence, and must be recognised and worshipped accordingly.[34] We can find God in what the Qur'ān describes as the "deep darkness" of land and sea, and in the winds that He causes to blow, in the nourishment He has created for us, and in the endless regeneration of new life.[35] We find God in the endlessly recurring cycle of night and day. Just as only God can lead us to the truth, only God is capable of creating light and ordering darkness.[36] In His wisdom, God created the day for work and the night for rest, a "daily miracle," for if we were compelled to rest all the time in the darkness we would not have the scope to develop all our capabilities, while if we were compelled to work all the time we would be tired. Asad compares this cycle to that of our lives as faithful worshippers. While it is essential to worship God and pray to Him, we can also "rest" from this in the form of attending to the requirements of our lives here on earth, in the course of which we must also be good and strive to do His will. The day will come when all of this will be behind us, and we will be called before God to be judged by Him.[37]

Through His acts of Divine Creation, the universe is filled with the love of God and the energy of divine love resonates throughout it.[38] Human be-

---

33 Q. 3:27; 6:95,10:31, 30:19.
34 Q. 27:62.
35 Q. 27:63-4.
36 Q. 28:71-2.
37 Ali, 1934, 1141, note 3399.
38 Chittick, 2013, 80.

ings, the only creatures in God's Creation capable of understanding, can see in it God's infinite mercy at work, for He has created this world with everything we need to survive and flourish, and He continues to create and sustain, while His hand gently leads all of Creation towards its destiny.[39] In Creation, we find both witnesses to and proof of God's oneness and supremacy,[40] and of His special plan for humanity, for which the heavens and the earth have been arranged to provide everything necessary for life;[41] Creation shows us everything we need to know about God, His plans for us in the universe, and the nature of our relationship with Him.[42]

The Qur'ān reminds us in many passages of the need to observe, reflect and think about the way in which Creation invites us to discover God for ourselves.[43] In God's creations, especially humans, we see aspects of His divine qualities, although these are only ever found in a perfect form in God Himself.[44] At various points in the Qur'ān, God speaks of creating humankind, highlighting our special role in Creation and the fact that God is there to guide us at all times, while one day we will be returned to Him.[45]

As God is the ultimate being and Creator of all, it logically follows that He is perfect in His individuality. But what does this mean? In *Creative Evolution*, Bergson shows us that, in most cases, individuality is not absolute. Even in the case of women and men, the pinnacle of God's Creation, nobody truly exists as a simple individual. We are all dependent on other people and things at all periods of our lives. In particular, we are drawn to come together as couples to create children, which is something that no human can accomplish alone, and as children we are utterly dependent on our parents. The human organism is not designed to live completely separately. Instead, in the

---

39 Rahman, 1989, 7.
40 Madigan, 2006, 81.
41 Q. 14:32-3.
42 Madigan, 2006, 83.
43 Rahman, 1989, 11; Q. 67:3.
44 Madigan, 2006, 82.
45 For example, Q. 23:11 and Q. 75:36-40.

case of God, who is peerless and eternal, a pure and true state of individuality is reached,[46] for God has no need to seek completion in another being and, being eternal, no need for reproduction. As our Creator, He can simply bring into existence any being that He wishes. This essential oneness is highlighted in the Qur'ān as one of the most important elements of God, and represents a major theological difference between Islam and Christianity, which otherwise share many ideas about the perfection and eternal nature of the deity Whom both faiths worship.

As creatures who have been blessed by God with the capacity to think and reason, human beings can observe and learn the rules of nature and use this knowledge in the pursuit of sustenance or comfort, as in the case of agriculture and science. Indeed, God encourages us to use our gifts to understand His Creation better. Nature, for its part, simply is incapable of violating His law.[47] Alone of all the creations breathed into existence by God, only humans have the capacity to know the law of God, and yet choose to disobey it – which means that only humans have the capacity to consciously choose to follow God's law, and worship Him.

Diverse religious faiths around the world have devised particular conceptions of God, many of which seem very different to that espoused by Islam. Some cultures are polytheistic, and worship many gods, and others tend towards pantheism, or the idea that God is "in" everything. Others, such as the faith followed in ancient Greece, devised the notion of the universe as cyclical and essentially without purpose.[48] Islam, however, recognises God's hand and purpose in all of Creation, but considers Him to be a discrete individual, who can be sensed through His work, but who stands alone in His utter perfection.

Like Islam, Judaism and Christianity associate God with light, and there are many metaphors that make this connection which, if not read carefully, might lead one astray from the notion of God as individual. For

---

46 Bergson, 1911, 14.
47 Rahman, 1989, 13.
48 Rahman, 1989, 8.

example, while God can be sensed through the "Light of the heaven and the earth ... [He is] Light upon Light and He guides to His Light whom He wills,"[49] He is not "in" it; like all of Creation, the light is of Him, and not vice versa, because everything in the universe comes from God. Conversely, those who would seek to act against God and His plan for the world are compared to "multiple darknesses."[50] Today, with the benefit of our understanding of modern physics as revealed by generations of scientific endeavour, we can understand these metaphors more completely than our ancestors ever could (just one of many indications of the timeless relevance of the Qur'ān). Now we know that the speed of light is the fastest thing in the world, and that this basic truth is the same, regardless of who is observing, and what other things might be moving around them. In a world in which almost nothing is constant, the light that we see is the closest thing to approximate God, as it is unique, and incomparable. We can thus understand the metaphor as describing God's quality as both absolute and absolutely individual.

The Qur'ān clarifies that God, "the All-Hearing, the All-Seeing,"[51] is unique and separate from all created things:

> He is neither a substance (jawhar), a composite body (jism), nor an accident ('arad), He is the first, with nothing before Him, the last, nothing that can be said to come after Him. Sublimely exalted above anything that men may devise by way of definition.[52]

In Islam, the concepts of "natural" and "supernatural" are a false dichotomy. Because God is responsible for all Creation, and because everything that exists, everything that happens, and everything that might one day exist or happen, results from God's creative activity, everything is natural, and simply

---

49 Q. 24:35.
50 Q. 24:40.
51 Q. 42:11.
52 Q. 112:4.

part of God's great plan and His wonderfully complex, fully integrated reality. From our limited perspective, some aspects of this reality are easier to perceive than others, but that does not warrant the quarantining of the less accessible aspects into a separate category designated "supernatural." The Qur'ān refers to those aspects of reality that we can perceive as the "observable sphere of Being," as opposed to those that are beyond our ability to perceive and are known, therefore, as the "non-observable sphere."[53]

Unlike God, human beings and all the other creatures devised by Him live just for a little while on earth.[54] Thus, when we recognise God and worship Him, we are freed from the inevitability of death to embrace the possibility of resurrection to be with Him in the next life, which is beyond Creation and our earthly understanding.[55]

God in His Infinity

As the mortal beings that we are, we might be inclined to consider the idea of the individual to imply someone or something that will one day reach the end of its life. After all, we humans will all one day perish, just like the other living beings we see around us. How, then, can we understand God as an individual, when we also know that He is infinite, with no beginning or end? The fact is that our comprehension of infinity is, ordinarily, limited. With reference to God, we do not speak of spatial infinity, because God cannot be limited, spatially or in any other way.[56] This quality of infinity is also unique to God:

> He is all-enveloping, literally infinite, and He *alone* is infinite. All else carries in the very texture of its being the hallmark of its finitude and creatureliness.[57]

---

53 Asad, 1987, 138.
54 Q. 55:26-7.
55 Asad, 1984, 585, note 60.
56 Iqbal, 1989, 50-2.
57 Rahman, 1989, 4.

God's Knowledge

Within Islamic scholarship, two of the most widely discussed attributes of God are His knowledge and His power. One interpretation of the situation is that God knows Himself, and as the source of all Creation, also knows all things by default, as it were. Because He knows all, and He is the source of all. God alone is all-knowing, and the beings of His Creation can only know as much as He has chosen to reveal to them.[58] According to this view, "knowledge" and Creation are essentially equivalent.

Human beings have come to know about God through the revelations of the prophets, particularly Muhammad, but without God even these holy men are nothing, for all prophets were both guided by and to God, from whom all knowledge ultimately springs.[59] The Qur'ān describes God as revealing His teaching by means of the messages He has sent via His prophets, in His holy books (particularly the Qur'ān) and by giving us guidance. When times are difficult and we are in a state of moral crisis, we need this access to God's message and knowledge more than ever.[60] In His wisdom, God has sent prophetic messages to His people in diverse historical and cultural contexts, culminating in the perfection of His message as revealed to Muhammad and expounded in the Qur'ān. In each case of God's revelation, the message was provided in a language and format that made it accessible to the people of the day. These messages, embodying God's truth, reveal not just His knowledge, but also the means to obtain salvation and life everlasting, and they are equally applicable to all human beings, regardless of where they come from.[61]

Without knowledge, omnipotence would be a mere force of nature. But the Qur'ān sees in nature a great level of order, in which forces align to create a world with form and substance. As nature is but God's Creation, the Qur'ān views God's omnipotence as intimately bound to His wisdom. Thus, God's awesome power is revealed to those who look for it in the order, regularity

---

58 Madigan, 2006, 82.
59 Chittick, 2013, 68.
60 Rahman, 1989, 9.
61 Chittick, 2013, 77-8.

and design encompassed in nature, as in the natural cycles of life, as discussed above. God is seen as holding all the goodness in the world, while wrongdoing is the sole remit of men and women, who often suffer terribly as a result of their own actions.[62]

A second interpretation argues that God knows all things, with all of their differences, precisely because His knowledge is creative in nature. In His knowledge of Himself, His knowledge of everything else is automatically implied as well. In the Qur'ān, metaphors of writing and record-keeping are often used to describe God's knowledge of everything that happens in the universe.[63]

The Islamic scholar Ibn Sina maintained that God's knowledge cannot derive from outside things, because this would imply His dependence on something other than Himself, and that His knowledge would also change from one moment to another. As we have already established, God is a complete individual, Who never depends on any other entity, and His knowledge is complete and perfect.

In reality, God's knowledge is not impacted by things and events in the material world, because everything comes from God's knowledge in the first place, and He knows everything down to the last detail, including when and where every event will take place, and the role that each and every living being will play in causing it to happen, as well as the consequences of every action taken.[64]

We learn as children that God sees and knows all, but what does this mean? It can be hard to grasp this concept, limited as we are by our imperfect human senses. God sees and hears everything that happens at once, in what has been described as "one indivisible act of perception." Our understanding and experience of time are not the same as God's, and simply do not approximate it in any way. The Qur'ān describes Divine time as the "Mother of Books."[65] All of history, liberated from the sequential time that we experience

---

62 Iqbal, 1989, 64.
63 Madigan, 2006, 86.
64 Rahman, 1975, 146-51.
65 Q. 3:7; 13:39; 43:4.

as human beings, is seen by God as a "now" that transcends past, present and future. In this context, God knows and sees all, and His knowledge differs radically from ours, as we are limited to our own experience, and the information we can glean from other flawed human beings, none of whom can ever comprehend more than an infinitesimal fraction of all that God understands. God, who created everything, and sees and hears everything, has a perspective incomparable to any other. For God, the universe, with its contents, is not "other," as it originates in Him. In God, the acts of creating and knowing are one and the same. It is only from our perspective as human beings that Creation appears to be a particular moment in the lifespan of God. In a moment, God can see all of the events of history, past and present, as an eternal "now" that is beyond time[66] and certainly beyond the limitations of human understanding.

The world around us, and all of its contents – plants, animals, the seas and so forth – are intrinsic to God's Creation, just as our characters as individual humans are intrinsic to us. As the Qur'ān phrases it, nature, God's Creation, is "the habit of God."[67] By striving to understand nature, we are given some insight into God and His works.[68] The Arabic term for God's truth, *haqq*, implies not just truth per se, but also what is real, appropriate, correct and just. This truth is precisely the knowledge that we mortals need in order to access God's salvation.[69]

God as our Guide and Judge

God is the sole being with knowledge in its true and absolute sense, and we human beings can only strive to glimpse and understand a fragment of this. For this reason, God acts as our guide, helping us to understand the world that He has created for us, and to navigate it in ways espoused by Him.

---

66 Iqbal, 1989, 60.
67 Q. 33:62; 35:43; 40:85; 48:23.
68 Iqbal, 1989, 45.
69 Chittick, 2013, 70.

In His wisdom, God created us humans as imperfect, forgetful and ignorant. However, we are also blessed with free will and with sufficient knowledge to realise that our only route to salvation is by accepting the guidance of our creator,[70] with "guidance" understood in the Islamic context as "the knowledge that saves" and the universal truth of God's message as revealed through the Qur'ān.[71] As He is the one Who created us and knows all, God is the only guide we can truly trust,[72] and we must allow ourselves to be led by Him.[73]

The Qur'ān provides extensive explicit guidance in all areas of life, including legislative material that can be applied to every aspect of human existence, such as marriage and family life, diet, warfare, and more.[74] By accepting this guidance, we make it easier for ourselves to live according to God's word.

As our guide, God is, above all, merciful. This quality is frequently referenced in the Qur'ān, which often refers to Him as "all-Merciful" and "ever-Merciful," and in which He is described by Muhammad as more merciful to His people than a mother is to her children and as wanting nothing but the best for them.[75] In her boundless love for her children, a mother displays no more than the tiniest fraction of the great love that God has for the beings of His Creation.

Providing us with His divine guidance throughout our lives, God is also the ultimate judge of human behaviour, and He is utterly just. In creating the world, God has provided us with a testing ground where we can live out our lives and, ultimately, be rewarded or punished for the ways in which we have behaved.[76] God, being merciful, will always be more inclined to forgive than to condemn.[77]

---

70 Chittick, 2013, 71.
71 Chittick, 2013, 74.
72 Q. 25:31.
73 Q. 2:157.
74 Madigan, 2006, 93.
75 Chittick, 2013, 71-2.
76 Q. 45:22; 11:7.
77 For example, Q. 2:173; 20:82; 4:43.

The Conception of God

It is also important to remember that, while God is endlessly merciful, He does expect those who have heard His message to accept it. The Qur'ān makes this clear in many passages. Through the Qur'ān, God speaks warmly of the faithful, who worship Him and acknowledge His hand in creating the world around them, such as the prophet Abraham, who is quoted as asserting, "... I have set my face, firmly and truly, towards Him who created the heavens and the earth, and never shall I give partners to God."[78] Abraham lived among the Chaldean people, who had acquired great knowledge of astronomy by the standards of the day. By embracing faith in God, however, Abraham was able to see that the amazing sights in the sky above him were something much more wonderful than he had ever imagined, and an integral part of God's Creation. Whereas some people foolishly worshipped the stars and the sun in the sky, imagining them to have a life of their own, Abraham understood that this animism was no more than rank superstition, and that the stars and all the other celestial bodies have no powers of their own, and simply do God's bidding in their orbit. Without the energy of the sun, there would be no life here on Earth, but our thanks and praise are due to the One who created it, and not the object itself. Without the pale light cast by the moon, we would be in darkness at night, and again thanks and praise are due to the One who created it. There is no sense in worshipping anything that comes from God, when He alone deserves our thanks and praise. In faith in God, we can find our redemption from the fear and darkness of superstition.[79] However, despite the fact that God's Creation and all it contains speaks loudly of His greatness,[80] human beings all too often wilfully choose to ignore the manifold examples of God's Creation and sovereignty, and do not worship Him as He deserves and demands.[81]

---

78 Q. 6:76-9.
79 Ali, 1934, 361-2.
80 Q. 13:15; Q. 16:49; Q. 22:18.
81 Q. 17:44.

Change and Constancy, Space and Time

For us, as living beings who are born, mature, grow old and die, change is a constant and a fundamental aspect of who and what we are. Throughout the short period of our time on earth, things change for us in many ways, and on a daily basis we lurch from one state of change to another. This condition of imperfection is our reality and all we know, so it can be very difficult for us to grasp the concept of a Creator who is forever unchanging. In this context, people are tempted to ask what change means for God, and how He experiences it. However, God, who has always existed, and always will, can never change. His quality of perfection, transcending all human concerns, means that the notion of change simply cannot be applied to Him. Whereas our lives are characterised by continuous change, God's existence takes place in the realm of constancy, from which He engages in His work of continuous Creation. Unlike us mortals, who need sleep, God never rests, and does not experience tiredness.[82] The only sense in which we can understand God to "change" is insofar as He is constantly involved in the astonishing act of Creation. God's life, if we can use the term "life," is an unending journey of revelation, with no "beginning," "middle" or "end." While we, in our small ways, are also engaged in a journey, ours inevitably has an end in sight, and there is always the risk that we might fail. God's journey of Creation is perfection by its very nature, and involves His unfailing engagement with the process of Creation in the context of the infinite creative possibilities that reside in Him, and that are directed by Him with supreme rationality.[83]

How are we to understand the difficult question of "where" God is? It is difficult for the limited human consciousness to conceive of a being who is not rooted in a particular place, as we must always be. The Qur'ān addresses this issue on various occasions, pointing out that God is at all times aware of what is on the earth and in the heavens that He created, that He always knows what is being discussed between any combination of human individuals,[84]

---

82 Q. 50:38; 2:255.
83 Iqbal, 1989, 47-8.
84 Q. 58:7.

The Conception of God

and that nothing ever happens on earth without God being aware of it, right down to the smallest event one can imagine.[85]

The Qur'ān is of necessity written in a human language, for us to read, listen to, and understand, but it is essential to remember that mere words cannot do justice to God, and that terms that imply nearness, contact or togetherness do not have the same implication when they are applied to God as when they are used to discuss material objects or beings. Just as our soul's contact with every aspect of our being is real, but at the same time intangible, so is God invariably part of us and everything we do. God is not limited by location, and can be everywhere at the same time.[86] When we look for God, we find Him in His Own Creation, which shows us in so many ways that life and everything we see were breathed into existence by a power engaging in conscious planning. Or, as the Qur'ān puts it, "God is His Own Witness."[87] Human beings, who have been given superiority over all other aspects of God's Creation, should understand that God knows everything that happens in their lives. Describing Himself as even closer to them than their own "neck-vein,"[88] God speaks through the Qur'ān to remind people that He is aware of everything, even their most intimate thoughts, and with them always. He hears human beings when they cry out for help and He provides them with succour. With all of the gifts that have been bestowed on us by God, we can never truly be independent from Him, as we owe Him everything we have. How foolish it would be, therefore, to forget Him.[89]

---

85 Q. 10:61.
86 Iqbal, 1989, 108.
87 Q. 3:18.
88 Q. 50:16.
89 Ali, 1934, 1107.

CHAPTER 2

The Creation of the Heavens and the Earth

> He it is who has created for you all that is on earth, and has applied His design to the heavens and fashioned them into seven heavens; He alone has full knowledge of everything.[1]

AS WE HAVE already discussed, in His Creation of the universe, God reveals Himself to us every day, in a multitude of ways. God is perceptible to us all, every day, in the wonders of His Creation. In the Qur'ān, He makes the majesty of this Creation evident, stating that His decision to make everything was not "idle play," and pointing out that if He needed a "pastime," He would have found one within Himself and would have had no need to create the universe that is our home.[2]

Of course, prior to Islam, the Arabs had their own ideas about Creation and were familiar to varying degrees with the teachings of the Jews and Christians, who had received earlier revelations from God. However, the pre-Islam Arabs did not yet have any true understanding of these revelations' significance to human life, and rather believed that God had created human beings and then stood back from them, leaving them to the mercy of an obscurely understood fate thought to determine what happened to each person over the course of their life.[3]

---

1 Q. 2:29.
2 Q. 21:16-7.
3 Idleman Smith and Yazbeck Haddad, 2002, 2.

Of God, but not in God

Without God, the universe would not exist. But why did God create the universe and how can we understand that it comes from him, but is at the same time separate? If God had needed the "pastime" referred to above, He would have found one within His Self, and there would have been no need to create the universe. Moreover, as it would have been within His Self, it would have shared his quality of being infinite. But every living creature created by God has its own lifespan. It comes into being, gets old, and dies. Even mountains, which can seem to be immutable to us from the perspective of our short lives, were once created and are now subject to the forces of erosion and may one day cease to exist. The impermanence of every aspect of the universe clarifies that it cannot be seen as a simple "projection" of the Creator, Who has always existed, and always will,[4] but as the deliberate, physical expression of His will.

The Old Testament provides a simple narrative outlining the general sequence in which Creation took place. However, instead of providing a chronological narrative of this type, the Qur'ān references Creation in multiple instances and diverse contexts throughout the book. These scattered passages all deal with different aspects of Creation, providing different levels of detail. A close reading of the Qur'ān is necessary in order to arrive at a full picture. The Qur'ān takes a similar "scattered" approach to the discussion of many topics.

In the first instance, it is important to highlight that there are, in fact, many similarities between the simple account of Creation provided in the Old Testament and the more sophisticated treatment the same topic receives in the Qur'ān, which was received and written down several hundred years later. Both texts state, for example, that God's initial period of Creation took place over a time frame of six days. Jews and Christians further believe that, after working for six days, God rested on the seventh. This is why they observe an obligatory day of rest, which for Jews is Saturday and for Christians Sunday,

---

4 Asad, 1984, 489.

when work is restricted and time is given to rest and worship. Traditionally, this description of "days" is taken literally in these faiths, and assumed to correspond to six calendar days as we experience them as humans on earth – as twenty-four hours or the time it takes for the planet to rotate through day and night.

The Qur'ān, as well as the Old Testament, considers the act of Creation as one in which God simply states that something will exist, and so it does. The idea of things coming into being out of nothing in an instant response to God's command is an effective image for articulating God's immense power, before which there is no resistance from anything. The verse thus expresses that the willed thing is brought into existence by God without any trouble or delay, for when He wishes it, His will is invariably acted upon by everything in Creation.[5]

An examination of the Qur'ān reveals great subtleties in its accounts of Creation, accommodated by the nuanced nature of the Arabic language. For example, the term "samā," which can be translated as either "heaven" or "sky," can also be applied to anything that is spread above any other thing. This term can be used to describe the skies, which appear to the human eye to be spread above the earth, and it is often employed in this manner. However, it can also be used in a wider sense, with the implication of an overarching "cosmic system." The Qur'ān makes reference to the term "seven heavens." Read literally, this suggests that heaven has seven divisions or areas, but in Arabic (as in some other Semitic languages), "seven" can also be used as a term to imply "several," just as "seventy" means many. With this understanding, we can see that the Qur'ān states that there is not just one cosmic system, but many. In this way, it reminds us of our individual smallness and insignificance when we compare ourselves with the majesty and complexity of God's Creation.[6]

---

5 Asad, 1984, 732, notes 7-13.
6 Asad, 1984, 8, note 20.

What is Creation for?

As God is perfect, eternal, and infinitely wise, we must assume that He had a purpose in creating the universe. The Qur'ān confirms this in many passages, stating that every single aspect of Creation, no matter how minute, is part of His eternal plan. Everything has a grand meaning, and nothing ever comes into being as a result of mere happenstance.[7] Moreover, as sentient, intelligent beings, we humans are in a unique position insofar as we can understand and appreciate all the wonders that God has created to provide for all our needs and those of all our fellow beings. Nature provides us with nutritious food in abundance, has given us the sun and the moon to shine down upon us and guide our path, and the intelligence and ability to use features of His Creation in a wide range of ways.[8]

The Qur'ān makes frequent reference to the cyclical nature of Creation, and employs as metaphor many examples from nature. One of these potent examples is that of water, on which all life depends. The great oceans that traverse the globe are composed of water, on which our ships can sail and bring goods and people all around the world. Ocean water evaporates and rises into the sky, where it forms the clouds that we see above us and that so often move us emotionally with their beauty. These clouds deposit water in the form of rain onto our fields, watering the crops we sow and filling lakes and rivers, which flow back into the seas and oceans, returning us to the beginning of the cycle. Each aspect of this journey is an aspect of the life-giving and -nourishing qualities of God's Creation!

Furthermore, the Qur'ān's bold statement that every living thing created by God is made of water represents a simple scientific truth that is, as occurs so often, more complex than it first appears, and certainly more complex than Muhammad and his contemporaries would have been able to understand at the time of revelation. Today, we know that all living matter originated in a maritime environment, that water is the only liquid that embodies the special properties necessary for life to emerge and develop within, and that the

---

7 Q. 10:5; 3:191; 38:27.
8 Q. 14:32-33.

building block of every living cell, plant or animal, known as protoplasm, is largely composed of water, meaning that all living things depend on it.

In the absolutely necessity of water to life, we glimpse the overall plan that unites all Creation and, in the process, obtain some insight into God's uniqueness. Everything we see around us has a beginning and an end, and depends on specific aspects of God's Creation simply to exist. Knowing what we do, it is clear that no living creature could feasibly have evolved out of nothing and that "nothingness" is a meaningless idea. While we may begin to understand some of the evolutionary processes originally described in the Qur'ān, a rational view forces us to accept a primary cause of life Whose power is beyond the limits of our understanding![9]

Of course, as well as providing us with every single thing we need in the material sense, the universe also satisfies us in a spiritual way, in the profound emotional response we have to examples of natural beauty. Anyone with the wisdom to see and the humility to accept finds in Creation countless examples of God's bounty![10]

The Qur'ān reminds us frequently of the perfect beauty we find in Creation, and indeed all we need to do to see is to look around, because even in the most squalid urban environment there is always something natural and beautiful to admire. Nature is resilient, as anyone who has seen a fragile flower growing through tough concrete can attest. While everything created by God has its utility, there is also beauty everywhere to be seen, sometimes in surprising places. For example, whereas night is often described in negative terms in many traditional cultures – as a time of unseen dangers, crime and unfathomable darkness when anything awful might happen – the Qur'ān points out that there is also much of great beauty to be seen and appreciated during the hours of darkness. All we need to do is raise our eyes to the heavens, and the majesty of Creation is spread out before us in the form of the countless stars and planets, only a few of which we can see from our vantage point on earth, while we rely on the sun for warmth and light here on our little

---

9 Asad, 1984, 232; 491-2.
10 Ali, 1934, 66.

planet, and while generations of navigators had no more than the moon and stars to guide their way.

Of course, once in a while we are forced to confront natural disasters, such as earthquakes, tornadoes, floods, and so forth. While these events can seem devastating at the time, humankind survives, adapts to and learns from each and every episode.

The Special Place of Humanity in Creation

Human beings cannot even dream of attaining a fraction of the power and wisdom of God. They were created by Him from clay and put on the earth, each to live for a period of time specified by God. However, as the descendants of the original humans, God has appointed us to oversee the world He made for us.[11] While this is a great honour, it is also an immense responsibility, for alone of all the creatures of God's Creation, we must one day account for all the decisions we have taken during our time here on Earth:

> He has made all that He has created good. And He began the Creation of man from clay, then made his offspring from a drop of fluid despised, then He formed him and breathed into him of His spirit. And He gave you hearing and sight and feeling, though you gave little thanks. They say, When are we lost in the earth, will we be created anew? And they deny the meeting with their Lord. But you say: The angel of death, who has charge over you, and you will be returned to your Lord.[12]

In creating men and women, God has given each of them the means to live a good life and has placed them in a position of honour above all other living creatures.[13] With our God-given talents, we can create vessels with which we

---

11 Q. 2: 29-30.
12 Idleman Smith and Yazbeck Haddad, 2002, 11-2; Q. 32: 7-11.
13 Q. 2:31.

can travel the seas (and, in recent generations, the skies), and in farming and animal husbandry we can harness the natural laws created by God to provide ourselves with sustenance.[14] In all of this, we find God's hand at work. Indeed, even in our ability as humans to use our minds and hands in the creations of technological solutions to our challenges, we see evidence of God. The Qur'ān implores us to use our powers of reason to see and understand the nature of Creation, and all that God has done for us.

Time in Creation

The scholar Fakhruddīn Rāzi devoted considerable attention to the question of time, but failed to reach any conclusion, stating bluntly, "Until now, I have not been able to discover anything really true with regard to the nature of time."

In general, the Qur'ān does not suggest a specific sequence of time between one act of Creation and another, but there is an exception in the following verses:

> (O Men!) Are you more difficult to create than the heaven which He has built? High has He reared its vault and formed it in accordance with what it was meant to be; and He has made dark its night and brought forth its light of day. And after that, the earth: wide has He spread its expanse, and has caused its waters to come out of it, and its pasture, and has made the mountains firm: (all this) as a means of livelihood for you and your animals.[15]

In this passage, the Qur'ān is very clear in stating that God created the earth and made it so that humans could use it for agriculture during a specific period of time before He created the cyclical nature of day and night. We can further see that there is a distinction to be made between the sky and

---

14 Q. 2:164.
15 Q. 79:27-33.

The Creation of the Heavens and the Earth

its contents, and the earth on which we live. The implication in the passages above is that the earth (by which we mean the planet Earth) already existed before God made it suitable for agriculture, and therefore before He created the skies.

The Qur'ān clarifies that there was a time when the universe was a singular entity. It describes God tearing asunder this entity to create the heavens and earth as distinct realms of being.[16] While bearing in mind the necessary humility in understanding that many of today's scientific certainties will be tomorrow's debunked theories, it is also important to point out that this understanding of a singular origin of the universe is consistent with modern science's understanding that everything in the universe originated in hydrogen, which was gradually consolidated and became the individual stars and planets that fill the universe – just one of which is home to humankind!

The Qur'ān also refers to "days," possibly in part to highlight the continuity between the messages received by Muhammad and those received by God's earlier prophets.[17] However, the term "yawm" in Arabic, which is often translated as "day," is actually used in that language to mean "aeon," which can refer to any sort of period in time, either long or short. Thus, where the Qur'ān says, "Verily, Your Sustainer is God, who has created the heavens and the earth in six aeons, and is established on the throne of His almightiness,"[18] this need not be read as indicating six days in the way in which we typically understand the term, as six periods of twenty-four hours each, but rather as an undefined period of time.

The Qur'ān refers on various occasions to the might of God as revealed in his Creation of the earth, stating that He who "created the earth in two aeons" cannot be denied, for there is no one to rival Him,[19] that He created the mountains that tower over us and gave us the means to feed ourselves in

---

16 Q. 21:30.
17 Bucaille, 2003, 142-3.
18 Q. 7:54.
19 Q. 41:9.

four aeons,[20] (giving us a total of six days of Creation, as discussed above) and applied His will to both the skies and the earth, which obey Him in everything.[21] It is clear that the universe, which had a beginning in time and required a period of time to be created, is contrasted with God Himself, Who is timeless and infinite. Moreover, the Qur'ān makes it clear that Creation was not a one-off exercise, but is an ongoing process, of which the initial six days was merely the start. In the cyclical nature of Creation, we witness God's constant invigilation and ongoing Creation on a daily basis.[22]

The Qur'ān refers to God's ability to plan with reference to the skies, pointing out that He has created the sun (which radiates light) and the moon (which reflects light) in such a way that human beings can use them to calculate the passage of time.[23] The respective terms for radiant and reflected light both indicate God's intention and planning in His Creation, implying that He had a specific purpose in mind and that absolutely nothing that comes into being or exists in the universe should be seen as "accidental."

Nature can be described in a temporal way, as a series of events that take place within the context of God's ongoing creative flow. Our perception of these events as human beings divides them up into distinct periods of time because this is consistent with our experience. This temporal quality of nature is frequently emphasised in the Qur'ān, which reveals it not as a series of moments that might be visualised as a series of beads strung along a necklace, but as a complex whole in which the past is carried into the present, and the future is always there as a possibility waiting to be discovered. The Qur'ān describes this holistic understanding of time as "destiny," a word that has often been profoundly misunderstood in both Islamic and non-Islamic contexts. Destiny is properly understood simply as time before its many possibilities have been disclosed to human observers. In this context, we can understand the following verses:

---

20 Q. 41:10.
21 Q. 41:11.
22 Ali, 1934, 413, note 1032.
23 Q. 10:5.

> Extol the glory of your Sustainer's name, the All-Highest, who creates (all things), and thereupon forms it in accordance with what it is meant to be. And who determines the nature (of all that exists), and thereupon guides it (towards its fulfilment).[24]

This implies that God gives Creation inner constancy and the ability to function as it should, so that it is always adapted for what will come next.

> God created all things and assigned to each its destiny, and our ordaining (a thing and its coming into being) is but one (act), like the twinkling of an eye.[25]

This means that the moment God wills something into existence, it simply exists. There is no delay between one thing and the other, while the following verse indicates that God has given each element of existence its own function:

> He to whom the dominion over the heavens and the earth belongs, and who begets no offspring, and has no partner in His dominion: for it is He who creates every thing and determines its nature in accordance with (His own) design.[26]

If we understand that Creation is not just a series of unique beings and geographical features, but a collective whole that has integrity as such, we can see it as a sort of forever-growing organism, in which we are all essential parts. There are no limitations other than those prescribed by God Himself.[27] The simple fact is that there was nothing before He created the universe, each element of which will, one day, return to Him. Even "before" and "after" cannot really be understood in the simple way in which we typically use these terms,

---

24 Q. 87:1-3.
25 Q. 54:49-50.
26 Q. 25:2.
27 Q. 53:42.

because such reductive language tends to reduce God and the world to two separate things within space, when the reality is that everything is contained within God and dependent upon Him.

The complex matter of time has long been a subject of scholarly discussion in Islam. Tradition relates that the disciples of Saint Bā Yazid of Bistām once came to him and stated their view that there was clearly a moment of time when God existed, but nothing else, "before" as understood from the human perspective. The saint responded, "It is just the same now as it was then." The material world does not exist in parallel to God, with Him intervening from a distance, but consists of an ongoing act on the part of God that the human mind cannot help but see as a series of distinct things and periods of time; a complex understanding to grasp with our limited human imaginations.

Philosophically speaking, the emergence of Islamic scholarship represented the first major challenge to the idea of a "fixed" universe first mooted by Aristotle. The Ash'arite school of thought maintains that the world is composed of "jawāhir," which are tiny parts or atoms that cannot be subdivided; the essential building blocks of Creation. Because God's Creation is a continuous process, the absolute number of these tiny parts is infinite. New atoms are created in every moment, which means that the universe is in a continuous state of growth and expansion. As the Qur'ān states, "God adds to His Creation what He wills."[28] According to this view, prior to Creation these atoms are essentially dormant, part of God's innate creative energy. Their very existence can be described as God's creative energy embodied, and in coming together these elements create form and space in which opposing properties, such as life and death, or negative and positive energy, are coupled. In consequence, we are led to understand that all created things are subject to change, while each element of divine energy, no matter how small, has a presence of its own. This presence becomes more complex according to how these atoms are arranged, and they are at their most complex when they are manifested in human form.

---

28 Q. 35:1.

According to "Iraqi," the Sufi poet, there are infinite varieties of time along a spectrum from the material world to the purely spiritual. This view maintains that the material world experiences time that can be divided into past, present and future, whereas divine time, at the other end of the spectrum, having neither beginning nor end, simply cannot be understood in terms of sequence and change.[29]

God's Power Revealed in Creation

Many discussions of Creation in the Qur'ān point to God's extraordinary power, which is so great as to elude complete human understanding. Frequently this occurs in the context of passages that have become progressively clearer to scholars as our scientific endeavours have gradually revealed more to us about the mysteries of the universe. For example, today scientists know that hydrogen gas is a primal element, and that everything in the universe has evolved, and continues to evolve, from it. In the Qur'ān, which was revealed in the first instance to a prophet living in a pre-scientific age, this element is referred to as "smoke."

The Qur'ān makes reference to the heavens and the earth bowing to God's will and doing what He commands of them. Clearly, as they are simply elements of His Creation, by definition we are bound to see them as doing His will, while as none of the elements of Creation existed before God made them, it is obvious that they could not have chosen not to do His will at any point. We can read these references in an allegorical way, in the sense that they are utilised to show God's almighty power and in light of the term, "When God wills a thing to be, He but says unto it, 'Be'-and it is," which is repeated throughout the Qur'ān, and we can also understand them as indicating the fact that God's incredible power means that He is able to bring anything into existence with no trouble or delay, simply by commanding it.[30]

---

29 Iqbal, 1989, 52-60.
30 Yazicioglu, 2013, 23-4.

There are many examples throughout the Qur'ān of God's Creation being discussed allegorically. Clearly, when the Qur'ān states that God can make the heavens and earth "speak" this is not intended to be read in a literal sense, but is a literary and allegorical use of the term, as is any discussion of all the "things" in God's Creation worshipping him.[31] A literal understanding would require us to believe that the sky and the earth are alive in the same way as we humans, with intelligence and the ability to engage in conversation. With our God-given intelligence and unique ability to understand and worship God, we can clearly see that this is certainly not the case. Rather, such declarations should be read as figurative ways of discussing the awesome power of God and of understanding that, simply by existing, everything that He created gives testimony to His power.

Alongside these allegorical readings of God's power, there are also many straightforward references to it, which bluntly highlight His unique ability to do whatever He wishes. For example, the Qur'ān states that God has "raised the heavens" without the aid of any support visible to the human eye.[32] Here, we understand the term "heavens" ("samā" in Arabic) as indicating anything that is above us, and thus encompassing the sky that we can perceive above us, including any clouds that we might see, and the vast cosmic space in which all celestial bodies, including ours, are contained.

Certainly, in God's Creation we find not just a million reasons to worship Him and give Him praise, but glimpses of the reality and majesty of our Creator Himself!

---

31 Q. 17:44.
32 Q. 13:2.

CHAPTER 3

❖ ❖ ❖

The Creation of Human Beings

ALONE OF GOD'S Creation on Earth, humans are a very special species. Nonetheless, in most respects, they have more in common with other living entities than otherwise. Like all other living beings, they have a specific lifespan and will age, become frail and die. They are vulnerable not just to the weakening effects of aging, but also to the predations of viruses, germs, and other natural agents of disease and destruction. This is our biological reality, and not a single one of us can escape it, not matter how we delude ourselves. In other respects, we humans are very different to all other creatures, as we are capable of understanding, at least to some limited extent, the majesty and wonder of He who created us. We are also unique in that, alone of Creation, those among us who have lived in a way that has pleased God will be called to join Him in the afterlife on the Day of Resurrection and will receive our eternal reward with Him. God, who is ever-merciful, promises His people that He will always provide them with what they need to live, asking for nothing in return other than that they acknowledge and worship Him.[1]

The Qur'ān describes the creation of humanity as follows:

> Indeed, We create man out of the essence of clay, and then We cause him to remain as a drop of sperm in (the womb's) firm keeping, and then We create out of the drop of sperm a germ-cell, and then We create out of the germ-cell an embryonic lump, and then We create within the embryonic lump bones, and then We clothe the bones with

---

1 Q. 51:56-9.

flesh – and then We bring (all) this into being as a new Creation: hallowed, therefore, is God, the best of creators. And then, behold! After all this, you are destined to die. And then, behold, you shall be raised from the dead on resurrection day.[2]

It is striking to note the way in which this text describes the development of a foetus in its mother's womb. The Qur'ān also describes how God infused something of his own spirit into the fleshly body of humanity, described as "breathing His spirit" into His new creation.[3]

According to the Qur'ān, God created the angels before He created humanity, and the angels were not pleased with what they saw, to the extent of arguing against God's decision to make this new species and place it above all others.[4] The angels argued that, in human beings, God had created a species that would "work mischief on the earth and shed blood," comparing humans unfavourably to themselves, who would "sing Your glories and exalt your utter holiness." God did not deny that humans would "work mischief" but simply replied to the angels, "I know what you do not know,"[5] indicating that He had a special plan for humanity. After He had created human beings, God ordered His angels to bow down before them, and all of them, bar Iblis (whom we will discuss in Chapter Four), did so,[6] despite their initial misgivings.

Islamic scholars have debated over passages that use the term "nafs" which can refer to a soul, a spirit, a mind, a person, and so on. Many have interpreted it as meaning simply a human individual in the singular and have thus read many passages as referring specifically to Adam, who is described as the first man. Others believe that it should be generally translated as "human being"

---

2 Q. 23:12-16; 4:1.
3 Q. 15:29; 32:9; 38:72.
4 Q. 38:69; 2:30.
5 Rahman, 1989, 17; Q. 2:30.
6 Q. 2:34; Q. 15:31; Q. 17:61; Q. 38:74.

and that when God is depicted as issuing directions, He is speaking to all of humanity.[7]

Why Did God Create Human Beings?

When we ask ourselves why God created us as sentient beings, we find the answer in the Qur'ān. God is described as having imparted to Adam "the names of all things," which indicates that He gifted humanity with the power of critical thought, and with the ability to distinguish between what is true and what is false. Strikingly, the Qur'ān describes the angels as lacking the capacity for creative knowledge, which was gifted to humanity by God.[8] Clearly, humans' capacity for abstract thought and speech, which has made it possible for us to form great civilisations, sets us firmly apart even from the living creatures whom we most closely resemble. Considering this, we humans – who have been blessed by God with so many gifts – cannot make excuses for failing to recognise that God exists and that He is exalted above all things. The Qur'ān states:

> O MANKIND! Be conscious of your Sustainer, Who has created you out of one living entity, and out of it created its mate, and out of the two spread abroad a multitude of men and women. And remain conscious of God, in Whose name you demand (your rights) from one another, and of these ties of kinship. Verily, God is ever watchful over you.[9]

The purpose of humanity, then, is to live well and serve God as He has outlined for us in the Qur'ān. We are aware of God's existence, and we have the linguistic and intellectual capacity to reason about and discuss all of the implications of this. As a result, we can choose to do our best to live according

---

7 Ridā, 1999, 262-7.
8 Rahman, 1989, 18.
9 Q. 4:1.

to His will. This is what the Qur'ān refers to when it speaks of worship. Moreover, in worshipping God, we do not provide Him with what He needs, but rather we provide *ourselves* with spiritual nourishment, what we need to live happy and healthy lives, for God's laws for us are designed only for our own good. By surrendering ourselves to God's will, we can acquire a deeper understanding of precisely what it is, and in that way, find ourselves becoming closer to God.[10]

God also created human beings to reign over nature, which He has made specifically for them.[11] However, this position of authority should not be interpreted as humans having a "right" to simply take from nature for their own needs without giving a thought to the consequences of their actions. Rather, it is also a momentous responsibility that each of us should take extremely seriously. Humans have a duty of care to watch over the world that has been given to them by their benevolent Creator, a world that contains everything they will ever need for their material existence, and abundant beauty to nourish their spirits. Thus, the Qur'ān can be claimed as the world's earliest treatise on environmentalism, among many other things.

The Nature of Humanity

The Qur'ān makes frequent reference to the fact of humanity having been created out of "clay" or "dust."[12] This highlights both our very humble origins, which we share with all other living beings, and the scientific fact of our composition in a range of substances that are also found in a wide variety of settings, including in their elemental form, on Earth. In the description of humans as being made of "dried clay that emits a sound"[13] we find a reference to the fact that, alone of all other living creatures, we have the capacity to express

---

10 Asad, 1984, 806, note 38.
11 Q. 14:32-3.
12 Q. 15:26.
13 Q. 55:14.

The Creation of Human Beings

ourselves with rational speech, as well as a hint of our inherent fragility.[14] The Qur'ān describes the clay from which we are made as being altered in composition and formed into shape, indicating the ways in which our physical forms have evolved and changed in the context of God's Creation. Unlike some concepts of humanity, which draw a clear distinction between mind and body, Islam does not view humans in terms of this binary opposition, but rather sees the mind and the body coming together as a discrete whole.[15]

Here on Earth, we humans are often painfully (and frequently problematically) aware of differences of ethnicity and race. However, the Qur'ān makes it more than clear that all human beings are equal, and all are equally loved by God. A far more fundamental distinction than that between ethnic and racial groups is that of gender. Clearly, God has made human beings both female and male, who together form the totality of humanity. When the Qur'ān refers to a "mate," this can refer equally to males as to females, and does not imply a subservient role. Men and women are *each other's* mates or counterparts, and they matter equally to God. Each, furthermore, has been created from the same substance and, together, they sit in a position of supremacy over the rest of the natural world.[16]

Men and women are described in the Qur'ān as having been created to hold a position of authority above other living creatures on Earth.[17] We are described as "inheritors" of the Earth. God also describes how some humans have been given authority over others, and that each will be judged according to his or her capacity.[18] In other words, a great deal more will be expected of someone with a particularly high level of intelligence or many more talents than others, simply because they have been given so many gifts and capabilities by God and are in a good position to understand His messages to humanity. Yet we are all created to serve God in our own unique way, according to

---

14 Rāzi, n.d. 179-90.
15 Rahman, 1989, 17.
16 Ridā, 1999, 179-80.
17 Q. 2:30.
18 Q. 6:165.

the particular gifts and talents that we have been given; God does not love the talented more than those of us who do not seem to excel in any particular way.

The "Fall" of Humankind

The Qur'ān (like the Torah) describes humanity's original fall from grace in the garden in which Adam and Eve were created. God directed them to eat whatever they wished, but to avoid a particular tree. Satan told them that God had forbidden them to eat the fruit of this tree, because if they did they would become angels, or live forever, and He made them aware of their state of nakedness.[19] As we know, they did eat from the tree, and they were cast out of the Garden of Eden.

The story of the Fall of Man is an ancient one that was well-known long before the Qur'ān was received and written down. Certainly, the Qur'ān often makes use of elements of folklore and popular culture that were current in Muhammad's day, as well as earlier Scriptures, the better to make its message understandable. So how can we understand the story of the fall in an Islamic context? Firstly, it is crucial to note that when the Qur'ān uses such stories, it rarely proposes them as actual historical narratives that tell the literal truth. Instead, it explores them as carriers of useful moral or philosophical lessons that can be applied to everyone. This approach is highlighted by the fact that, when it deals with material that is essentially legendary in nature, it refrains from mentioning specific locations or historical personages that would limit it to a particular moment in time.

Those familiar with the story of the Fall of Man from Genesis, which is sacred to both the Jews and the Christians, will soon see significant differences in how the story is told in the Qur'ān; differences that clearly indicate the intention behind its inclusion. In the Qur'ān, Eve is not described as having been formed out of man's rib, and there is no mention of Satan appearing in the form of a snake. The original man and woman are not referred to by

---

19 Q. 7:19-20.

their given names, but with terms that indicate that the story should be read as applying to *all* human beings.[20] In this way, we can understand the story of Creation, as revealed in the Qur'ān, to be, above all, an allegory.

The Qur'ān discusses the story of the Fall in terms of two grand chapters, one of which it describes as "the tree" and the other as relating to the "tree of eternity" and the "kingdom that faileth not."[21] It describes the putative first woman and first man as both being led astray by Satan, who sets about sowing doubt in their minds. Adam and his wife tasted the fruit of both trees. Conversely, in the version in Genesis, they taste the fruit of the tree of life only, and are driven out of the Garden of Eden immediately after this first act of disobedience, after which God places angels and a flaming sword, turning on all sides, at the eastern side of the garden, to keep the tree of life safe.

When we hear of the nakedness of Adam and Eve, and their shame when they realised it, we can understand this as an allegorical description of how human beings lived before they became sufficiently conscious to realise that they have the power to choose between two or more actions, which brings with it the capacity to choose to do evil. Regardless of how tempting evil-doing may seem at the time, the consequences of it are invariably dreadful. Thus, we can see that the story of the Fall is really a narrative of human existence.

The description of the original "garden" from which the first people are supposed to have "fallen" should be read allegorically. The Qur'ān clearly states that human beings belong on Earth, rather than as having been "banished" there,[22] and that Earth is a wonderful gift from God that can never be seen as a punishment. The garden should not be confused with heaven or the afterlife, which is described in the Qur'ān as the place "wherein the righteous will pass to one another the cup which shall engender no light discourse, no motive to sin,"[23] and as a place where the righteous will never feel tired, and

---

20 Iqbal, 1989, 65-6.
21 Q. 20:120.
22 Q. 71:17-8.
23 Q. 52:23.

where they will stay forever.[24] The term "Jannat" is used in the Qur'ān to describe both the original garden and the afterlife, with the former described as a place "where there is neither hunger, nor thirst, neither heat nor nakedness."[25] This can be interpreted as implying an early stage of human social development, before human beings were capable of feeling or expressing the desires and intellectual curiosity that would one day lead to the development of the many sophisticated cultures and civilisations that make our world such a fascinating place to live in, and that continue to steer our path towards the future. In the early days, human beings, who were still in a primitive state of development, did not even realise that evil existed, and did not understand the implications of making a choice between one behaviour and another. Like any other living being, they simply followed their instincts and were intellectually incapable of making profound moral decisions – and therefore incapable of being judged by the same standards as modern humans.

As humans became increasingly self-aware, a state symbolised in the story of the loss of innocence as recorded in the Qur'ān and other holy scriptures, they ceased to live purely according to their basic instincts, and became thinking creatures capable of distinguishing between right and wrong and of making moral decisions accordingly. The Fall is often misunderstood and described in purely negative terms but, looking at it more deeply, we can see that this rise in self-consciousness was actually an opportunity for human beings to enter a new stage of development, as they became capable of making moral choices. God has given all humans free will and the capacity to choose to act either rightly or wrongly. This is part of the gift that sets us apart from all other living beings,[26] and we should cherish it. Far from referring to sinfulness in the way in which we usually understand the term, the story of the Fall is about our species' transition through the ages from simplicity to complexity; "a kind of waking from the dream of nature."[27] In the process, we gradually

---

24 Q. 15:48.
25 Q. 20:118-9.
26 Asad, 1984, 205.
27 Iqbal, 1999, 68.

became able to perceive the hand of God in the world around us, and capable of understanding His message as revealed to us via His prophets.

At this point, it should be abundantly clear that some traditional views of the Fall as indicating women's inferiority to men are certainly false. First of all, the term "Adam" is used to indicate *all* of humanity, and thus refers to both women and men equally. Secondly, unlike the Book of Genesis, which is sacred to Christians and Jews, it does not depict Eve as a temptress, solely or largely to blame for the introduction of sin to the world. In the Qur'ān, women are described as the equals of men, and as no lesser in the eyes of God. In God's plan for humanity, humans of all types and both genders were created by God to live together on this earth according to His rules for them. God honours most those people who live according to His will, regardless of whether they are male or female.[28]

The first acts of disobedience to God's law were also first acts of enacting free will, which is why the Qur'ān describes them as having been forgiven by God.[29] Doing good becomes much more meaningful when free will enters the equation and, in this context, committing sinful acts also bears another meaning. Although we are used to seeing good and evil as polar opposites, it is more useful to envision them as, together, forming part of a whole. Similarly, although the story of the Fall deals with humankind's disobedience, the true implications of the story are much more complex than first appears. The first humans' disobedience can also be read as their search for knowledge, and their desire to have power of their own, including the power to bear children. The positioning of the narrative is also telling, coming as it does immediately after verses that describe humankind's superiority, as compared to the angels, in remembering the names of the things in God's Creation.[30]

God has made us all capable of living virtuously and as He wants, and has given us all the physical and mental qualities we need to honour Him, both

---

28 Barlas, 2006, 259-60.
29 Q. 2:35-7, 20:120-2.
30 Q. 2:31-4.

during worship and in the way we live. When the day comes, He will judge each and every one of us according to how we have lived.[31]

Our Place on Earth

A very important distinction between Genesis and the Qur'ān is found in the description of the Earth following the Fall. The Genesis describes the Earth as having been cursed because of humankind's disobedience,[32] but the Qur'ān is very clear in describing the Earth in extremely positive terms, as the place created by God as a home and a haven for human beings, and as a "source of profit" to him.[33] It states that, because the Earth is such a wonderful place, human beings ought to be thankful to God and give Him praise, for example in the following verses:

> (O Men) We have given you a place on earth, and appointed thereon means of livelihood for you: (yet) how seldom are you grateful.[34]
>
> And the earth – We have spread it out wide, and placed on it mountains firm, and caused every kind to grow on it in balanced manner. And provided thereon means of livelihood for you as well as for all whose providers you are not.[35]

The Qur'ān does not consider our beautiful Earth to be an ante-chamber in which men and women are doomed to spend their mortal lives in penance for an act of original sin, but a beautiful gift that has been given to humankind, containing all we need to flourish, in both the material and the spiritual sense.

---

31 Q. 21:35.
32 Genesis, iii, 17.
33 Q. 2:36, 7:24.
34 Q. 7:10.
35 Q. 15:19-20.

All living creatures pass through a life cycle, and human beings are no exception. We are born, we grow up, we get old and we die.[36] This process is described in detail in the Qur'ān, which asserts, in God's own voice, that death is a simple reality of the life that God has established. While there is nothing to stop God changing the nature of our existence, and causing us to exist in another manner, we should be aware of the extraordinary miracle of our own existence.[37]

God's relationship with human beings is described as a "covenant," referring to our social and spiritual obligations towards God, and towards other human beings, all of which arise from faith in God. Previously, God had entered into covenant with His people, but they had failed to observe His holy law, and it had lapsed.[38] But all people are born with the natural ability to perceive God in the world around them, and together with what they learn in the Qur'ān, every mentally fit person is capable of bearing testimony to his own actions before God.[39]

The Qur'ān states:

> When your Sustainer brought forth their offspring from the loins of the Children of Adam and made them bear witness about themselves, He said: "Am I not your Lord?" and they said, "Yes we bear witness." So you cannot say on the day of resurrection, "We were not aware of this," or, "It was our forefathers who, before us, ascribed partners to God, and we are only the descendants who came after them; will you destroy us because of the deeds of those who invented falsehood."[40]

---

36 Asad, 1984, 941.
37 Q. 56:60-2.
38 Q. 20:115; 20: 121.
39 Affi, 2016, 26-7.
40 Q. 7:172-3.

Death, the Great Leveller

The great prophets, including Muhammad and Jesus, will die in the same way as ordinary women and men, for as well as being the voice of God on Earth, they are flesh and blood human beings, prone to exactly the same frailties and weaknesses as others. In the Qur'ān God speaks to Jesus, saying: "Verily, I shall cause thee to die, and shall exalt thee unto Me."[41] This refers to the fact that, like all of the prophets He sent to Earth, God elevated Jesus to the realm of His special Grace.[42] The Qur'ān also quotes Jesus as referring to his own death in the past tense, bolstering this view. It stresses the mortality of Muhammad, stating that he is "only" an apostle and that all other apostles died in their time.[43] The reference to Muhammad's mortality occurs in the context of text about the Battle of Uhud, at which he was briefly rumoured to be dead, causing many of the Muslim soldiers to abandon their positions. When Muhammad did eventually die, years later, the first Caliph Abū Bakr responded to Muslims' fear that Islam might end without its prophet, stating:

> Behold, whoever has worshipped Muhammad may know that Muhammad has died, but whoever worshipped God may know that God is ever-living, and never dies, all confusion was stilled.[44]

After death, but before judgement, people are considered to be in a place or state referred to as "Barzakh," which means a partition or barrier. This is a complicated concept, referred to in the Qur'ān with reference to biological facts that we are not yet capable of understanding. However, we do know that, from here, it is impossible to return to earth.[45] We know from the Qur'ān, and indeed from our own lived experience as thinking human beings capable of seeing the world around us, and endeavouring to understand it, that every-

---

41 Q. 3:55.
42 Q. 5:117.
43 Q. 3:144.
44 Asad, 1984, 89, note 104.
45 Q. 23:99-100; 84:18-9.

thing in Creation is in a constant state of flux. At every moment, everything is in the process of shifting from one state to another. Humans alone will one day be resurrected, and humans alone are capable of understanding their mortality and eventual fate. Barzakh is not simply a state of waiting, but one in which what remains of the human being, the ego or spirit, is given the opportunity to occasionally glimpse aspects of the new reality that is awaiting, and to prepare for it. It is a period of ongoing struggle that may be easier for some, and more difficult for others. Each spirit will continue to struggle until it achieves its own resurrection.[46]

Death and the Afterlife

Considering the incredible fact that God has chosen to give us life in our current form, and has placed us here on Earth to spend our days, it is clear that He can give us any form He chooses when our life here is over. With our limited human imaginations, we cannot even begin to envision what the afterlife will be like, but it certainly will be very different to everything we know now. Certainly, considering that we are creatures who took many millions of years to evolve to reach our current state, it is impossible to think that God would simply discard us when we reach the end of our time here on Earth. Rather, He has plans for each and every one of us.

We have no guaranteed right to immortality with God, but our lives here on earth offer us many opportunities to make decisions and behave in a way that will either support or act against this coming to pass. We are all candidates for everlasting life in heaven, which we can only achieve by means of our own efforts.[47]

Revealingly, the Qur'ān refers to death as something that God has "created" rather than the mere absence of life.[48] This clearly shows that death as we experience it here on Earth is not simply synonymous with a lack of

---

46 Iqbal, 1989, 96.
47 Iqbal, 1989, 95.
48 Q. 67:1-2.

existence, but is a positive state. Islamic scholars have interpreted the relevant verse as indicating conditions prior to Creation, when no plants or animals existed, and also to the state we will be in after our death here on Earth and prior to our transition to the afterlife. While we cannot even begin to imagine what the afterlife will be like, the Qurʾān does tell us that we will become a new type of Creation that we cannot currently understand; a sort of new body that grows out of the way we have lived on Earth:

> By the soul and He Who hath balanced it, and hath shown to it the ways of wickedness and piety, blessed is he who hath made it grow and undone is he who hath corrupted it.[49]

The Qurʾān sometimes refers to death as akin to sleep. In both cases, the body is apparently unconscious,[50] although we can only wake from death into everlasting life, and cannot return to life on Earth. Those who died after living virtuous lives will be gathered up by the angels and received joyfully into the afterlife[51] where they will be returned to God.[52] Those who were sinners throughout their lives, continuing to act against God, and not repenting of their evil ways, will experience terrible suffering in the afterlife in retribution for having failed to acknowledge the truth during their life on Earth. Using allegorical language, the Qurʾān describes the angels beating them on their faces and backs, and stating that they will experience suffering through fire.[53] (We will be discussing the afterlife in much more detail at a later stage in this book).

The Theory of Evolution, first expressed coherently in the nineteenth century, introduced a note of despondency to much scientific and popular discussion about the destiny of humankind. This relates to the fact that, in all

---

49 Q. 91:7-9.
50 Q. 39:42.
51 Q. 16:32.
52 Q. 32:11.
53 Q. 8:50, 47:27.

our arrogance, we modern humans often assume that our current mental and physical states of being are evolution's finest product, that we will not evolve any further, and that death, understood as a biological event, has no positive implications. But scientific understanding – which itself is a gift of God – should bring us hope and joy, rather than depression and sadness. Consider the lines of the great poet Rūmi:

> First man appeared in the class of inorganic things. Next he passed therefrom into that of plants. For years he lived as one of the plants, remembering naught of his inorganic state so different. And when he passed from the vegetative to the animal state, he had no remembrance of his state as a plant, except the inclination he felt to the world of plants, especially at the time of spring and sweet-flowers, like the inclination of infants towards their mothers, which know not the cause of their inclination to the breast. Again the great Creator, as you know, drew man out of the animal into human state, thus man passed from one order of nature to another, till he became wise and knowing and strong as he is now, of his first souls he has now no remembrance, and he will be again changed from his present soul.[54]

---

54 Cited in Iqbal, 1989, 97.

CHAPTER 4

Satan and Evil

THE ISSUE OF why a loving and merciful God, who created us, this world, and everything we see in it, would allow evil to exist has long been a thorny topic for theologians and philosophers from diverse cultural and theological backgrounds, and none more so than Islam. Very fundamental questions are asked: If God loves us, why does He allow evil to exist at all? If God is all-powerful, why does He permit Satan's existence, when this seems to threaten the very fabric of His wonderful Creation and entices women and men, the most important of all of God's creatures, to commit evil acts? If God hates it when we sin, then why has He created the circumstances that make this possible?

It is a matter of simple observation to state that God's love and omnipotence appear to be at odds with the presence of evil in the world,[1] to the extent that some have argued that the presence of evil in the world constitutes "proof" that God does not exist at all.[2] Yet we know from the bountiful evidence in Creation, from our own experience of faith, and from the word of God as revealed to Muhammad, that God is with us always, sees everything, and loves and cares for us. So, how are we supposed to understand the uncomfortable fact of the presence of evil, and how can we integrate this understanding into the broader picture of Islam, and into our own lives?

---

1 Mackie, 1999, 41.
2 Swinburn, 1999, 52.

The Jinn and the Origins of Evil

In referencing the origins of evil, the Qur'ān uses terminology that would have been very familiar to the Arabs of Muhammad's day, referring to the "jinn," which were thought to be spirits who engaged in evil upon earth. For the Arabs of the day, the term was used to mean "demons" in a broad sense. However, in order to understand it in the sacred context of the Qur'ān, we need to set aside this folkloric understanding and reach for the more sophisticated level of knowledge that emerges from the study of Islam. Although jinn in pre-Islamic folklore and in the Qur'ān have the same name, they are not one and the same by any means. In the Qur'ān, the term "jinn" should be read as coming from the verb "janna," which refers to things that are concealed by or covered with darkness. This can be used in an ordinary, non-supernatural sense, for example to describe someone as being in the dark at night[3] (and remember how very dark things were in the days before electricity; powerful as darkness is as a metaphor today, it was much more so before the invention of electricity). This verb is also used to imply darkness that is intense or confusing, and everything that cannot be perceived with the human senses, but which is nonetheless real.

In the Qur'ān, God refers to having created the spirit jinn before He made human beings. He contrasts them with human beings on the grounds that people were fashioned out of clay, and out of "dark slime,"[4] while the jinn were created "out of a confusing flame of fire,"[5] "out of the fire of scorching winds," and "out of fire."[6] Thus, humans and jinn are posited as approximately equivalent in some ways, but very different, to one another. The jinn can thus be understood as a sort of parallel species to humankind.[7] In the Qur'ān, God stresses that the jinn are not bodily creatures, but creatures of a spiritual nature who exist in an extra-corporeal realm. Collectively, they are referred to

---

3 Q. 6:76.
4 Q. 15:26.
5 Q. 55:15.
6 Q. 7:12; 38:76.
7 Rahman, 1989, 121.

as al-jānn, a collective noun that refers to these forces or beings.[8] God's message, as purveyed by Muhammad, is of relevance to both populations.[9] They are implicitly compared in the verse that states that, "Even if all mankind and jinn came together to produce something like this Qur'ān, they could not produce anything like it, however much they helped each other."[10]

The jinn are most commonly presented as spiritual forces that human beings cannot perceive with their senses, a term that includes the idea of satanic forces.[11] In some contexts, the jinn can also be understood to be angels or angelic forces, which are also imperceptible to the senses and which are revealed to us only insofar as we can sometimes perceive the effects they have had on our world, and not in any direct way. Thus, the jinn are not by any means to be associated exclusively with the notion of evil. Both humans and jinn are called to follow God and do His bidding.

There are hadith in which Muhammad describes angels as having been created out of light, an interesting point seen with respect to the parallels between light and fire, which are clearly closely related, and which are often discussed in the context of the same verse.[12] Some Islamic scholars consider the Qur'ān to often use the words "light" and "fire" interchangeably.

The jinn are described in the Qur'ān as having been made before the Creation of human beings.[13] The Qur'ān refers to the fact that, unable to directly observe jinn, humans often attribute powers akin to God's to them, although this interpretation is false.[14] Just because we cannot see the jinn does not mean that they have the ability to carry out the great acts of Creation, or other great acts, that belong to God alone. The Qur'ān actually describes the jinn themselves as stating that some of them had listened to God's word and

---

8 Q. 15:26-7.
9 Rahman, 1989, 122.
10 Q. 17:88.
11 Q. 15:17.
12 For example, Q. 27:8.
13 Q; 15:27; 7:38; 34:41; 6:100.
14 Asad, 1984, 692, note 67; Q. 37:158.

become Muslims, while some others had not;[15] another point of comparison between the jinn and human beings. Overall, while the Qur'ān describes the jinn as having been created out of fire rather than clay, and while they are depicted as having certain qualities and powers that humans do not, such as the ability to remain invisible, in many ways they resemble human beings, in particular in the fact that they were created by God and are obliged to listen to and heed His message.[16]

As well as being used to refer to spiritual beings, the term jinn is sometimes used to describe other phenomena that are not usually perceptible to human beings, but which are nonetheless possessed of intelligence. In this sense of the word, the reality is that we may not be capable of completely understanding what is meant by the term, or at least not in this lifetime. This is a reminder that our senses are inherently limited, and that therefore our inability to see or perceive something is by no means proof that it does not exist.[17] A further, occasional usage of the word is to mean "unseen people," indicating people who are generally perfectly visible and normal, but who cannot be seen by the person central to the matter at hand. We see an example of this usage in the following verse, which appears to refer to people of the Jewish faith[18]:

> AND LO! We caused a group of unseen beings to incline towards thee, (O Muhammad) so that they might give ear to the Qur'an: and so, as soon as they became aware of it, they said (unto one another), "Listen in Silence!" And when (the recitation) was ended, they returned to their people as warners. They said: "O our people! Behold, we have been listening to a revelation bestowed from on high after (that of) Moses, confirming the truth of whatever there still remains (of the Torah): it guides towards the truth, and onto a straight way."[19]

---

15 Rahman, 1989, 122.
16 Rahman, 1989, 122.
17 Asad, 1984, 994.
18 Asad, 1984, 775, note 39.
19 Q. 46:29-30.

The Qur'ān refers in various contexts to entire realms that are beyond our ability to perceive. God is referred to as "Sustainer of all the worlds," suggesting that there are worlds parallel to the one in which we live that we cannot see or experience, even if these different dimensions impact on one another in ways that we cannot experience directly or understand. Given the fact that the universe is infinite in size, it is reasonable to assume that on this planet, or on another one, there may be living creatures whose make-up is so different to ours that we cannot really sense them at all under ordinary circumstances. Consider the fact that folklore around the world relates stories of ghosts, manifestations and encounters with otherworldly beings. Knowing the little that we do about the jinn, could it be that these are simple attempts to understand moments when our paths crossed with another of the worlds created by God? Until we become capable of perceiving these other beings in some way, the word "jinn" can also be used to describe them.

While, as should be clear, the jinn are in no way intrinsically evil, the Qur'ān represents them as being more prone to sinful acts than humans, and it is from among their population that true evil sprang near the dawn of human time.

Iblis, Satan, the Fallen Angel

References to the jinn having been made by God out of fire are often with respect to the named spirit, Iblis. Iblis was originally a jinn, and, as such, he coexisted with human beings, even though he had been created long before Adam was.[20] The Qur'ān tells the story of how God ordered the angels to "Prostrate yourselves before Adam" after his initial Creation of humankind, with the implication that human beings were to be considered special among other beings of His Creation, above even the angels. All of the angels did as they were told bar Iblis, who refused on the grounds that this new being, a human, was foolish, had been made of clay, and did not deserve to be regarded

---

20 Rahman, 1989, 123.

as important.[21] Indeed, the Qur'ān does describe Adam as having been created out of stinking, base matter.[22] This apparently offended Iblis, who had been created out of fire, and considered himself far superior to humankind.[23] The Qur'ān describes Iblis as exercising his free will and choosing to disobey God's command,[24] because of his belief that God had created him superior to Adam[25] and that it was therefore unseemly of God to expect him to pay obeisance to humankind. To some extent, Iblis can be seen as a tragic figure insofar as his refusal to bow to humanity seems somewhat justified,[26] in light of the fact that the original humans were indeed made of stinking mud.[27] This suggests a much more complex ideology around sin than a simple binary one.[28]

Iblis stated that if he were left to his devices until Resurrection Day, he would lead the descendants of Adam astray and ensure that the majority of them obeyed him blindly rather than following the dictates of their Creator.[29] In this account, in which Adam should be read as standing in for all of humankind rather than simply as a solitary figure, we see the origins of Satan and his role in leading weak and foolish human beings astray, tempting them away from the "straight path" created by God for them with the intention that they should follow it, and join him in heaven after the Day of Judgement. Satan is clearly portrayed as a trouble-maker who brings nothing but discord and problems to the Earth, and who acts against the best interests of human beings.[30]

---

21 Q. 7:12.
22 Q. 15:26.
23 Bodman, 2011, 203.
24 Rahman, 1989, 121.
25 Rahman, 1989, 124.
26 Bodman, 2011, 24
27 Q 15:26; 15:28.
28 Bodman, 2011, 35.
29 Q. 17:62.
30 Q. 17:53.

The Ultimate Reward: Eschatology in the Qur'ān

For many Muslims, the terms "Iblis" and "Satan" are used interchangeably, and in everyday language both refer to the Devil or Satan. Taken from a more academic perspective, however, they have distinct meanings whereby "Iblis" refers to the manifestation of evil, while "Satan" refers to the agent who carries out evil deeds. The origins of the name "Iblis" have been the subject of much scholarly debate over the years. Linguists from the west have often posited the idea that the term may originate in the Greek word "diābolos," from which "devil" was derived. Variations on this Greek term are still found in many European languages. However, there is scant evidence in favour of this strongly Eurocentric view, while there is much to suggest that many of the motifs and concepts embedded in Greek lore actually sprang from the South-Arabian civilisation that preceded the heights of Greek culture. It seems more than likely that the term "diābolos" actually comes from an ancient Arabic term for Fallen Angel, which springs from the verb "ablasa," which indicates despair, the loss of hope, or being broken-spirited. Some linguists point to the fact that the noun "diābnolos," used as "slanderer," comes from the verb "diāballen," which means "to throw (something) across." However, given the fact that Greeks tended to adapt foreign names to their own language, it seems likely that when they heard the word "Iblis," they identified it with the familiar term "diābnolos."[31]

The Qur'ān makes frequent reference to Iblis, who is invariably described as an enemy of humankind, and as despised by God for his disobedience. When he refused to prostrate himself before Adam, as God had instructed him to do, God described him as "arrogant" and ordered him to leave, stating, "among the humiliated shalt thou be!"[32] Iblis requested a "respite" from God's judgement until the Day of Resurrection, which was granted, and asserted his intention of lying "in ambush" along the "straight way" that God had created for human beings, stating:

---

31 Asad, 1984, 204.
32 Q. 7:13.

And shall most certainly fall upon them openly as well as in a manner beyond their ken, and from their right and from their left; and most of them Thou wilt find ungrateful.[33]

In response to Iblis's assertion of his intention to lie in wait for human beings and to lead them astray, God banishes him, referring to him as "disgraced and disowned" and states that He will "fill hell" with anyone who follows him.[34] In this respect, the story of Iblis appears to be the story of someone who defies His Lord and who will be duly punished as a result, as well as a cautionary tale, warning human beings of the fate that awaits them in the afterlife if they do not do as they have been instructed by God.

At a first glance, Iblis/Satan appears to be a direct adversary of God. However, the Qur'ān also states on multiple occasions that nothing can happen unless God wills it. It points out that every prophet sent by God has had to deal with the forces of evil, manifested both as humans who spoke out against them and as spirits who spread delusions. This could not have happened without God's knowledge.[35] Clearly, then, while Iblis defied God and stated his intention of leading human beings astray, this was part of a greater plan that came from God Himself, for if He had willed it, God would have ensured that Iblis simply could not defy him.

Some philosophers have suggested that the presence of evil in the world is a condition of the presence of God, and that without evil, there could be no corresponding good,[36] for doing good would be essentially meaningless if there was nothing to compare it to. As God is omnipotent, this is clearly a false conclusion to draw, for God alone determines what exists and what does not, and thus, of necessity, antedates evil. So why did God permit Iblis to defy him, and to continue carrying out his intention of leading people astray?

---

33 Q. 7:17.
34 Q. 7:18.
35 Q. 6:112.
36 Mackie, 1999, 43.

The Qur'ān describes the nuanced role of Satan (Iblis) in its discussion of what will happen on the Day of Judgement, when each human being who has ever lived will stand before God and will be judged by Him on the basis of how he or she conducted themselves during their lifetime. On that momentous occasion, Satan will point out that God promised His people many things, which have come true, and that Iblis also promised much, but that his promises were meaningless. While he has the intention of leading people astray, ultimately his power comes not from him but from them, for they themselves decided to follow him and his empty promises rather than God, and they themselves decided that his power was comparable to God's. These people, who commit acts of evil rather than the good deeds commanded by God, will suffer terribly in consequence,[37] and all the blame will be theirs. On the Day of Judgement, when humankind is finally shown the truth and made aware of all of their actions, including the sins committed, those who are condemned to hell will attempt to justify why they had committed sins, on the grounds that part of their inner selves ('qārin' – intimate companion) guided them to do so.[38] Commenting on this matter, Asad said:

> ... "his intimate companion" where it may be taken as denoting man's moral consciousness, in the present instance, the "speaker" is obviously its counterpart, namely, the complex of the sinner's instinctive urges and inordinate, unrestrained appetites summarized in the term 'sā'iq' (that which drives) and often symbolized as shaytān ("Satan" or "Satanic forces").[39]

Iblis makes many promises to human beings, but the Qur'ān reveals that he never seeks to justify humans' belief that he is in any way the equal of God. Conversely, where the Qur'ān depicts him as speaking, he refers to God as "Sustainer," in a clear admission of God's supreme power over him and all

---

37 Q. 14:22.
38 Q. 50:21-7.
39 Asad, 1984, 799, note 19.

other creatures.[40] Indeed, he is quoted as saying "I fear God"[41] and never states that he is God's equal.[42] (an absurd idea). Iblis's own, very limited, power comes from his attempts to make human beings' decisions to engage in sinful behaviour seem "goodly to them."[43] Because of their own weakness, and the decisions they take to ignore God's commands, they are persuaded that they are right to do whatever they want, for their own selfish reasons. By thus following Satan's path, they implicitly suggest that Satan's blandishments are as meaningful and important as the messages sent by God.[44] In this way they insult God twice; once by refusing to follow His path, and again by suggesting that a lesser being should be considered with the same respect and awe as He.

In the Qur'ān, God Himself states that Satan has no power beyond that given to him by the mortals who decide to follow his path and not the righteous one provided by God,[45] and he asserts His authority, stating that it is His will that Satan has no power to entice those who are truly aware of God and His message to us. Even though Satan apparently rebelled against God, this was part of God's master plan for the world. Satan fulfils the role of giving human beings the opportunity to exercise the free will that is their gift from their Creator and, in so doing, to choose whether to live good lives, or lives full of evil-doing. Satan poses no threat whatsoever to God, whose power is beyond understanding, and who could vanquish him in a moment, but his intentions are to lead human beings astray, so human beings have within their ability the capacity to reject or be won over by him.[46]

Thus, we can see the presence of Satan among us as part of God's eternal plan: "Art thou not aware that We have let loose all (manner of) satanic forces upon those who deny the truth – (force) that impel them (towards sin) with

---

40 Q. 15:36; 8:48; 59:16.
41 Q. 8:48; 59:16.
42 Q. 7:20.
43 Q. 6:43; 8:48; 16:63; 27:24; 29:38.
44 Asad, 1984, 375-6.
45 Q. 15:39-43.
46 Rahman, 1989, 123.

strong impulsion."[47] Islamic scholars believe that this verse refers to the capacity of human beings to exercise free will and choose to follow either God or Satan. The same human beings are given ample warnings by God that they should not follow Satan, who is described as their "foe," who will ensure that those who follow him will end up in hell,[48] and as a being whose only desire is to cause problems and hatred among human populations, while enticing them away from worshipping God.[49] Typical verses read as follows:

> O you who believe! do not follow the footsteps of Satan for whosoever follows his footsteps, he commands obscenity and evil, and but for God's favour upon you and His mercy, none of you could ever be pure, but God purifies whomsoever He wills – He is hearing and knowing.[50]

And:

> O children of Adam! let not Satan seduce you, just as he caused your ancestors to be expelled from the Garden by rending them away from their clothing in order to expose their private parts—indeed, he and his ilk see you whence you do not see them; We have made Satan's friends of the unbelievers.[51]

The Qur'ān also contrasts God's commands and will, which are always reasonable and rational, with the promises of Satan, which are irrational and are embedded in superstition or in engaging in practices that are bad for us, such as consuming alcohol or drugs, or gambling. While these practices may seem alluring at first, they make us unwell, both physically and spiritually. They are

---

47 Q. 19:83.
48 Q. 2:208; 43:62; 35:6.
49 Q. 5:91.
50 Q. 24:21.
51 Q. 7:27.

practices that will lead us towards poverty and ill-health, and that will impact negatively on our families, while those who follow God's law can be assured that He will forgive them for their weaknesses and bless them with His bounty and with everlasting life.[52] As God wants nothing more than the best for us, clearly, He does not want us to engage in behaviours that do us no good.

We need look no further than the Qur'ān for advice and counsel on this matter, for the book provides us with many warnings about Satan and his intentions for us, summed up in the following verse: "Satan is your enemy, so take him for your enemy."[53] It is important to remember that Satan is essentially weak in comparison with the awesome powers of God. He can never force anyone to commit evil acts, but can only tempt them, while God can make anyone do whatever He wishes. Human beings alone are the ones to decide how they plan to live their lives because they have been blessed with free will. The onus is on men and women to make wise and godly choices in the face of this temptation.[54]

The Nature of Evil

Many people, scholars, clerics and laymen, have struggled with the knowledge that their ever-loving God could countenance the presence of evil among the creatures who represent His most cherished Creation. Islamic tradition speaks of the early Muslims, grappling with this very issue, who asked Muhammad about the nature of evil. Muhammad is said to have replied that there were "satans" among human beings, and that they were even more evil than those found among the spirits. For Muhammad, true evil lay, above all, in those who refused to listen to the voice of God as revealed to His prophet and, even worse, attempted to lead others astray. In Islam in general, the concept of evil is a complex one; more so than in its sister faiths of Judaism and Christianity,

---

52 Q. 2:268.
53 Q. 35:6.
54 Rahman, 1989, 127.

which tend to see good and evil in very simple binary terms,[55] and to present Satan, the personification of evil, almost as if he were as powerful as God Himself[56] – an idea that is utterly ludicrous to scholars and thoughtful followers of Islam, who believe that, as God created everything, nothing can compare to Him.

In discussing the nature of evil, the Qur'ān makes it clear that the root of evil lies in ignoring God's message and choosing to follow Satan instead.[57] It makes reference to the folly and evil of worshipping idols, using imagery associated with practices common among pre-Islam Arabs, when cattle were often sacrificed to false gods in acts that introduced "corruption" to God's perfect universe,[58] and were therefore evil in and of themselves, as attempts to interfere with God's plan.[59] Choosing idolatry when one has had the opportunity to hear God's message to the world is clearly an example of following Satan's path, rather than the creator's.

People often think of evil in terms of what people do, but it often lies more in what we decide *not* to do, when we make the conscious decision not to do as God has instructed. Satan tempts us not to engage in charity and good deeds, filling us with doubt about the wisdom of doing so, and suggesting that doing good will make us poor. Evil promises selfishness, greed and self-indulgence, while God urges us to act with kindness, mercy and charity towards our fellow human beings, and shows us that true generosity never goes unrewarded. Those who are truly wise will choose God's path, while those who succumb to their own inner weakness are likely to be tempted to commit evil through their own omissions,[60] and will certainly be abandoned by Satan, who will be quick to point out that he never claimed to be God,

---

55 Bodman, 2011, 103.
56 Bodman, 2011, 105.
57 Q. 3:175.
58 Q. 4:119.
59 Abduh, 1999, 345-7.
60 Ali, 1934, 123.

whom he fears.[61] Satan's only power lies in the fact of human weakness, for he can only lead when people let him into their hearts and refuse to heed the word of God.

In denying God through their words and deeds, by disobeying Him and wandering far from the path of righteousness that He has provided us, humans are committing evil. Thus, evil is the absence of good, and a counterpart to it, but it is also a great deal more.[62] Evil is a matter of choice and free will, and the conscious decision on the part of individual women and men to turn their backs on God and act in opposition to His wishes and His wisdom. This conscious evil can be referred to as moral evil,[63] with the clear implication that it is a choice, and a deliberate turning away from the path of justice. Decision-making tends to create behavioural patterns in our lives. Each time we carry out an evil act, it makes it easier for us to do this again the next time, and each time we carry out an act of goodness, the path is paved towards further goodness in the future.[64]

Western scholars have sometimes associated evil with difficult aspects of life, such as pain and suffering, which is contrasted with "good," seen as pleasure and happiness.[65] To do so is to miss the point, however. As flesh-and-blood creatures, we are part of God's Creation, and our time on earth is inherently limited. In this context, death and disease are part of the picture. Death cannot be seen as evil, because it is simply the passing from one state to the next.[66] Disease cannot be seen as evil, because it comes from nature, and because being ill continues to present us with many opportunities to do good, in how we react to our trying circumstances, or in giving people the opportunity to respond to those who are unwell with God-given compassion.[67]

---

61 Q. 59:16; 8:48; 14:22; Ali, 1934, 1722.
62 Mackie, 1999, 44.
63 Swinburne, 1999, 53.
64 Swinburne, 1999, 55.
65 Mackie, 1999, 46.
66 Swinburne, 1999, 52.
67 Swinburne, 1999, 60.

True evil lies in the moral realm, when men and women are confronted with decisions to be made, and choose the path away from God, rather than the one that will lead them directly to Him.

Avoiding Evil

While the question of the presence of evil in a perfect universe is a perplexing one, avoiding evil is a simple matter, and God has given us many opportunities to follow His path. In this, we humans are unique, for we alone have been given the ability and responsibility to make our moral decisions between good and evil.[68]

Even before Muhammad brought His message in all its perfection in the form of the Qur'ān, God had provided His people with prophets, such as Moses and Jesus, who had brought His truth before them, teaching them the correct way to behave, and instructing them to worship the God Who had created them. Those who exercised their free will and refused to listen engaged in evil-doing, while those who heeded God's word avoided contact with evil, and pleased Him.[69]

Free will, which allows us to engage in evil, can just as easily be exercised in deliberately choosing to do good and follow God's law.[70] God, in all His wisdom, has created us with the innate capacity to choose whether to follow Him or listen to the false promises of Satan. After all, what meaning could we possibly ascribe to virtuous acts that we had not chosen to engage in, but that we simply enacted as though we were puppets, carrying out God's will without even thinking about it?

Our world is full of occasions when we must choose between the right and the wrong path. Those of us who ensure that we are at all times on guard against the perils of moral danger are less likely to commit evil, for we are alert

---

68 Rahman, 1989, 123.
69 Q. 22:52.
70 Mackie, 1999, 48.

to the ways in which Satan works against us:⁷¹ "Indeed, upon my servants you will be able to exercise no influence, but only those errant ones who follow you."⁷²

If we find ourselves tempted by Satan and his promises, the answer is simple: by turning to God and seeking refuge with Him, we will find the truth that will set us free,⁷³ because Satan has no power over those who follow God, and recognise that only God is all-powerful.⁷⁴ While God will certainly punish those who choose to follow Satan despite the many opportunities He has given us to stay on the right path, His earnest wish for us is to avoid evil, do good, and live forever with Him.⁷⁵ He is loving and merciful, and His desire is for His people to choose wisely, live righteously, and come home to Him on the Day of Resurrection.

We will start to find our inner strength, in which our ability to resist evil lies, when we recognise our inherent weakness. By embracing humility and the overarching power of God, we can avoid committing acts of evil, and dedicate ourselves to Him, from Whom all goodness flows.⁷⁶

---

71 Rahman, 1989, 124.
72 Q. 15:42; 17:65.
73 Q. 7:200; 43:36; 23:97-98.
74 Q. 16:98-100.
75 Q. 43:36-38; 41:25.
76 Asad, 1984, 345, note 53.

CHAPTER 5

❖ ❖ ❖

The Signs of the Hour

A RANGE OF religions discuss the matter of the end of the world, a subject matter known in theology as "eschatology," a term that was first coined in the sixteenth century to describe the scholarly discussion of the end of the world.[1] None have ever managed to pinpoint the likely time for this event with any precision. Since the beginning, Christians have predicted that the end of the world is an inevitability, and have made this a central pillar of their belief system. Numerous splinter groups of major world religions have had the experience of predicting the timing of the Day of Judgement at various points in history, only to see its supposed date coming and going with nothing of note happening at all – frequently to the great embarrassment of those who had predicted it most fervently. Famously, the Zoroastrians made a precise prediction as to when the world was going to end, and then had to reinterpret their scriptures when it did not happen! Here, we will explore the urgent matter of what Islam has to say on the subject.

The End of the World

Like many other major world religions, Islam discusses the matter of the end of the world. In fact, along with belief in God, revelation, the prophets and the angels, holding a belief in the inevitability of a "last day" is actually one of the five essential tenets of the Islamic faith, while as much as ten percent of the Qur'ān discusses this essential and urgent matter.[2] In absolute terms,

---

1 Definition provided by Webster's Online Dictionary.
2 Lange, 2016, 37.

the amount of space used in the Qur'ān to discuss matters of eschatology is greater than that dedicated to discussing the prophets.[3] Clearly, then, the discussion of this important topic is actually fundamental to Islamic thought. Therefore, an understanding of the implications is essential to anyone interested in understanding Islam.

In its intense focus on themes of judgement and the afterlife, the Qur'ān has much in common with Christianity.[4] Themes of judgement, heaven and hell are particularly strong in the earlier revelations received by Muhammad, when he was still in Mecca.[5] (Later revelations were received during his time in Medina, another city in Arabia, where the early Muslim community lived after leaving Mecca and as they became more established as a faith group and a community.) At first, those who heard Muhammad's speak were confused by the Qur'ān's descriptions of rewards offered in the afterlife, and thought that he was referring to material goods that they could enjoy while they were still alive.[6] Some critics ridiculed Muhammad's message of everlasting life with one such, named Ubayy, crumbling a dry bone in his hand and sarcastically ordering Muhammad to bring it back to life.[7] It took some time before the earliest Muslims could fully understand the implications of the Qur'ān's teaching about life in the next world, and they are depicted as struggling with the idea of resurrection[8] and asking Muhammad how it could be that humans could be brought back to life, saying, "When we are bones and mortal remains, will we be raised up in some flesh creation?"[9]

Although Qur'ān discusses the end of the world in some detail, and asserts that human beings certainly will be born again, it gives no indication of when this event is likely to take place, underlining the fact that only God

---

3 Tottoli, 2006, 475.
4 Buck, 2006, 30.
5 Madigan, 2006, 90; Neuwirth, 2006, 104.
6 Rustomji, 2008, 10.
7 Rustomji, 2008, 13.
8 Saeed, 2006, 43.
9 Q. 17:19.

knows when His Day of Judgement will happen. However, if members of the early Islamic community could know that, after more than fourteen centuries, modern Muslims are still waiting for the signs that will tell them that the end of time is approaching, they would be very surprised![10] The Qur'ān makes it perfectly clear that nobody, not even God's messenger Muhammad, knows when the end of the world will actually happen. It addresses Muhammad directly, saying:

> They question you (Muhammad) about the hour (Resurrection Day), when will it come to pass? But how could you tell anything about it? Only your Lord knows when it will come. Your duty is but to warn those who fear it. It will be on the day when they see it, as if they had tarried but a single evening or at most till the following morn.[11]

Regardless of how much human beings speculate, they will not know when the Day of Judgement is coming until it actually happens. There is, however, no doubt that the end of the world *will* come, and that it will take place at the precise time that has already been determined by God. Clearly, the implications are that we have a responsibility to be prepared for the Day of Judgement at all times, and that everything we do in our lives should ensure that we are always ready to meet He who created us. This view is also taken in the Christian scriptures, for example in the following verse:

> But of that day and that Hour knoweth no man, no, not the angels which are in heaven, neither the Son, but the Father. Take ye heed, watch and pray, for ye know not when the time is.[12]

A well-known hadith represents a Bedouin asking Muhammad about when the end of the world will come. Muhammad did not attempt to answer, but

---

10 Idleman Smith and Yazbeck Haddad 2002, 65-6.
11 Abu-Hamdiyyah, 2000, 55; Q. 79:42-6. See also Q. 7:187-8.
12 Mark xiii, 32-3.

affirmed that it would certainly happen one day, and asked what the man had done to prepare himself for it. Underlining the message of that one should always be ready for the Day of Judgement, the Qur'ān affirms that as only God knows, it could start at any moment.[13] It is perfectly clear in pointing out that, in this life, we are living simply in what it describes as a "temporary abode" whose duration will be fleeting in comparison to the eternal afterlife.[14] For these reasons, we should all ensure that we are *always* ready to meet our Creator. When that happens, it will not matter if we were female or male, rich or poor, black or white, because the only important thing will be how we have conducted ourselves during our lives.

Signs and Portents

According to various traditions (but not to the Qur'ān, which should be viewed as the ultimate authority on such matters as the last, and ultimate, book of revelation sent to humanity via one of God's prophets), important signs indicating the imminent arrival of the Day of Judgement are as follows:

1. A false messiah will come, and will last on Earth for forty days.
2. Jesus will return to earth, kill the false messiah and establish taxes, after which the Earth will experience a time of abundance.
3. Gog and Magog will appear on Earth, bringing with them corruption, drought and famine.
4. The "beast of the Earth" will appear.
5. The sun will rise in the west.

What are we to make of these varied traditions? Simply, they were invented by storytellers over the years and cannot be compared to the revelations received by Muhammad, and recorded in the Qur'ān. Even a brief exploration of them reveals that they make no sense, and are folkloric elements that cannot be

---

13 Q. 33:63.
14 Lange, 2016, 38.

taken seriously, as entertaining as they may be. For example, we know from history, and it is mentioned in several places in the Qur'ān, that Jesus died many years before Muhammad was born and was a mortal being, who cannot "return to earth" in any normal sense of the term.[15] Jesus was an important prophet and he is held in great esteem by Islam, but he was not, as some believe, the son of God, while God alone will determine the form and outcome of the Day of Judgement.

However, the Qur'ān does discuss the things that will happen as part of the process involved in the end of the world. Collectively, these signs are known as ishārāt as-sā'ah, and they are cited in numerous verses as constituting proof of God's supremacy over the Earth and all it contains. Some of the most dramatic of the Qur'ānic verses that discuss the end of the world describe events that will destroy the Earth and devastate the natural process and cycles of nature to which we are so accustomed that most of us barely give them a second thought. They describe a dreadful vision, of a world in which the sun has been darkened, the stars have lost their light, the mountains have vanished, "the she-camel big with young, about to give birth, are left untended" (in other words, are neglected by their owners when they are at their most vulnerable), when all the animals gather together, when the seas boil over, when all humans are expected to account for their deeds, when "the girl-child that was buried alive is made to ask, for what crime she had been slain," when the deeds of human beings are examined, heaven becomes visible and the flames of hell are burning bright.[16] Clearly, the Qur'ān is painting a picture of the world when the laws of nature as we understand them no longer function. Everything we know and understand will disappear, and the world of the spirit will be revealed before us.

It is telling that this scene starts with the sun, for without the sun there can be no life. The most remote celestial body in our solar system, the sun provides us with the light, heat and energy that we and all other living beings require to survive. In the hours of darkness, we can see the faint light

---

15 Q. 61:6; 3:55; 5:117.
16 Q. 81:1-14.

emanated from the billions of other stars in the sky, and we have learned to use these stars for the purpose of navigation.[17] These, too, will simply disappear as though they had never been there at all. Here on Earth, the mountains that appear so massive and eternal will simply vanish "as if they had been a mirage,"[18] and will be scattered far and wide, leaving the earth "level and bare."[19] The Earth, and indeed the whole universe as we humans have always understood it, will be utterly changed.[20] Thereafter, because the world will become completely unfamiliar to us, beyond anything that we have ever experienced, or can even imagine, all discussion is carried out in allegorical terms.[21] As all this turmoil takes place, the very oceans will "boil over" and cover all the landmarks on Earth. As we experience them, the oceans typically observe the laws of nature, interrupted only occasionally by a relatively minor (in apocalyptic terms) unusual event, such as the devastating tsunami of 2004. The destruction of the natural world as we know it will be so complete as the Day of Judgement approaches that even the apparently eternal waters of the ocean will cease to behave as we expect or have experienced in the past.[22]

It is interesting to note that the Day of Judgement is described in the Qur'ān essentially as reversing the order of Creation. The heavens, which the Qur'ān describes as consisting of seven layers, are removed, rolled up, and destroyed. The stars fall and become dark, and the sun and moon are covered by darkness,[23] as the sky is "cleft asunder."[24] This description of the end of the world, which is described in rich, lyrical language, can be understood both literally and allegorically. The stars will "fall" (in other words, we will not be able to see them from our vantage point on earth) but also, we will see the

---

17 Q. 6:97.
18 Q. 78:20.
19 Q. 20:105-7.
20 Q. 14:48.
21 Asad 1984, 380, note 63.
22 Ali, 1934, 1904-5.
23 Q. 75:9.
24 Q. 82:1-3.

sudden irrelevance of those things that in our everyday life we associated with honour, wealth, and comfort. In darkness, then, the Earth steadily breaks up, its mountains are levelled and the planet is reduced to dust in its totality, while bodies of water come together, mingling salt and fresh water as the ocean fills the planet. At some point, every living thing will perish, leaving nothing but God at the heart of the universe.[25] Thus, the Day of Judgement will be a terrifying event, for the virtuous as much as for the sinful.

Eschatology and Modern Understanding

Some contemporary scholars and scientists have tried to bring together Qur'ānic teaching with what we have learned of the world through scientific enterprise. In this light, some have tried to understand the natural phenomena described in the Qur'ān in a scientific way, looking at what we know about the atmosphere, the nature of magnetic forces, and life. We often find that the Qur'ān demonstrates an understanding of the reality of the natural world that was only uncovered by science many centuries after its revelation.[26] In this light, how are we to interpret what the Qur'ān has to say about the end of the world? Simply put, the Qur'ān has demonstrated its scientific understanding and veracity on multiple occasions. Even if, to sceptical modern ears, its account of the ways in which the end of the world will come to pass seem improbable, who are we to doubt it, when it has been proven correct time and time again?

At the time of writing, we are witnessing the devastating result of our species' environmental mismanagement of the beautiful world that God created for us, and that contains everything we need to live healthy, and happy lives. As individuals, as communities, and as nations, we would do well to heed the lessons for life embedded in the Qur'ān and abide by them to the absolute best of our ability.

---

25 Q. 28:88; 55:26-7.
26 Idleman Smith and Yazbeck Haddad, 2002, 128.

CHAPTER 6

❖ ❖ ❖

The Ultimate Abode

IN ALL OF His revelations to humanity, God has taken pains to remind human beings that the Earth on which they live is just a temporary dwelling place that He has created for them and that, even if they fear death, they should know that the next life will be "better and more enduring,"[1] and utterly incomparable to anything that they can even imagine with their limited human understanding. This simple fact is at the heart of what the Qur'ān teaches, and provides a context for all of its other messages. It is the motivation behind the work that the most diligent Muslim scholars carry out in their quest to better understand God and His Creation. In this way, they are given the opportunity to achieve true happiness, or the essence of what it means to be truly human.[2]

The Qur'ān points out that this message was brought to humanity not just by the prophet Muhammad, but also by earlier prophets such as Abraham, Moses, and Jesus. Thus, we can see that humanity was given many opportunities to learn the truth about God's intentions for them and their ultimate destiny, and that this crucial message has required reiteration at diverse points in history. We can also clearly see that the fundamental elements of faith are shared among Islam, Christianity and Judaism, all of which subscribe to some of God's most basic messages. This fact is recognised by the Qur'ān, which refers to Christians and Jews as "people of the book" in multiple passages and urges Muslims to respect them so long as they observe the teachings sent to them by God. Indeed, the Qur'ān indicates that God intentionally

---
1 Q. 87:16-9.
2 Chittick, 1994, 158.

created human beings in a range of faith and ethnic groups, bound to adhere to slightly different laws when it comes to their behaviour:

> And unto thee (O Prophet) have we vouchsafed this divine writ, setting forth the truth, confirming the truth of whatever there still remains of earlier revelations and determining what is true therein. Judge, then, between the followers of earlier revelation in accordance with what God has bestowed from on high, and do not follow their errant views, forsaking the truth that has come unto thee. Unto everyone one of you have We appointed a (different) law and way of life. And if God had so willed, He could surely have made you all one single community: but (He willed it otherwise) in order to test you by means of what He has vouchsafed unto you. Vie, then, with one another in doing good works! Unto God you all must return; and then He will make you truly understand all that on which you were wont to differ.[3]

However, while the so-called New Testament, which tells the story of Jesus, also refers to the next world and incorporates ideas about the Day of Judgement, it differs from the other texts insofar as it tells the story of Jesus in the third person, rather than relating the message of God as received by him as a prophet. The Qur'ān, which is the most recent, and the ultimate, book of revelation, contains all we need to know about God's plans for humanity. While, from the very start of revelation, Muhammad had been perfectly clear in recognising and honouring the fact that the Jews and the Christians had both previously received word from God, and are in many respects kindred spirits to Muslims, he was also clear in establishing Islam as a whole new faith that built on, rather than merely developing from, what had gone before.[4] In other words, Islam is not a mere complementary faith, but a new set of answers to the eternal questions posed by humankind.

---

3 Q. 5:48.
4 Rahman, 1989, 163.

The Ultimate Abode

News of Heaven Received by Muhammad

Clearly, God's message about heaven and the hereafter was received as a revelation by the prophet Muhammad, who did not hesitate to pass on the good news to his followers. In the Qur'ān, Muhammad is instructed to tell his wives that if all they want is to enjoy a comfortable life now, God would provide them with one, but that if they truly worship God and listen to His word as revealed to Muhammad, they will be amply rewarded in the next life.[5] To put this into some historical context, this revelation was received at a time when life had started to get easier for the young Muslim community, which suffered terrible persecution (up to and including torture and death) in its very early days. They had managed to win the agricultural Khaybar area, and the poverty and uncertainty of the early days had started to recede as they became gradually more prosperous and less vulnerable to attack from more powerful groups. Some Muslim families even began to become wealthy. However, to the consternation of Muhammad's wives, their lives remained quite harsh and difficult, because Muhammad insisted that he and his family should make do with just the basics because of his belief that they should not enjoy a standard of living greater than that of the poorest of his followers. Understandably, Muhammad's wives could not immediately understand why they had to live in such a humble manner, when other Muslim women were beginning to enjoy relative comfort, and it rankled with them to have to "make do" when other people were prospering all around them. Why, they reasoned, should they be punished because they were married to the Prophet? God's revelation, as mentioned above, clarified that the best thing they could do was to choose God and to live with Him in the next life, rather than striving to obtain material possessions in the here and now. As they came to understand His message, these women, among the earliest Muslims and the closest to Muhammad, came ever closer to God as they swore to do their best to ensure that they would live with Him in the next world.[6]

---

5 Q. 33:28-9.
6 Asad, 1984, 644.

The Ultimate Reward: Eschatology in the Qur'ān

Throughout the Qur'ān, heaven and earth are not discussed separately, but in relation to one another, to underline the fact that neither exists in a vacuum, and that each is an aspect of God's Creation, and of His divine plan. Even the words that are used to describe each place or state of being make sense only in juxtaposition, such as "the first and the last" or "the nearer and the farther." Heaven is never discussed as a discrete topic, as we are given to understand that believing in the afterlife is a basic tenet of Islam. To believe in God is to know that He has plans for us that extend far beyond this world. God describes his world and its transitory pleasures as "a play and a passing delight" and "a beautiful show." He points out that everything that we know eventually dies and withers, while God and His eternal forgiveness will last forever.[7] This is not to say that God is suggesting that we should despise our beautiful world or look down on it as something that is incomparable to what will come next. After all, He created it for us, it is our home, and it has a higher purpose.[8] The problem is that so many people live their lives without giving a moment's thought to the fact that God has created so many wonderful things for them and has given them more opportunities than they can count to please and serve Him. Rather than using this life to prepare for their eternal reward, many people use it to play, to waste their time with pointless frivolities, and to try to accumulate as much wealth as they can during their brief lifetimes, as if they thought that they would be able to bring it with them when they die. Just as all life eventually withers and turns to dust, so will all humanity, and those who have not used their time on earth wisely, to give praise and thanks to God and live in a way that pleases Him, will not join Him in the next life,[9] as they have shown through their own actions that they are not worthy of doing so.

---

7 Q. 57:20.
8 Q. 38:27; 23:115.
9 Ali, 1934, 1695; Q. 30:7.

Heaven as a Reward for the Just

One of the clearest, and most fundamental, messages of the Qur'ān is that we will be rewarded in the next life for the way in which we have conducted ourselves in this one, and that true salvation will be given to the just in the next life.[10] God is giving and merciful to all of us in this life, but only those who conduct themselves as He wishes will be rewarded in the next. Those who live according to His holy law, and who devote themselves to and worship Him will be given more in the afterlife than they can ever imagine, while those who work ceaselessly for material gain in this world may earn what they are looking for (although they may not) but will not be given any special treatment in the afterlife.[11] In this way, the concept of heaven remains at the forefront of the person's mind throughout their lifetime, providing them with a guiding force that makes it easier for them to live as God wants them to.[12]

The Qur'ān reminds us that the many wonderful things that God has blessed us with on earth are merely for our temporary pleasure, and that the reward that awaits the righteous and the just in the afterlife is far greater, and will last forever rather than just for a fleeting moment in time, as we experience our lives here on earth. Those who do not engage in sinful actions, who forgive those who offend them, who are charitable towards those who are needy, and who are steadfast in praying to the God who created them; these are the ones who will receive their eternal reward in heaven.[13] Whether or not they were able to accumulate wealth in this life will matter not at all compared to whether or not they strove to be just and fair in everything they did. The Qur'ān frequently exhorts humankind to behave as God wishes them to. It is also perfectly clear in laying down His law and explaining exactly what God expects of His people, while reminding us that anything we experience in this life, whether pleasurable or challenging, is temporary and represents a mere moment in time compared to eternity.

---

10 Khalil, 2013, 3.
11 Q. 42:20.
12 Rustomji, 2008, 40.
13 Q. 42:36-9.

The Ultimate Reward: Eschatology in the Qur'ān

How can we recognise those who live according to God's law, and how can we nourish those qualities in ourselves? The Islamic scholar Yusuf Ali has outlined nine crucial characteristics of true believers:

1. They have faith in God.
2. Having faith in God, they also have trust in Him, and turn to God's holy law for guidance, rather than striving towards worldly values.
3. Although no human is entirely without sin, they avoid committing grievous sins and always conduct themselves in a decent manner.
4. Even when they are treated very badly by others, they are always ready to forgive.
5. They are always open to see and contemplate God's signs, to listen to the word of God and to do their best to follow His path.
6. They regularly pray to and praise God.
7. In life, they conduct themselves in an open manner, and make important decisions together with people of interest. For instance, decisions concerning the household are made between husband and wife, while decisions concerning business affairs are made between business partners, and so forth.
8. They are charitable towards those who are less well-off than themselves.
9. When they are mistreated, they are brave and stand up for their rights within the limits provided to them by God.[14]

Material versus Eternal Reward

Throughout the Qur'ān, God contrasts our life in the here and now with what He has prepared for us next. He draws our attention not just to the material things that delight us, such as wealth and fine belongings, but also to the joy that parents find in their children. Even the extraordinary love and pride that parents find in their offspring is as nothing compared to the reward we

---

14 Ali, 1934, 1486-7.

will receive for good deeds, which the Qur'ān describes as the fruit that lasts forever.[15]

God warns us against allowing ourselves to care more about our material possessions and our relationships with the important people in our lives than about Him, just as He warned Muhammad's wives against longing for comfort at the expense of virtue. As He is the beginning and the end, our primary relationship is with Him and we should never forget it.[16] This is not to say that God wishes us to renounce all pleasure in the many wonderful things He has provided to us. Quite the reverse. Ever merciful, and ever bountiful, God is happy for us to take pleasure in the earthly delights, so long as we recognise Him as the ultimate creator of all things. All God asks in return is that we obey His holy law, and give just a fraction of what He has given us to the causes of charity and justice.

The Qur'ān states that the wonderful things that God has given us also provide us with the opportunity to show our true selves.[17] In the attitudes that we adopt towards the material objects and the many gifts bestowed on us by God, we are given the opportunity to show Him what we are made of. If we have been blessed with material riches, we can choose whether or not to give generously to charity, and whether or not to treat our employees with kindness and justice. In such decision-making, we show our true selves and we grant ourselves the possibility of true spiritual growth.

Almost invariably, when people refuse to listen to and believe in God's message, the underlying reason is their obsessive attachment to the material things of this world, together with an unwarranted pride in what they – having closed their eyes to God – like to consider their own great achievements.[18]

While it can be tempting to consider that those who enjoy great wealth and privilege in this world are the lucky ones, real wealth, and real privilege, will be the lot of those who strive at all times to do good in this world, as

---

15 Q. 18:46.
16 Q. 9:24.
17 Q. 18:7.
18 Asad, 1984, 438, note 5.

they will be the ones who will live with God in the next.[19] Knowing this, why would any of us consider ourselves satisfied with what we can receive now, when self-sacrifice and good deeds will earn us benefits that we can only begin to imagine in the next life?[20] It seems absurd to imagine that frivolities such as high end cars or fancy jewellery can compare in any way with the wonders that await us, if we live in a way that pleases God.

The life story of Muhammad reveals some examples of people who were tempted to indulge in their own comforts rather than following the word of God. In one instance, Muhammad received news that the Byzantines, who then led a great empire, had become unsettled by how quickly Islam was growing in Arabia, and had put together an army to fight against the early Muslims, whom they had identified as a threat to their way of life and supremacy in the region. This left the Muslims with two choices: Either they could go with Muhammad to defend themselves and their beliefs, or they could stay put in the hope that it would all blow over. Some of them objected to travelling in the heat of the summer and on the grounds that they would miss the harvest, and would have to endure a year of hardship as a result. The message for them was that it is better to endure a little hardship now in exchange for unceasing reward with God in heaven. In this context, they were brought to understand that enduring a trek in the heat, or failing to gather all of this year's harvest in a timely manner, was little to ask of a people who had been offered an eternal reward with God in heaven and who had His promise that He would protect them.

We are too easily dazzled by the apparent glamour of worldly accomplishments, to the extent that we often fail to see such things for what they really are. In the Qur'ān, God urges us to look beyond surface appearances to see the truth, and to ponder why some foolish humans imagine that they have acquired mastery over the world and everything in it, when in reality God alone created the world, and continues to cherish and nourish it.[21] We fool ourselves

---

19 Q. 16:30.
20 Q. 9:38.
21 Q.10:24, 18:45.

if we believe that we can control even our little corner of the world, because nothing can happen without God's knowledge, and our ability to manipulate the world around us is strictly limited.

Conversely, those who live for God, and who are prepared to eschew the material pleasures of this life in exchange for eternity with Him, will be granted their wish.[22] For each of us, this can mean critically exploring the material things that we find most attractive, with a view to becoming free from our obsessions and better able to engage in self-sacrifice. When we do so, we know that God sees and hears all of our efforts, and that He will remember how hard we tried to live in the manner He desires.[23]

It is interesting to note that God reminds us that we should not care more about our "clan" that we do about Him. At the time of revelation, Arab society was organised around tribal units to which people owed their fealty. Today, most big societies are no longer tribal, but in modern times we can understand this teaching to denote the idea of the nation or national identity. All around the world, and throughout history, we have seen countless tragic examples of the awful things that happen when people put their national identity before anything else. Consider the appalling outcomes of the rise of Nazism in Germany, or the devastating massacres that took place in Rwanda, for example. In each case, the origin of these atrocities is found in the irrational belief that one group of people is inherently "better," and thus entitled to "more" than another. Sometimes these ideas are dressed up in false scientific theories that claim that certain racial or ethnic groups are more talented than others and thus deserve the right to decide others' fate. And yet what could be more stupid than to imagine that one group of people is inherently better than any other, simply because it follows a particular flag into battle, or speaks a particular language or looks a particular way? After all, we have all been placed on this earth by the same Creator, who loves us all equally, and wants only the best for us. At a time in which obsessive nationalism is once more on the march around the world, while our ability to create weapons of

---

22 Q. 4:74-7.
23 Q. 4:13.

mass destruction is greater than at any point in history, this message is more timely than ever. We must all remember that there are no nations, no tribes and no families in the afterlife and that, here on earth, there is much more to unite us than to divide us. We are all God's people and we will all be judged on an equal basis, depending on how we have conducted ourselves in life, as individuals and as societies.

While it can be difficult, with our limited human imaginations, to comprehend the enormity and majesty of the next world, if we trust in God and do our best to live as He has taught us, one day we will truly understand.

All are Truly Equal

Here on earth, it can sometimes seem that we were not all created equal. After all, some people are much wealthier than others, some are luckier, and some enjoy great health while others suffer. Some children are born into wealthy families and enjoy immense privilege from the moment they draw breath, while others are born into poverty and endure hardship from the start. Some are blessed with great natural talents of the intellect, and others struggle in this area all their lives. However, we all need to remember how important to is to bear in mind that our lives on earth are genuinely just fleeting moments in comparison to eternity, and that nobody, no matter how powerful, can bring any of their riches with them to the next world, while all of us are called by God to do whatever we can to ensure that the world is as equal as possible[24]. Rich and poor, male and female, nobody is truly capable of judging us but God. God, who has made everything for our benefit, certainly cannot be bribed, as unscrupulous officials in this lifetime may be:

> And leave to themselves all those who, beguiled by the life of this world, have made play and passing delights their religion, but remind

---

24 Sonn, 2006, 11.

them herewith that (in the life come) every human being shall be held in pledge for whatever wrong he has done, and shall have none to protect him from God, and none to intercede for him; and though he offer any conceivable ransom, it shall not be accepted from him.[25]

Above all, this verse reminds us of the fundamental equality of all women and men, which is a central tenet to Islam, despite the fact that Muhammad received his revelations in the context of an intensely patriarchal society in which any other form of social organisation was effectively unimaginable. The Qur'ān is perfectly clear in stating that men and women are utterly equal in the eyes of God, and that all who conduct themselves as He has dictated shall be blessed with their eternal reward in heaven:

> Those who have surrendered to God of males and females, those who believe in males and females, those who are sincere of males and females, those who are truthful of males and females, those who are patient of males and females, those who fear God of males and females, those who preserve their private parts [from indecency] of males and females, those who remember God often of males and females—God has prepared for them forgiveness and great reward.[26]

Indeed, the major division between people, as related in the Qur'ān, is not made on the basis of their gender, but according to how they live their lives on earth.

What, then, of the difference between the poor and the wealthy? While there is nothing wrong with material success per se, the Qur'ān is clear in stating that an obsession with material riches to the exclusion of developing a close relationship with God is certainly a bad thing. In other words, what really matters is not whether one is wealthy or not, but how one both chases

---

25 Q. 6:70, 7:51.
26 Q. 4: 124; 40:40; 16:97.

wealth and, on achieving it, manages it.[27] If we are wealthy, but live our lives well and use our wealth to further God's work – for example, by giving to charity – that is well and good. However, far too many become obsessed with wealth for its own sake, to the extent that it blinds them from seeing their true purpose in life and understanding that life is short compared to the eternity that they will spend in the afterlife. The Qur'ān refers to some of the wealthy traders of Mecca as being aware of the material things of life, but choosing to ignore the fact of God and His eternal existence. Here on earth, some people become utterly obsessed with material gain, to the point of treating materialism as their religion. But when the great day comes, all will be assessed by God according to their individual merits and demerits, and not on the basis of what possessions they managed to accumulate during their lifetimes. During our lives in earth, the Qur'ān also states that societies that allow themselves to sink into a moral torpor will tend to decline in prosperity, while those that maintain a clear understanding of God's message will tend to prosper.[28] Who could possibly imagine that God, the creator of everything we see around us, would ever be impressed by material possessions? On the Day of Judgement, regardless of whether we were rich or poor, successful or humble, all of those who have lived as God wishes will be brought before him and given their eternal reward with Him.[29] When that happens, those who spent their lifetimes convinced that material possessions were the only thing that would bring them true happiness will realise how utterly, and tragically, wrong they actually were. As an aside, it is important to note that while material poverty is certainly no barrier to salvation or eternal happiness, nor is it in any way a guarantee of it. What really matters is not whether we were rich or poor, but how we conducted ourselves during our lives.

In heaven, everyone who has earned the great honour of living there will be "rich" and happy. Of course, heavenly "riches" are not like riches here on

---

27 Rahman, 1989, 58.
28 Q. 20:124.
29 Q. 3:14-5.

earth. The Qur'ān describes this blissful state using language and analogies that would have resonated with the early Muslims, listing the sort of things that they would have prized and cherished in their lives: children, horses, land, and gold and silver. Of course, these descriptions of the afterlife should not be taken literally, but understood as a way of communicating with people in a particular place and time in their own language. Were the Qur'ān to be revealed today, to a contemporary listenership, we can assume that the analogies used would be drawn from our own experience too.

The fundamental equality of all in the afterlife is also underlined in the instructions in the Qur'ān that even prophets, who receive God's message and provide it to ordinary men and women, will be judged equally, and will not be given special treatment unless they have conducted themselves fairly and virtuously in their lives on earth.[30] Throughout the Qur'ān, any instructions that are given to the prophets should also be taken as applying to their followers, too. The prophets are instructed that, during their lifetimes, they have no right to keep slaves in the normal course of events, and that even prisoners taken in times of war should be released as soon as the war is over.[31] These instructions were given in a range of contexts, including that of the captives seized by the Muslim army at the Battle of Badr, which was one of the great breakthrough events in early Islamic history. While some of Muhammad's followers felt that the captives should be put to death in revenge for the ways in which they had conducted themselves in the past, and for rejecting the teachings of Islam, Abū Bakr, one of Muhammad's closest companions, realised that it would be better to forgive them, and in this way, give them the opportunity to realise the wonderful truth of Islam. As this action was exactly what God had ordered, as He is ever merciful, both the captors and the captives were given a chance to live out their lives and face their judgement from God on an equal footing.[32] The truth is that God grants

---

30 Q. 7:6-7.
31 Q. 47:4; 8:67-68.
32 Asad, 1984, 251, note 73.

all of us many opportunities to repent, change our ways, and come closer to Him and to our eternal reward.[33] Thus, it matters not to God whether we lose wars or win them, or succeed or fail to thrive in this life, because what really matters is how we conduct ourselves, and whether or not we deserve to pass from this life to His heavenly home.

---

33 Q. 8:70.

CHAPTER 7

Resurrection

IN ISLAM, THE promise that death is not the final act, and that human beings will be raised up by God and given a new life on the Day of Judgement, is a central element of theology and faith, and one that informs every other aspect of Islamic theology, thinking and guidance. The Qur'ān discusses the important topic of resurrection in great detail, describing it in vivid and colourful ways, as in the following verse:

> When trumpet is blown with a single blast and the earth and the mountains are lifted up and crushed with a single blow, then, on that Day, the terror shall come to pass, and heaven shall be split, for upon that Day it shall be very frail.[1]

The trumpet referred to here will be blown by the angel Israfil. The Qur'ān states that the trumpet will be blown again when the period of resurrection has come to an end:

> The Trumpet will (just) be sounded, when all that are in the heavens and on earth will swoon, except such as it will please Allah (to attempt). Then will a second one be sounded, when, behold, they will be standing and looking on.[2]

---

1 Q. 69:13-16; 74:8; 6:73; 23:101.
2 Q. 39:68.

Clearly, the reference here to the trumpet should be interpreted as a metaphor, and not as a literal description of someone blowing a trumpet. The reference to the first trumpet, when everything on the earth and in the heavens shall "swoon" is a way of indicating that all life as we know it today will come to an end, will simply cease to be, while the ways in which the laws of nature are observed will be utterly changed from what we know today. We should read the reference to the second trumpet blast as describing the Creation of a new world, completely different to anything we have ever seen before, and mentioned in the Qur'ān as follows: "The earth shall be changed into another earth, as shall be the heavens."[3]

What will this new world be like? While there is much that we cannot currently know, the Qur'ān explains that the new world that will come into being at this time will be very unlike the current one. It will be without death, inequality or injustice, all of which are unavoidable now. Into this new environment, every human being who has ever lived will be resurrected, and this is where they will be judged by God.[4] In other words, the "end of the world" does not in any way mean the annihilation of the universe, but its transformation into an utterly new form that we are not yet capable of understanding or imagining.[5] To understand how God's Creation can thus be utterly changed, it may help to envision an unfired clay pot being broken down and rendered again into a completely different form. The substance has not changed, but the form and purpose of the object are different.

The Qur'ān clearly asserts God's ability to do whatever He wills, including bringing people back to life, as will occur when resurrection takes place and the dead are returned to life so that they can stand before God to receive His judgement:

> Are, then, they (who deny the life to come) not aware that God, who has created the heavens and the earth and never been wearied by their

---

3 Q. 14:48.
4 Ali, 1934, 1417-8; notes 4343-4.
5 Asad, 1984, 482, note 90.

Creation, has also the power to bring the dead back to life? Yea, verily, He has the power to will anything.[6]

The Qur'ān is completely clear and unequivocal in its statements that assert that God has promised us everlasting life with Him, and that His promise is, by definition, realisable and true. Because of this, we are honour bound to listen to God's holy message, to be punished when we utter falsehoods, and to live in a way that shows our commitment to personal responsibility for our actions here on earth. Put simply, a belief in the absolute truth and inevitability of resurrection is essential, and to fail to believe is to fail to accept God's truth as it is revealed to and for us in the Qur'ān. Above all, this failure is a great personal loss for each person who refuses to listen to God's word, for they are depriving themselves of the greatest joy imaginable.

Understanding Resurrection

Whereas Islam and Christianity both subscribe to a belief in resurrection, and hold this belief to be a fundamental tenet of their theologies, there are key differences in how resurrection is viewed by the respective faiths. Christians tend towards a belief in the actual resurrection of the person as they were during their earthly lives, in their original bodies, restored from the grave to be essentially unchanged from how the individuals were in life. Islam, however, argues that resurrection is part of the natural cycle of life as conceived by God and that (as we will discuss) our bodies will be composed of different substances suited to their new environment. It also suggests that all living beings, and not just humans, shall be gathered unto God in the end, in "the ultimate manifestation of God's power in nature":[7]

> Although there is no beast that walks on earth and no bird that flies on its two wings which is not (God's) creature like yourselves; no

---

6 Q. 46:33.
7 Zebiri, 2006, 279.

single thing have We neglected in Our decree. And once again: Unto their Sustainer shall they all be gathered.[8]

Only humans – who alone of God's Creation are capable of abstract, moral thought – shall be judged according to how they have conducted themselves during their lives. Because of our higher intelligence, we are capable of looking at nature and finding in it multiple signs and proofs of God and all His works. We can also develop this gift by striving to use our observations to better understand the role of God in creating and sustaining the universe. We are also capable of making moral decisions with respect to how we treat others, and with respect to our relationship with God. For all these reasons, the implications of resurrection are extremely far-reaching for all human beings, as we will see in the next and subsequent chapters.

The Qur'ān tacitly accepts that resurrection is a difficult doctrine to understand. It points to God's great, and demonstrated, powers, to reassure the faithful that not only is God capable of resurrecting the deceased, but He has promised to do so, eliminating all doubt about the matter. It states:

> O men! If you are in doubt as to the truth of resurrection (remember that) verily, We have created you out of dust, then out of a drop of sperm. All this (happens) because God alone is the Ultimate Truth, and because He alone brings the dead to life, and because He has the power to will anything.[9]

The holy book also discusses the rejection of the doctrine of resurrection by contemporaries of Muhammad's. It appears that many of those who heard him speak struggled to understand the concept of resurrection, which seemed very alien to them at the time, and even swore oaths stating, "Never will God raise from the dead anyone who has died."[10] The pagan Arabs of Muhammad's

---

8 Q. 6:38.
9 Q. 22:5-6.
10 Q.16:38.

time were much given to swearing oaths. Their strongest oaths were sworn by the Supreme God, while less important oaths were sworn according to lesser gods, their ancestors, or possessions or other items that they valued greatly. Their feeling was that, while there might well be a Supreme God, there was no reason to suppose that He would resurrect them after death, and that, even if He could, there was no reason to assume that He would want to. It must be borne in mind that, while the idea of resurrection was familiar to Christians at the time, it was a completely new concept for the pagan Arabs. Consequently, many of them found it painfully difficult to comprehend and closed their minds to it. They felt that Muhammad's insistence that they would be reborn into an afterlife was nonsense, while at the same time, and paradoxically, were roused to anger by his news that non-believers could not enter heaven if they had been given the chance to hear the truth as it had been revealed to the Prophet, and had chosen to reject it. The Qur'ān systematically refuted all of their arguments in a calm and rational fashion, using examples from nature, and especially from embryology, to argue that not only could God resurrect people after death, but that He certainly would do so.[11]

In various verses in the Qur'ān, we are reminded that humanity was originally created out of dust.[12] We are thus reminded that, in a purely physical way, we have much in common with the rest of God's Creation on earth. Modern science has been able to confirm what the Qur'ān has always asserted: that is, that everything on earth is composed of the same relatively small number of essential compounds. We were created out of dust, we will return to dust after death and, on the Day of Judgement, God will cause us to emerge from it in resurrection as we assume our new bodily forms. In scientific terms, we see a description of how all of our bodies are composed of elementary substances found naturally on earth, and how Creation itself embodies proof of God's majesty, of the fleetingness of life, and the promise of resurrection in the future.

---

11 Affi, 2016, 15-6.
12 For example, Q. 71:17-18; 20:55.

The Ultimate Reward: Eschatology in the Qur'ān

It is important to understand the distinction between immortality and life after death. Immortality belongs only to God, Who is eternal, having no beginning and no end, whereas all of the life created by Him is temporary by its very nature. Different creatures have diverse life spans, but they all share the fact that their lifespans on earth are bound to come to an end at some point. Although we all therefore have a beginning and an end, there is life beyond the "end" – albeit a very different type of life to that we experienced during our short time on earth. This is what is meant by resurrection, and it is in this new life that we will receive our reward or punishment.

Because we are intrinsically unable to understand what the next life will be like, the Qur'ān typically discusses our existence in the next world in allegorical terms, using its characteristically rich language. Using terms and concepts that are familiar to us from this life, the Qur'ān provides us with the opportunity to catch a glimpse of the glories (or indeed the torments) that await us in the next. Resurrection clearly implies a new life, but this does not mean, in any way, that we will inhabit the same bodies that we owned on earth, or that our new lives will be in any way the same or even similar. The resurrection to which the Qur'ān refers is the resurrection of the human personality or character. Until we have experienced this for ourselves, there is no way for us to understand what our new bodies will look like, or of what substance they will be composed. What we *do* know is that life will not return to the flesh-and-blood bodies that we used during our time here on earth. Today, although scholars of Islam differ on many details, almost all agree that we will be corporeal beings after resurrection, with vanishingly few subscribing to the idea that we will be purely spiritual creatures. The scholar Maulana Muhammad Ali states that there can be no soul without a body, but that our bodies will change, saying, "If the very earth and heaven have changed at the Resurrection, how can the human body remain the same?"[13] The theologian Shāh Walī Allāh believed that resurrection will involve the placing of the spiritual element of humanity into a body suited to its new environment, a view

---

13 Cited in Idelman Smith and Yazbeck Haddad, 2002, 133.

supported by the Qur'ān.¹⁴ The Qur'ān also discusses the scientific fact of decomposition. We all know that the body disintegrates after death – in other words, its gradual return to the dust from whence it came. Because there will be effectively no body to resurrect when this process has been completed, resurrection will be akin to a new wave of Creation, in which the original spirit is retained, but the body is created anew.¹⁵ In this way, resurrection is not an "external event" in which the human spirit is simply placed in another body:

> The resurrection, therefore, is not an external event. It is the consummation of a life-process within the ego. Whether individual or universal, it is nothing more than a kind of stock-taking of the ego's past achievements and his future possibilities.¹⁶

Rather, it is a natural element of a process of life in which the spirit is itself involved in its own rebirth, much as a baby is involved in its own springing forth from its mother's body, while God assesses the deeds of the human individual involved during their life on earth, and decides what his or her fate shall be.¹⁷

The bodies that we will inhabit after resurrection might look like the ones we have now, but they will be made up of a completely different substance, and they will be capable of experiencing pleasure and joy in ways that we cannot even begin to understand on the basis of current experience. The bodies we have now were designed by God for the purpose of living on earth, and in this context, they are perfect. After resurrection, He will design for us bodies that are made for the purpose of living forever in heaven with Him,¹⁸ and they will be equally perfect in that new context.

As resurrection will take place on the Day of Judgement, what is the fate of the uncountable millions who have died many years before this occurs?

---

14 Q. 50:3-4.
15 Q. 10:4; 21:104; 30:11; 85:13.
16 Iqbal, 1989, 96.
17 Iqbal, 1989, 96-8.
18 Khan, 1962, 185.

Effectively, their consciousness will enter into a sort of sleep or fugue state at the time of their deaths, and the time they have spent in the grave will seem fleeting to them: "And on the Day when He shall gather them (it will seem to them) as if they had not tarried (on earth) longer than an hour of a day, knowing one another."[19] Moreover, their time on earth, and the many and complex relationships that they had with others during that time, will seem like nothing but a short moment in comparison with the vast duration of eternal life, in which all of these relationships are redefined,[20] and in which each individual will be judged according to his or her own merits and flaws.

The Qur'ān uses language in a range of creative ways to bring the message of the Day of Judgement to the people. In certain passages, it discusses it in the present or past tense, with the intention of underlining its inevitability and the fact that it could simply happen at any time. It vividly describes how everything that we take for granted as the natural order of things will simply disappear and cease to exist. God's trumpet call will herald first the absolute interruption of nature as we know it, and then the final obliteration of all life on earth, leaving only God as judge and decision-maker,[21] and as the one who gives new life to "bones that have crumbled to dust"[22] In this moment, we shall finally have the capacity to completely understand the concept of God's almightiness, hitherto eclipsed from view by the limited nature of human understanding. To date, even the most advanced efforts of the world's top scientists have failed to explain the mystery of life, and nobody has ever been able to extend life indefinitely. Yet all around us we see proofs of God's hand at work: when the earth creates abundant vegetable matter, and when this vegetable matter supports all manner of animal life. This life can seem to die during a drought, or during a long, hard winter, and yet the rain falls, or spring returns, and life is born again in one of the most astonishing miracles of the everyday:

---

19 Q. 10:45.
20 Q. 79:46; 23:101.
21 Idleman Smith and Yazbeck Haddad, 2002, 71.
22 Q. 36:78-81.

You see the earth lifeless, but when We pour down rain on it, it is stirred to life, it swells, and it produces every kind of beautiful growth… it is He who gives life to the dead, and it is He who has power over all things.[23]

Just as plants and all the life they support appear to die, only to be reborn when the environmental situation changes, our human consciousness can sink into oblivion, only to be reborn into its new existence at the moment of God's appointed hour.[24]

Human Consciousness in this Life and the Next

Stated simply, the doctrine of resurrection refers to the fact that our human minds and distinct human consciousness will continue from this life to the next, and that we will experience this as an unbroken continuum of existence, because we will not experience the passage of time between our deaths and our rebirth. Our bodies will be very different in their composition and nature after the Day of Judgement, but our essential humanness, and the special, personal qualities that make us unique, will stay the same. The Qur'ān is extremely clear in outlining this continuity, and it affirms the implication that we will continue to bear moral responsibility for how we have lived even when we have passed into our new existence. One big change will be that our capacities for perception will be much greater, with the result that we will become ever more keenly aware of how we are responsible for everything we did during our time on earth. Considering this in the context of the many statements in the Qur'ān about the joy or suffering we will experience in the next life places the responsibility for our actions firmly on our own shoulders. We are used to hearing "heaven" and "hell" being discussed in terms of reward and punishment, but while this is broadly true, it fails to capture the complexity of the situation. Life after death is not just the opening of a new

---

23 Zebiri, 2006, 278; Q. 22:5-6.
24 Ali, 1934, 1181.

chapter, but a development, a growth, from our past existence, in which we will continue to live in a new way, but on a much higher level, than before. It may be that new goals for further development will be presented to us at that stage but, simply put, we will not know this until we have reached the new phase of our lives, and any speculation about this matter now is no more than guesswork.[25]

Moving beyond the Qur'ān, authenticated Islamic traditions may give us some hints at the nature of life in the next world. Apparently, on various occasions Muhammad stated that everyone in heaven will be restored to youth and to a virginal state, regardless of how old and decrepit they had become.

Refuting Doubters

How can we explain the reluctance of those who have heard the good news from God to accept the idea of resurrection? By definition, rejecting the idea of resurrection also means rejecting the idea of God being our ultimate judge or arbiter. It indicates an attitude that does not accept the possibility of anything beyond our immediate, and immensely limited, ability to observe it. This attitude is associated with an obsession with the material aspects of life, and with a prideful approach that will not allow the essential humility of belief in God's sovereignty over us all. God is merciful, and He offers everyone who is prepared to listen the chance to live according to His wishes and thus offers them the potential for eternal life in Heaven. He also warns those who are given every opportunity to heed His word that if they continue refusing to listen, they will suffer from their sins. In the Qur'ān, doubters are described as asking Muhammad, "Shall we be raised up and also our forefathers?" to which the prophet answers: "Yes, and you will be humiliated!"[26]

As we have seen, Muhammad had to deal in his lifetime with those who doubted the doctrine of resurrection that he preached, and who further

---

25 Asad, 1987, 148-9.
26 Q. 36:78-9.

Resurrection

doubted the very idea of a final Judgement. In fact, the doctrine of resurrection was one of the aspects of Qur'ānic teaching that troubled the people of Mecca the most. They even demanded that this teaching be removed from the Qur'ān, as they found it entirely incompatible with their world view.[27] They stated that they had come across similar teachings, presumably from Jews and Christians, and that the very idea of resurrection was nothing more than "a fiction of the earlier communities,"[28] that they simply refused to entertain. All these years later, there are still many who will not accept this teaching, despite the fact that Creation offers us abundant proofs of God's existence and His mercy. The Qur'ān itself discusses the incredulity of true believers when they are forced to deal with those who reject the manifold proofs of God, as well as the idea that we will be restored to life after death.[29] What is even more puzzling is that there are those who do profess to believe in God, and yet reject His teaching of eternal life. Truly, this makes absolutely no sense. If they can look around them at this wonderful world and see the hand of God in Creation, how can they deny that God has the capacity to bring about resurrection and eternal life? If He has made the universe, our world, and all that we see in nature, who are we to doubt that He can continue to do whatever He wishes and grant us all existence when death brings an end to our brief time on earth? Consider that the ability to reproduce here on earth is a natural gift awarded us by God and not something that we created ourselves. Surely, when we think about His awesome powers, we can understand that He who created human beings in the first place can also cause them to return to life. In the Qur'ān, the verb which means "to bring forth" is used to describe children emerging from their mothers' wombs,[30] plants from the earth, and people from this life to the next at the point of resurrection.

---

27 Rahman, 1989, 115.
28 Q. 23:82; 27:67-8.
29 Q. 13:5; 32:10.
30 Q. 16:78.

The Qur'ān provides us with the logical arguments that we need to refute those who reject the doctrine of resurrection and eternal life. It poses the question: "Could We, then, be (thought of as being) worn out by the first Creation?"[31] It then answers it, by stating that not only can God effect a second Creation, but He finds it even easier than He did the first time: "And He it is who creates (all life) in the first instance, and then brings it forth anew, and most easy is this for Him,"[32] and, speaking in God's voice, "Out of it (the earth) We created you and into it We shall make you return and from it We will bring you out another time."[33]

The Qur'ān provides us with a vivid description of the experience of deniers of resurrection when the Day of Judgement comes. On that day, God is described as saying to them: "And now, indeed, you have come unto Us in a lonely state, even as We created you in the first instance."[34] These simple words evoke a powerful image of these lost souls, bereft without their unfounded certainties, standing before God in the realisation that they were utterly wrong, and that they have nobody to blame but themselves.

Those who continue to reject the Qur'ān's teaching about resurrection are rejecting not just that specific doctrine, but also the Qur'ān itself and the teachings of not just Muhammad, but the other prophets who came before him with the good news of God's promise. From start to finish, the Qur'ān references the essential belief in the next world as a crucial aspect of faith that no true Muslim can deny. It asserts that, on the day when the world ends, all the dead will be gathered together, and none will be left out, including the doubters, with "no true understanding of God."[35] God, who is ever-merciful, repeatedly exhorts those who are inclined to doubt to heed His message, urging them to think for themselves and accept that

---

31 Q. 50:15.
32 Q. 30:27.
33 Q. 20:55; 71:17-18.
34 Q. 6:94; 18:47-8; 19:95.
35 Q. 39:67.

Resurrection

they are His Creation and will be brought before Him with the fullness of time.[36]

God's Promise

> He (it is who) brings forth the living out of that which is dead, and brings forth the dead out of that which is alive, and gives life to the earth after it had been lifeless: and even thus will you be brought forth (from death to life).[37]

Above all, Resurrection is God's promise to us. When we pass from this world to the next, we will be living the reality of His commitment, which means that those of us who live according to His teachings, as revealed in the Qur'ān and in other books of revelation, have nothing to fear from death at all. For them, their new beginning will bring only nearness to God and joy that cannot be expressed within the limits of human language. On the Day of Resurrection, those who have truly done their best to live according to the will of God will be greeted by His angels, who will state that they are experiencing their Day of Triumph, and that as God made all of Creation in the first instance, so is He doing it anew, as He promised from the start.[38]

Sentient living beings fear death, but death is unavoidable and a perfectly natural feature of life. We humans often try to distract ourselves from this fear by focusing on material possessions and well-being. We are tempted to spend our lives in a continuous race towards what we think are the pleasures of existence, but seeking pleasure for its own reward is never fulfilling in the long run, and is a pointless exercise when one considers the incomparable glories of life everlasting, as promised by God. It is only in the next life that we will realise the full extent of our destiny, for this is when it will be revealed to us:

---

36 Q. 56:60-2.
37 Q. 30:19.
38 Q. 21:103-4.

"Only on the Day of Resurrection will you be requited in full for whatever you have done… for the life of this world is nothing but an enjoyment of self-delusion."[39] On that great day all of us, including the prophets – who are as mortal as anyone else – will be judged according to their deeds in this lifetime, and will be made privy to the awesome powers of God.

---

39 Q. 3:185.

CHAPTER 8

❖ ❖ ❖

The Day of Judgement

A STRONG AND abiding belief in the Day of Judgement is a central tenet of Islam, one of the five pillars of the faith,[1] and as such as a non-negotiable element for all observant Muslims.[2] Indicative of its centrality to Islamic teaching is the abundance of surahs from the very earliest days of revelation, when Muhammad was in Mecca and the faith was in the most fundamental level of development. Clearly, it was crucial above all to communicate this message very clearly to the early believers.[3]

Many of the Meccans, hearing Muhammad preach, rejected his message of the Last Day in particular for a long time,[4] in response to which the Qur'ān offered surahs such as "God made the heavens and the earth in truth, so that each soul could be rewarded for what it earned,"[5] and "And it is He who created the heavens and the earth in six days – and his throne was upon the water – that he might test you, as to which of you is best in conduct."[6] Throughout the Qur'ān, many passages stress the importance of understanding and believing in the concept of the Day of Judgement, when each human being ever created will receive their reward or their punishment.

---

1 Lange, 2016, 37.
2 Rahman, 1968, 32-3.
3 Saeed, 2006, 45.
4 Neuwirth, 206, 151.
5 Q, 45:22.
6 Q. 11:7.

In the Qur'ān, the Day of Judgement is referred to variously as the Last Day,[7] the Hour,[8] the Day of Resurrection,[9] and the Day of Reckoning. On the Day of Judgement, the world as we know it destroyed, God will unfurl the scrolls that record all the good and evil deeds of each and every human being who has ever walked the earth. The many generations who lived and died before this day will have been asleep, and will not have experienced the passage of time during this period, regardless of how brief or how long. Now they will be awoken, and called upon to account for their deeds during their lifetimes.[10] This is what is meant by Judgement, and it is the logical conclusion of God's Creation of human beings as intelligent creatures with free will that we can use to decide how we will conduct ourselves during the limited period of our lives on earth. While, clearly, God wishes above all for us to behave in certain ways, He has no means of compelling us to do so, and simply observes our conduct on earth until the Day of Judgement takes place.

The Qur'ān's descriptions of what will become of us in the afterlife provide us with consistent teaching as to the importance of respecting the divine authority of God, and of acknowledging the consequences of our own actions.[11] The Last Judgement is as an essential element of belief for a number of core reasons:[12]

- The behaviour of human beings must, of necessity, be judged by God to ensure that everyone is treated fairly, because our limited experience on earth does not provide the opportunity for fairness to be extended to all – we have all seen how some people behave very badly and yet prosper, while others remain poor and destitute through no fault of their own.

---

7 Q. 2:8.
8 Q. 6:31.
9 Q. 21:47.
10 Lange, 2016, 39.
11 Buck, 2006, 30.
12 Rahman, 1989, 116.

- The knowledge that our human story has a clearly defined end that we will all experience gives each of us the motivation we need to strive to live as well as we can during our lives on earth, provided we listen to the word of God, for we do not know when our lives will end, and must strive at all times to do our best to live according to God's wishes for us.
- Conflicts of interest, injustices, and disputes need to be settled, and they are not always settled during the course of our earthly existence, leaving a door open for them to be dealt with at the time of the end of the world.

The Nature of Judgement

In our earthly lives, we may think that the things we have done are secrets, but at the end of the world, when we are exposed to the nature of true reality, every secret, whether good or bad, will be an open book as God places it on display before us all, and our consciousness expands until it is capable of understanding the information that we are being presented with. Every time we did or failed to do something good, or committed an evil act, will be completely visible, and the condition of our soul will be plain for all to see. Nothing can be hidden, not even our innermost thoughts,[13] or those sins that we engaged in when we were sure that nobody was watching. Believers and unbelievers alike will realise that everything the apostles (and the Qur'ān confirms that God has sent this message to many of His prophets over the years, not just Muhammad, the final and ultimate prophet)[14] said about judgement and resurrection is true.[15] This is the moment when "every human will be shaken into a unique and unprecedented self-awareness of his deeds."[16] When this happens, we will view before us both hell, which will burn more brightly

---

13 Q. 100: 9-10.
14 Khorchide and Hartmann, 2014, 24.
15 Rubin, 2006, 243.
16 Rahman, 1989, 106.

than the fiercest flame, and God's garden or heaven, which we will see clearly before any of us have reached it. Imagine how tantalising this will be for those who doubted God's word during their lifetimes!

The Qur'ān describes how, once the process of judgement has started, all the creatures created by God will "fall down senseless" and how, when we find ourselves finally standing before God, Who will be seated before us in judgement, we will begin to understand His truth as never before. Bathed in the bright light of God, a record of the deeds carried out by each of us in life will be "laid bare" as everyone, including God's own prophets, will face His judgement.[17] The prophets, like those to whom they preached during their brief lifetimes on earth, will testify even against themselves on the Day of Judgement, admitting the truth about the way they behaved on earth,[18] and recording every single moment in which they behaved in a way that displeased God. Once again, this is a telling reminder of the fact that God's messengers, while enormously important to our cultural and spiritual development, are not gods but mere mortals like the rest of us, and that they will be judged accordingly.

Many verses in the Qur'ān refer to this Last Day, when "man will recall what he had been striving for,"[19] while it describes the good and evil receiving scrolls detailing their good deeds in their right and left hands, respectively,[20] tapping into ancient beliefs that associate the right with goodness, and the left with evil.[21] The Qur'ān also describes the weighing of our deeds on a scale that measures them with incredible precision and determines whether the good outweigh the bad, or vice versa.[22]

The Qur'ān warns us to take seriously its message that the Day of Judgement is always approaching, commenting that, even though we will all

---

17 Q. 39:68-70.
18 Asad, 1984, 715.
19 Q. 79:34-5.
20 Q. 69:19-29.
21 Intriguingly, these beliefs are also embedded in the English language, in which the word "sinister" is derived from a word meaning "left."
22 Q. 101:6-8.

one day face our reckoning, we tend to be foolish and neglect to take it seriously, focusing instead on the transitory delights of everyday.[23] We should be mindful of the fact that God sent us His messenger Muhammad (and indeed the earlier prophets) to bring us the news of the Last Hour that awaits.[24] We should all live our lives each and every day in the knowledge that the Day of Judgement could come at any moment and that, in any case, its ultimate arrival is unavoidable, endeavouring to do nothing for which repentance is necessary, and repenting and making amends immediately whenever this does happen.[25]

Our Essential Judgement

On the Day of Judgement, each human being will stand alone. In this way, each individual will be called to account for his- or herself, in stark contrast to the way in which they conducted their lives in families, tribes, communities, or nations:[26]

> ... the day when a man shall flee from his brother, his mother and father, his wife and children – for every man on that day, shall have a preoccupation that will release him from all these.[27]

The Qur'ān describes how even women who are still suckling their children will forget their babies, while pregnant women will give birth, and all humanity will seem almost drunk or out of their minds as a result of their fear of God's imminent judgement on them.[28] These vivid descriptions highlight the essential loneliness of the process of judgement as each realises that they will

---

23 Q. 21:1-3.
24 Q. 79:42-5; 31:34.
25 Q. 47:18.
26 Q. 19:95.
27 Q. 80:34-7.
28 Q. 22:2.

be judged according to their individual merits, or lack thereof. It should be noted that this description is metaphorical, and should not be understood in a literal sense. On the Day of Judgement, nobody will be pregnant. The point is that if we humans were told that the Day of Judgement was imminent, and were capable of truly understanding this, we would be so shocked that pregnant women would miscarry, while others would not behave as they usually do.

The righteous, who do not doubt that they will be judged favourably by God, will not share the terrible grief experienced by those who have sinned against Him, but everyone will share a sense of dread for the incredible, and unimaginable, events that are about to unfold. The Qur'ān utilises an age-old Arabic turn of phrase for a day filled with terror that refers to "a day on which the locks of children turn grey."[29] Of course, as the Qur'ān stresses that children are without sin and cannot be held to account for what they do, it is clear that this phrase should be read allegorically.[30]

Regardless of how we tried to conceal our evil deeds, everything will be laid bare, with no place to hide. It will be utterly impossible for us to justify the petty things we did during our lifetimes to further our own material interests, even though we were flying in the face of everything God wanted. Faced with the overwhelming evidence that we ourselves provide, even those of us facing eternity in hell will be obliged to admit that we have left no possible alternative, and were the masters of our own destiny from the start.[31]

Islamic scholars such as Ibn Taymiyya have explained the sense of regret experienced by those who have been doomed to hell by referring to the fact that the reality of Muhammad's prophethood is accessible to anyone who is of sound mind and rational, and who reflects on the messages that he brought to humanity. Because of this, those who opted not to follow the Word of God, even though they had the opportunity to listen and obey, did so consciously

---

29 Q. 73:17.
30 Rāzi, n.d., 184.
31 Ali, 1934, 1992.

and deliberately.³² The Qur'ān describes this phenomenon in terms of God raising a veil from us, enabling us to see our life's deeds with a degree of clarity and sharpness that we have never used before, and to understand how we have often been driven by our own selfishness and laziness to follow our baser instincts into self-indulgence, indolence, and sin, rather than towards the light and wisdom of God.³³ For this reason, those who are condemned to hell are described in the Qur'ān as sadly lamenting, "If only we had listened, or reasoned, we would not be with the inhabitants of the burning fire."³⁴

While this process will be illuminating for us all, it will, understandably, be painfully difficult for those of us who have lived sinful lives, having chosen to ignore the word of God, and who are suddenly faced with the dread realisation that they now face an eternity of suffering for having failed to please the merciful God Who created them. The Qur'ān describes this devastation and heartbreak in powerful language, stating:

> And the record (of everyone's deeds) will be laid open; and thou wilt behold the guilty filled with dread at what (they see) therein; and they will exclaim; "Oh, woe unto us! What a record is this! It leaves out nothing, be it small or great, but takes everything into account."³⁵

In some ways, when we return to God on the Day of Judgement, we have regressed to the state in which we originally entered the world; "in a lonely state," with no possessions or material goods at all, as tiny, defenceless, naked infants without even the concept of possessions or material goods. Throughout our lifetimes, we have accumulated possessions and a network of friends and contacts, but all of this counts as nothing when it comes to creating a summation of our deeds. The Qur'ān states that "Indeed, all bonds between you (and your earthly life) are now severed, and all your former fancies have forsaken

---

32 Khalil, 2012, 77.
33 Q. 50:21-2.
34 Q. 67:10.
35 Q. 18:49.

you."³⁶ When we are returned to God's presence on the Day of Judgement, the only "possession" we have left is our past; the collective of every decision we have ever taken. All of our material possessions are gone, and any friendships or relationships that were valuable to us on earth have ceased to exist. Now, our only currency is the sum of good deeds that we carried out during our lifetime in the beautiful world that God created for each and every one of us.

As we live our earthly lives, we do well to remember that every day, and in each decision we make, however minor it seems at the time, we are creating our very own destiny that, on the Day of Judgement, will be laid out before us, showing us with glaring clarity everything that we have done for good or ill.³⁷ Today we may lie and dissemble, even to ourselves, and pretend that our evil deeds are not that important, or aggrandise what we believe to be our good deeds. We humans are very good at lying to ourselves and convincing ourselves that we have not really been as badly-behaved as we have. On the Day of Judgement, however, we will be unable to lie to ourselves anymore, and certainly we will not be able to conceal the truth from God, who knows and sees all. In this context, the Qur'ān speaks a great deal about destiny, which should be understood here not in the sense that each of us has a destiny from which we cannot escape, but insofar as each of us creates our own destiny in the decisions and actions that we take during our lifetimes on earth.

God has created us all as intelligent beings capable of making even very complex moral choices in extremely difficult circumstances. Thus, it is incumbent upon us to consider with each moral choice we make whether or not God would approve. This applies equally to deeds done as to deeds undone. In other words, refraining from carrying out an evil act, even when it is tempting to do so, or failing to carry out a good deed, even when we know we should, are both actions that form part of our overall tally, just as much as the active engagement in good or evil actions.³⁸

---

36 Q. 6:94.
37 Q. 17:13-4.
38 Asad, 1984, 420.

The Day of Judgement

Transformation on the Day of Judgement

Although the Qur'ān speaks of the destruction of this world as we know it, and of violent and dramatic changes to the very fabric of God's wondrous Creation, it is also clear that it is not referring to destruction in absolute terms. Rather, it is dealing with a theme of *transformation*. This is made clear in multiple verses that refer to Earth and the heavens being changed and turned into something new.[39] What comes next is, as yet, beyond our capacity to understand, but certainly it is part of God's overarching plans for His Creation and all that it contains. Knowing God as we do, as a merciful and loving Creator, we can be sure that His plans for this transformation will be extraordinary and beyond anything that we can currently imagine. We do know that this new earth will contain none of the injustice, inequality, darkness or evil of this one, and that all lies and pretences will cease to exist, while everything will be seen as it really is. In this transformed world, when "the earth shall be changed into another earth, as shall be the heavens"[40] those who have lived as God wishes will find true happiness. The transformed, and utterly different, nature of Creation after Judgement is generally discussed in the Qur'ān using rich, allegorical language that appeals to the emotions, reflecting the simple reality that, because it is beyond the bounds of human experience, no language on earth is currently capable of describing it.[41]

With none of their earthly possessions, God's people will stand before Him, having "come forth in haste from their graves, as if racing towards a goalpost."[42] While this does not mean that they will *literally* appear before God in the form that they have taken within their graves, it clearly evokes the idea of resurrection and the sense of inevitability and urgency associated with it. All of those who have been exposed to God's word as revealed to His prophets will have heard teachings about the Day of Judgement on many occasions throughout their lives. Now, finally, they will see all of these teachings

---

39 For example, Q. 14:48; 53:47; 34:7; 14:19; 35:16.
40 Q. 14:48.
41 Asad, 1984, 936, note 8.
42 Q. 70:43-4.

come to pass, and all of their deeds, good and bad, minor and major, will be revealed. The Qur'ān uses powerful, evocative language to describe this scenario, saying:

> On that day will all men come forward, cut off from one another, to be shown their (past) deeds. And so, he who shall have done an atom's weight of good, shall behold it; and he who shall have done an atom's weight of evil, shall behold it.[43]

We can understand the Day of Judgement as a great "sorting out." Whereas in this world, good and evil are inextricably interlinked, and frail human beings often delude themselves as to the true nature of their actions, on the Day of Judgement, our deeds will be meticulously sorted into good and evil. In life, negative qualities such as ignorance, discrimination, passion, spite, and selfishness can seem to intermingle with positive ones, including wisdom, justice, common sense, and love and compassion. Our interactions with others can be so complex and nuanced that it is not always immediately obvious whether virtue or vice is the overriding quality associated with them. On the Day of Judgement, they will be sorted out, one from the other.

The Judgement of Non-believers

How will God deal with those who were not Muslims? This thorny topic has been a subject of much debate among Islamic scholars over the years.

Clearly, as human beings lived on this earth for aeons before Muhammad received revelations from God, an uncountable number never had the chance to hear the Qur'ān, let alone adopt Islamic principles. Similarly, there are populations on earth today that have not had the opportunity to hear the Word of God. The Qur'ān makes it clear that each community of people will be judged according to how they lived within the context of their time, and

---

[43] Q. 99:6-8.

in accordance with the messages He has sent them, if any. Certainly, people from the past cannot be judged according to the same standards as those who have had the opportunity to hear God's message for themselves, and those who have never had the chance to hear the word of God cannot be treated as though they had. However, it should also be noted that there are some acts that are considered morally reprehensible by *all* thoughtful people. People who commit these heinous acts will be punished for them, and their lack of access to God's message will not be considered an acceptable mitigating factor on the Day of Judgement.[44]

As for Jews and Christians, who were in receipt of earlier revelations from God, they are to be judged according to the standards set out in their own revelations, as received by their prophets, which came from the same divine source as the Qur'ān, while the prophets themselves will be judged on how effectively they delivered God's message to His people.[45] Of Jews and Christians ("People of the Book") who have lived their lives in accordance with these scriptures, the Qur'ān states:

> The believers, the Jews, the Christians, and the Sabians – all those who believe in God and the Last Day and do good – will have their rewards with their Lord. No fear for them, nor will they grieve.[46]

In the Qur'ān, God asserts that He does not punish any people from a society that has not yet been given the opportunity to hear His word in the form of revelations received by a prophet.[47] Conversely, those who had the opportunity to hear the word of God from one of His messengers, and yet decided not to heed it, will be judged harshly, as they have no valid excuse for their choice.[48]

---

44 Khalil, 2012, 78.
45 Q. 7:6-7.
46 Q. 2:62.
47 Khalil, 2013, 5.
48 Q. 4:165.

Puzzling Descriptions of the Day of Judgement

Some of the descriptions of the Day of Judgement are puzzling to the modern reader, who does not necessarily understand the cultural context in which they were written and may wonder what these apparently obscure references and descriptions mean. Why, for example, are the animals described as huddling together? Some commentators believe that the animals are reacting in fear to the momentous things happening around them because they, like the humans, do not understand what is going on. Others have maintained that they will be compensated for the cruelties they have endured at the hands of human beings, and yet others that those beasts that were loved by human beings will be united with them in the afterlife, a view that is supported by a Qur'ānic verse that states that, "there is no beast that works on earth and no bird that flies on its two wings which is not (God's) creature like yourselves… unto their Sustainer shall they be gathered."[49] And what are we to make of references to the female child who was buried alive?[50] Prior to the advent of Islam, female infanticide, carried out by burying the new-born children alive in the desert sand, seems to have been relatively widespread. The reasons for this atrocity were the fear that female children would be an economic burden in the context of an intensely patriarchal society, or that they might be captured by an enemy tribe and bring shame and dishonour to their families by preferring their captors to their families of origin. While this appalling custom had some opponents even before Islam,[51] the Qur'ān firmly insisted on the essential equality of men and women from the start, and banned all such actions, denouncing them as grave sins. It describes these dreadful acts, and condemns them:

> For whenever any of them is given the glad tiding of (the birth of) a girl, his face darkens, and he is filled with suppressed anger. Avoiding

---

49 Q. 6:38.
50 Q. 81:8-9.
51 Notably Zayd ibn 'Amr ibn Nufayl, a cousin of 'Umar ibn al-Khattāb. Asad, 1984, 933, citing Fathu al-Bārī bi-Sharhi Sahīh al-Buikhārī, Cairo, 1348 H.

all people because of the evil of the glad tiding which he has received, (and debating within himself). Shall he keep this (child) despite the contempt – or shall he bury it in the dust? Oh, evil is whatever they decide.[52]

In the context of descriptions of the Day of Judgement, this is a clear reference to the fact that, ultimately, all sins will have to be answered for before God, who is the true arbiter of right and wrong. The murder of innocent little children, who have committed no crime, and whose only "offence" is being female in a world that privileges men and despises the women given life by God, and treasured by Him, was carried out for untold generations prior to the advent of Islam with the complete collusion of every level of society. At the end of the world, these voiceless, tiny victims of man's cruelty will be called to give evidence against their killers, and they will receive justice at long last, as well as their eternal reward, as the sinless beings that they are.[53]

Why does the Qur'ān single out she-camels for special mention? To understand this, we need to look to the social and economic environment of the time of revelation. In those days, the camel was hugely important as a beast of burden and as a source of food, and was, in fact, central to the Arabian economy. Camels were perfectly adapted to life in the desert, capable of storing water in their stomachs for days, of thriving even on a diet of dry desert bushes, and of carrying a heavy burden uncomplainingly. They provided meat and milk, and even their hair, wool and skin were widely used by the Arab peoples.[54] Camels were, therefore, essential to the economy, much-loved pets and valuable items of family property. Clearly, they were at their most valuable – and their most vulnerable – when they were about to give birth, and so they were always closely attended at those times. Ordinarily, nothing would have stopped an Arab family in Muhammad's day from taking great care of their precious camel. Yet when the Day of Judgement comes, and everything

---

52 Q. 16:57-9.
53 Ali, 1934, 1904.
54 Ali, 1934, 1945.

familiar disappears before our very eyes, even these most valuable and valued beasts will be ignored.

Punishment and Reward

We know that God will reward those who lived well, and punish those who did not, but how do we reconcile our knowledge of God as a merciful and loving Creator with that of the awful punishments that await those who do not please Him? This is one of the key arguments of non-believers, so it is important to understand how to answer their questions. Simply, we have free will, and this is one of our greatest gifts, for it separates us from all other living beings, and gives us the opportunity to consciously decide to please God in our daily lives. The Qur'ān makes special mention of free will as a special gift that has been granted to us by God:

> (I swear) by man's personality and that whereby it has been formed, God has engraved into it its evil and its good (whereby it can guard itself against moral peril). He who makes his personality pure, shall be successful, while he who corrupts us shall be in the loss.[55]

As Rahman puts it, "... man *ought* to follow his nature; this transformation of the *is* into *ought* is both the unique privilege and the unique risk of man. This is why it is so important for man to hearken and hearken well to his nature, despite the intrigues of Satan."[56]

All God wants of us is that we live in a way that is consistent with His holy law. He takes no joy in punishing those who have not lived according to His will. In fact, we need to understand this punishment clearly in the sense that it is simply the natural and inevitable consequence of the deeds of those involved. The Qur'ān states clearly that those who come before God having carried out good deeds will "gain further good therefrom," while those who

---

55 Rahman, 1989, 24; Q. 91:7-10.
56 Rahman, 1989, 24.

have carried out evil deeds "will not be requited with more than (the like of) what they have done."[57]

While our actions here on earth are brief, their inevitable consequences are very long. We see God's infinite mercy in the fact, recorded in the Qur'ān, that we will be rewarded tenfold for each good deed that we have carried out,[58] but that our punishment for evil deeds will simply be equivalent to what we have done,[59] and we will have to carry responsibility for our own fate.[60] Moreover, even those who have done evil, but who have genuinely repented and made amends in this lifetime, have the chance to access God's mercy, for He is always inclined to forgive, rather than to condemn, and He never gives any of us more than we can manage to deal with.[61] This mercy should not be conflated with the erroneous idea that God will forgive every sin we deliberately commit, in the expectation that He will do so. This is nothing but wishful thinking, and it is a dangerous road to go down.[62] As Rahman points out, this very idea rests on the infantilising of adults.[63] Of course, children cannot really be judged for what they do, as they are not yet capable of making moral decisions. Here on earth, we do not assume that competent adult men and women should be exempt from being judged when they do something wrong, because they have come of age and they are able to use their brains to make moral judgements. Why, then, would we expect God to treat adults as though they were children, and consider them incapable of making their own decisions, when He has created them as rational beings?

---

57 Q. 28:84; 27:89-90.
58 Q. 6:160; 40:40.
59 Q. 6:160; 10:27.
60 Q. 42:30.
61 Q. 23:62.
62 Q. 57:14.
63 Rahman, 1989, 9.

The Absolute Justice of God

God, Who is perfect and all-knowing, will administer justice on the Day of Judgement such that even those whose evil deeds outweigh their good will be forced to admit that He has been wise and fair and that they have left Him with no choice but to condemn them to the eternal torment that they so richly deserve. Each of us will be presented with a summation of our life's work, with nothing left out, and nothing misrepresented in even the slightest way. Those of us who will be granted entry to heaven will know—without pride or vanity—that we have been blessed by His grace because of our efforts to do good in this lifetime.

It is in order to be able to administer this justice perfectly that God has arranged for all our deeds to be recorded,[64] and He chastens those of us who doubt that He is aware of our every thought and deed, saying, "Or do they, perchance, think that We do not hear their hidden thoughts and their secret confabulation?"[65] We do well to remember that, regardless of how carefully we think we have concealed our nefarious plans, or our petty misdeeds, God sees and hears everything, and His angels are around us at all times, recording everything we do or omit to do in a flawless record of our lives. Because of this flawless record, none of us will be able to deny the evil deeds that we have engaged in. As the Qur'ān states, "On the Day when all secrets will be laid bare, and man will have neither strength nor helper,"[66] our actions will be judged according to the divine measure of absolute truth, and none of the advantages we enjoyed in life, such as wealth, status or influential friends, will make any difference whatsoever. We will not be able to use the culture we lived in, or the customs we were accustomed to, as an excuse for anything we did that failed to please God.[67]

The Qur'ān uses the term "harvest" to describe what will happen to us on the Day of Judgement, in the sense that we will reap whatever we sow, and

---

64 Q. 45:29.
65 Q. 43:80.
66 Q. 86:9-10.
67 Q. 53:39.

that our experience of the afterlife will be closely aligned to our behaviour. It is up to us whether we choose to spend eternity with God in heaven, with the possibility of continuous spiritual growth and development, or in hell, where we will be punished and forced to exist forever with the dreadful knowledge that our own foolish decisions have led to our being excluded from the presence of God for eternity. Those who have behaved in accordance with God's wishes, and who have truly repented for those sins that they did commit, will experience a sense of utter joy that is literally indescribable in everyday language, and completely beyond the realm of ordinary human understanding, summed up simply in the Qur'ān in simple, but beautifully evocative, language where it describes the faces of the true believers as "fresh with joy" and "looking at their Lord."[68]

Some critics may complain that life is unfair, and that some people's experience on earth is much more difficult than others' or that they have been challenged with more temptations. The simple fact is that God does not give anyone more than they can deal with. If we have been confronted with great temptations, it is because God knows that we have the inner strength to stay away from them, if only we choose to do so. If we are given great burdens to carry – sickness, poverty, or bereavement, for example – it is because God knows that we have the ability to transcend them and to stick to the straight path that He has laid out for us. Each of us is singly responsible for carrying and dealing with the challenges and burdens that are ours alone. We cannot ask for or expect another to help us with what God has sent us to deal with, because we alone are responsible and will be called upon to answer for it.[69] As the Qur'ān states:

> Whoever chooses to follow the right path, follows it but for his own good, and whoever goes astray, goes but astray to his own hurt; and no bearer of burdens shall be made to bear another's burden.[70]

---

68 Q. 75:22-3.
69 Q. 53:38.
70 Q. 17:15.

There is no option for transferring all or some of the burden to someone else. This essential law is mentioned at various points throughout the Qur'ān.[71]

It should be noted that, among other things, this is a clear rejection of the controversial Christian doctrine of "original sin," which maintains that every human is burdened with the sin of his or her remote ancestors from birth, as well as the idea that any individual's sins can be paid for through the sacrifice of a third party, such as saint or prophet. Clearly, then, the notion of the prophet Jesus "paying" for the sins of others by means of his own tragic death is sorely mistaken, as is the idea that an innocent new born child, a clean new soul, has to somehow pay for sins that were committed long before he or she was even conceived. Indeed, the idea of a new born being burdened with sin is ridiculous, and almost obscene, considered from an Islamic perspective. How could someone see a tiny baby, created and beloved by God, as a creature in need of redemption? Similarly, the Persian idea that the sins of mankind were redeemed by Mithras is absolutely without foundation. Moreover, it is clear that each human being must stand responsible for his or her own deeds, and cannot count on any sort of "mediation" (like the idea preached by the Roman Catholic Church) between themselves and the God Whom they will face on the great Day of Judgement:[72]

> And whatever (wrong) any human being commits rests upon himself alone, and no bearer of burdens shall be made to bear another's burden. And, in time, unto your Sustainer you all must return; and then, He will make you truly understand all that on which you were wont to differ."[73]

God created human beings to live within families, communities and tribes or nations. In life, these social divisions are of great importance to us all. Within the context of these manifold relationships, we all grow up, go about our daily

---

71 For example, Q. 6:164, 17:15, 35:18, 39:7.
72 Asad, 1984, 816, note 31, and 669, note 16.
73 Q. 6:164.

lives, and marry and have children of our own. These relationships are at the heart of society because God himself has created them to be so. Yet even these very important relationships, so fundamental to everything we do on earth, are irrelevant on the Day of Judgement, when each of us must stand alone:

> O men! Be conscious of your Sustainer, and stand in awe of the Day on which no parent will be of any avail to his child, nor a child will in the least avail his parent. Verily, God's promise is true indeed: let not, then, the life of this world delude you, and let not (your own) deceptive thoughts about God delude you.[74]

On the Day of Judgement, none of us will be able to help our loved ones, or stand in for them when it is their turn to account for themselves, for each of us will have to stand alone and responsible for our own behaviour.[75] The act of Judgement frees us from the limitations of the ethnic group or tribe to which we once belonged, while also allowing those who are granted entrance to heaven the possibility of spending eternity with the ones they love.[76] Indeed, those who have been sentenced by God to suffer in the hereafter for sins they committed will be in no position to bear anyone else's sorrows or torments, as they will have more than enough to deal with on their own:

> Verily, the Day of Distinction between the true and the (false) is the term appointed for all of them, the Day when no friend shall be of the least avail to his friend, and when none shall be succoured. Save those upon whom God will have bestowed His grace and mercy: for, verily, He alone is almighty, a dispenser of grace. (And they will be told) "This is the Day of Distinction (between the true and the false-the Day) which you were wont to call a lie!"[77]

---

74 Q. 31:33.
75 Q. 80:34-7; 82:18-9.
76 Rustomji, 2008, 5.
77 Q. 44:40-2; 37:21.

Instead, each of us will approach God, prostrate ourselves, and cast down our eyes as we are called upon to justify each of our actions during life,[78] whereupon the sinners will find that the idea that anything that is useful or easy can be justified in moral terms is nothing but a hollow lie. Indeed, anyone who denied God during their lives, having had the opportunity to come to Him, should note that even the good deeds they carried out will be as useless, "as ashes which the wind blows about fiercely on a stormy day"[79] This teaching, which occurs in the Qur'ān on just two occasions, refers to the deliberate rejection of God and His uniqueness, rather than to those who have not had the opportunity to come to Him. The second reference explores the theme in more detail:

> But as for those who are bent on denying the truth, their (good) deeds are like a mirage in the desert, which the thirsty supposes to be water – until, when he approaches it, he finds that it was nothing; instead, he finds (that) God (has always been present) with him, and that He will pay him his account in full – for God is swift in reckoning. Or (else, their deeds are) like the depths of darkness upon an abysmal sea, made yet more dark by wave billowing over wave, (black) clouds above it all; depths of darkness, layer upon layer, (so that) when one holds up his hand, he can hardly see it; for he to whom God gives no light, no light whatever has he.[80]

Knowing that God is merciful and wants nothing more than for us to live well and abide with Him in the afterlife, how are we supposed to reconcile this knowledge with the above verse? Quite simply, God refers here only to those who have had the opportunity to experience His light, who have been given ample opportunity to listen to His message, and who have rejected it through their own hubris and arrogance.

---

78 Q. 68:42-3.
79 Q. 14:18.
80 Q. 24:39-40.

The Day of Judgement

On the Day of Judgement, all of the people in the world will be divided into three groups[81]:

- Those who have lived according to God's wishes, "attaining to what is right."
- Those who allowed themselves to become "lost in evil."
- Those who were "the foremost in faith and good works" and who were always drawn close to God.

The terms "attaining to what is right" and "losing oneself in evil" are interesting cultural references to the pre-Islamic belief that future events could be predicted by watching how birds flew at particular times of the year. At the time, it was considered lucky when birds flew to the right, and unlucky when they flew to the left. As referenced briefly above, the ideas of "right" and "left" as "lucky" and "unlucky" were absorbed into the language, and were later adopted to indicate the concepts of "righteous" and "not righteous."

Those who are judged by God as righteous will find themselves immersed in bliss on the Day of Judgement. The Qur'ān uses the metaphor of a record of their lives being placed in their right hand, and depicts a righteous man as saying, "Come you all! Read this my record. Behold, I did know that (one day) I would have to face my account. And so he will find himself in a happy state of life."[82] The placement of his record in his right hand is a clear metaphor for the virtuous way in which he lived. Conversely, the unrighteous is depicted as having his record placed in his left hand, and as saying, "Oh, would that I had never been shown this my record, and neither known this my account. Oh, would that this (death of mine) had been the end of me. Of no avail to me is all that I have ever possessed, all my power of argument has died away from me."[83] The argument that is referred to here is that against divine judgement and the fate that this unrighteous person will face in hell. Even worse off is the

---

81 Q. 56:7-12.
82 Q. 69:18-22.
83 Q. 69:25-9.

sinner whose record is described as being given to him "behind his back," with the grim warning that, "he will in time pray for utter destruction."[84] Here, we clearly see that the sinner himself is absolutely horrified by his record, belatedly realising how utterly foolish and negligent he has been, and that he wishes more than anything that he did not have to see it.

The Qur'ān describes how sinners will attempt to escape their fate on the Day of Judgement, suggesting that, if they could, they would offer all their worldly goods to avoid experiencing the fires of hell. God will judge them fairly, as He judges everyone else.[85] The world as we know it will have been utterly transformed and will no longer be recognisable as the planet that we now call home, and relationships between sinful human beings will have been transformed into something hideous. Confronted with the consequences of what they have done, the sinners will desert even the people they cared for most, and attempt to offer them up as a ransom in exchange for escaping the dreadful fires of hell:

> But if those who are bent on evildoing possessed all that is on earth, and twice as much, they would surely offer it as ransom from the awful suffering (that will befall them) on the Day of Resurrection, for, something with which they had not reckoned before will (by then) have been made obvious to them by God. And obvious to them will have become the evil that they had wrought in life and thus shall they be overwhelmed by the very truth which they were wont to deride.[86]

The Qur'ān is perfectly clear in stating that the riches of the world are useless on the Day of Judgement – how can anyone imagine that He could bribe God, the creator and lord of everything in existence – and that there is nothing that could ever serve as ransom for those who lived and died while continuing

---

84 Q. 84:10-1.
85 Q. 10:54.
86 Q. 39:47-8; 70:10-4.

The Day of Judgement

to deny the truth.[87] The only path to salvation lies in doing good deeds and honouring God, whether one is rich or poor in this life.

Sinners are referred to as hiding their remorse, but the Qur'ān mentions in many different passages that sinners will express their remorse loudly and clearly on the last day. Here, it seems that the intended meaning is their simple inability to express the full depths of the remorse they are experiencing.[88] Unlike sinners, those whose behaviour in this world pleased God will be rewarded with happiness in the next life, characterised in the Qur'ān as heaven and again as a natural consequence of their behaviour, which in this case was pleasing to God:

> Of those who have responded to their Sustainer with a goodly response, and of those who did not respond to Him. (As for the latter,) if they possessed all that is on earth, and twice as much, they would surely offer it as ransom (on the Day of Judgement) a most evil reckoning awaits them, and their goal is hell; and how evil a resting-place![89]

The Qur'ān deals swiftly with those who would be tempted to argue that they committed evil deeds or did not worship God because they did not know that they should. It clearly states that God has provided us with "witnesses" who brought God's message to the people, thus making it impossible for evil-doers to plead ignorance of His law.[90] This refers to the fact that, on the Day of Judgement, God will call all of the prophets to whom He sent His message to testify that they had delivered it to the people. This testimony will clearly show that those who have pleaded ignorance are lying, having been given multiple opportunities to make the changes necessary to live in a way that pleases God.[91]

---

87 Q. 3:91; 57:15.
88 Asad, 1984, 300, note 77.
89 Q. 13:18, 5:36.
90 Q. 16:84.
91 Q. 77: 35-6.

Above all, it is essential to recognise that what happens in the next life is a completely natural consequence of what happens in this one. The Qur'an states that "whoever is blind (of heart) in this (world) will be blind in the life to come (as well), and still farther astray from the path (of truth)."[92] When the Qur'ān vividly describes the awfulness that awaits sinners in the next world, it is giving us a timely warning that our ultimate destiny is in our own hands. God has promised to reward us for all our good deeds, but to punish those who have refused to heed him despite the many opportunities he gave them to hear His teaching and come close to him.[93]

Nobody would wish to be a sinner on the Day of Judgement, when they are compared to the messengers and prophets whom God has sent to earth and found lacking,[94] whereupon they will wish they could be reduced to mere dust in order to escape the suffering that is in store for them. Nothing they can say or do will justify the way they have behaved, for God sees and knows all.[95] The Qur'ān metaphorically describes these people as being betrayed by their very own bodies, which are described as bearing witness against them.[96] This is a way of stating that there is never any point in trying to deceive God. These sinners are depicted as experiencing the sudden awakening of their moral conscience,[97] at a time when it is already far too late. In fact, this belated realisation that they have been acting against God throughout their lifetimes exacerbates, rather than improves, the extent to which they will be seen as guilty, given that they had already been gifted multiple opportunities to come to this realisation earlier, and rejected them all.[98] The Qur'ān goes further, to depict those who have died without ever repenting as being confronted on the Day of Judgement with a clear vision of their sins, each of

---

92 Q. 17:71-2.
93 Q. 4:40-2.
94 Rida, 1999, vol. 5, 89.
95 Q. 4:42.
96 Q. 41:20-2.
97 Q. 50:21; 23.
98 Asad, 1984, 798, note 16.

which is equivalent to a witness giving testimony, and forcing them to accept the reality of their guilt and their need for punishment. As Rahman states, each human being will be, "shaken into a unique and unprecedented awareness of his deeds."[99] This is consistent with the Qur'ān's teaching that our sins are, above all, wrongs committed against ourselves,[100] and that for peace to reign on earth, it is essential for human society to develop a sense of ethics, of right and wrong. We will not, then, be able to lay blame at the feet of others for the wrongdoings we have committed ourselves, and nor will we be able to escape our inevitable consequences, for there will be no one capable of coming to our aid, even if they wished to.[101]

When man's innermost thoughts, feeling and motivations are exposed, the implication is that their erstwhile claim that whatever is "expedient" is morally justifiable, shall be revealed as something indefensible and spiritually destructive. Instead, those who have made sacrifices for the cause of God and righteousness, rather than simply striving to accumulate as many possessions as possible, will be welcomed by God into heaven. Conversely, the evildoers will be unable to bargain with God, while there is nobody in a position to intercede on their behalf;[102] not their family members or even their own children.[103] Then, they will wish that the Day of Judgement could be delayed indefinitely, so that they can escape the inevitable reckoning and punishment.[104]

---

99 Rahman, 1989, 106.
100 Asad, 1984, 409, note 103.
101 Q. 40:17-8.
102 Q. 2:254.
103 Q. 60:3.
104 Q. 3:30.

CHAPTER 9

Miracles and the Miraculous Night Journey (Mi'rāj)

THROUGHOUT THE QUR'ĀN, God makes it abundantly clear that He created the earth and all it contains for the specific purpose of providing us humans with a home wherein we find all that we will ever need. In His wisdom, God has created us in the form of diverse races, groups and nations, and He has sent His message to various prophets at different points in history. The earth is not the natural abode for angelic beings – if it was, God would have sent an angel with his message.[1] Instead, He has sent us prophets in the form of men – ordinary, flesh and blood men – who have conveyed the Word of God to us in vernacular terms that we can understand and apply to our own lives.

Muhammad often faced criticism from his detractors, who queried why they could not see the angels he spoke of and suggested that, because he could not directly show them any such beings, he must be a fraud. The Qur'ān pointed out that angels will be revealed to humankind on the Day of Judgement, which is when we will finally be able to understand them, and it stated that some people are so determined to ignore God's truth that they would have rejected it even if God had sent His word in the form of writing on parchment.[2] It also makes it clear that humans are currently unable to understand the objective reality of angelic beings. Even if God had sent an angel to earth in a visible form, he would have appeared to be a human being,

---

1 Q. 17:95.
2 Q. 6:7-8.

and would made the doubters even more confused.[3] Giving the angel the appearance of a man would have been necessary, because our human minds are currently unable to perceive or comprehend angels in their real form.

Unbelievers often fail to truly understand the difference between spiritual things of God and the superstitious and unfounded beliefs that emerge from the minds of man. Because so many people worship false gods, and attribute divine powers to them, they often fail to understand that an angel is a very different sort of being. An angel is a being created by God that can never be perceived by weak humans who allow themselves to become obsessed with material wealth. So long as they remain so, they will never be able to truly understand the nature of God or of His angels. However, God is merciful, and He has given us all abundant chances to turn to Him and embrace His truth. We will all have the opportunity to see God's angels for ourselves on the Day of Judgement.

Miracles, the Prophets, and the Everyday

The very "ordinariness" of the prophets has sometimes been used by their critics in attempts to put them down by highlighting their status as apparently unexceptional human beings. In Muhammad's day, his detractors asked why he had not been given an "miraculous sign" from God to prove conclusively that he was everything he said. In doing so, the Qur'ān points out, they simply revealed their own ignorance, because God and all His mighty works are visible all around us, in the wonders of Creation, to anyone who opens his or her eyes sufficiently to see.[4]

The term "āyah" is used throughout the Qur'ān to mean "miracle," or an event that takes place even though it is not part of the natural order (in the sense of a happening that goes beyond the usual course of nature), but also a "sign" or "message," with the latter definition the most common by far. People often assume that a "miracle" is, by definition, a baffling and extraordinary

---

3 Q. 6:9.
4 Q. 6:37.

event, such as walking on water, or raising someone from the dead. Instead, miracles are actually more typically unusual messages from God, that may reveal a deep spiritual truth to us in a rich, symbolic manner that would have eluded us in a more ordinary setting.

Although human beings are often hungry for miracles that will show them the reality of God, they often fail to recognise the thousands of miracles that they encounter every day. There is no living creature on earth that was not created by God – and how miraculous is even the humblest of life forms![5] The term "ummah" implies a group of living creatures that have particular qualities in common, and it can be used for human communities (such as a tribe or a nation) and for other collectives of living beings, such as a group of animals. God calls on us all, collectively and individually, to observe His manifold miracles as they occur in nature all around us, and to use our observations as a way to understand Him better and to draw closer to Him.[6] Sadly, as the Qur'ān makes clear, there are many who essentially refuse to consider the evidence of God that is all around them; these are people of the same ilk as those, in Muhammad's day, who refused to listen to the prophet and take in the awesome reality of his message.[7] The great irony lies in the fact that all of those who doubt still live in and enjoy the beautiful world that God has made for us, in which not the slightest thing happens but for His decree.[8] The bitter truth is that those who doubt God and His messengers demand to see miracles to "prove" what they are told about, while ignoring the miracles that are beneath their noses every day. The Qur'ān reiterates that only God can perform miracles, while hardened unbelievers would reject one if it happened right in front of them.[9] Indeed, many people have rejected God's message, even when it was accompanied by miracles.[10]

---

5 Q. 6:38.
6 Asad, 1984, 177, note 30.
7 Q. 2:118; 7:203; 13:7, 27.
8 Q. 6:59.
9 Q. 6:109.
10 Q. 17:59.

Miracles and the Miraculous Night Journey (Mi'rāj)

As God can do everything, and Muhammad is His messenger, it is striking that Muhammad is, in general, not associated with miraculous events. In fact, in various places in the Qur'ān, the holy book emphasises that God did not empower Muhammad to perform miracles like those said to have been performed by earlier prophets. For Muhammad, and for the early Muslims, the Qur'ān itself was miracle enough, as it brought God's message to His people in a perfect form, clearly enunciated, relevant to human existence in every realm of life, and unchanging. Conversely, the earlier prophets tended to deliver messages that were less universal in nature, and more bound by the cultural and temporal environment in which they found themselves restricted by the level of social, spiritual and intellectual development of the people of the day. Because human societies were still less sophisticated than when Muhammad started to receive revelations, earlier prophets needed to use potent symbols, drawing on the notion of the miraculous, to alert the people to the importance of God's message. Instead, Muhammad lived at a time and in a social milieu when, thanks in part to the earlier revelations received by the Jews and Christians, society had become sufficiently mature to understand a complex ideology without resorting to such displays.[11] Furthermore, we should not assume from the many accounts of earlier prophets as performing miracles that these literally took place as they are often described in colloquial settings. Consider, for example, the case of Jesus, who is described as "turning water into wine." Rather than indicating that he literally turned water into wine, the reality – in truth far more moving and powerful – is that Jesus broke with the long-established traditions of a far from egalitarian society, and permitted all of those who were traditionally considered to be lesser people to engage directly with him and with God's message. Jesus's true miracle lay in his message of the essential equality of each and every human being, regardless of their gender, physical health, race, and so forth. Like Muhammad, Jesus's message was essentially a revolutionary one that plainly stated that all human beings are created equal, and that all are equally beloved by God.[12]

---

11 Asad 1984, 427-8, note 71.
12 Thiering, 1992, 34.

One of the problems that Muhammad had to face was the fact that the people of ancient Arabia had been primed by pre-Islamic belief systems and previous religious custom to expect that a "true" prophet would be able to make extraordinary things take place. The Qur'ān reports that many told him that they refused to believe that he was relating the Word of God until he caused the miraculous appearance of a spring of water from the ground, or created a luscious, fruit-bearing garden, showed them a house made out of gold, brought God and the angels literally in front of them to be seen, or even ascended to heaven.[13]

Muhammad was quick to clarify that he did indeed bring a miracle to the people, and that the miracle was the Qur'ān itself, with its far-reaching implications, and universal application. Moreover, notwithstanding the (often essentially folkloric) accounts of miracles performed by earlier prophets, he also made it clear that only God can truly perform miracles. Even if he had been able to (and he was but a man), Muhammad would not have enacted miracles, for such things belong to God and not to mere mortals. There is something deeply profound and moving about God's decision to choose from among the ordinary people the vessel for His messages to humanity.[14]

Notwithstanding the Qur'ān's insistence on Muhammad's status as an ordinary man who had been chosen by God to carry out a profoundly important task, one of the most intriguing elements of the Qur'ān refers to a deep mystic experience in which Muhammad travelled to Jerusalem, and then ascended into heaven in the company of the archangel Gabriel, where he met a number of the earlier prophets of God.[15] This journey in two parts is collectively known as the "night journey,"[16] as it took place in the course of a single night. During this experience, Muhammad was instructed to teach Muslims

---

13 Q. 17:90-3.
14 Q. 3:164; 7:35, 63,69; 9:128.
15 Asad, 1984, 996.
16 Colby, 2008, 15.

how to pray the Five Daily Prayers as an essential element of their faith.[17] This event is memorialised in the following verse:

> Limitless in His glory is He who transported His servant by night from the Inviolable House of Worship (at Mecca) to the Remote House of Worship (at Jerusalem) – the environs of which We had blessed – so that We might show him some of Our symbols; for, verily, He alone is all-hearing, all-seeing." And (thus, too,) We vouchsafed revelation unto Moses, and made it a guidance for the Children of Israel, (commanding them) "Do not ascribe to any but Me the power to determine your fate.[18]

The Context of the Journey

Muhammad's night journey began in Mecca, where he was living at the time, and brought him to Jerusalem (the part of the journey known as "Isra"), after which he ascended into heaven (the part of the journey known as "Mi'rāj"), and was made to travel through seven distinct layers of heaven before encountering God in paradise. The Qur'ān describes each layer of heaven as distinct from every other.[19] In this way, we should not interpret the word "heaven" as simply implying paradise. Muhammad's journey was unique. Although God had sent other prophets to bring His message to humanity before, He had never brought any of them to heaven during their lifetime.

How are we to correctly interpret the above verse describing Muhammad's journey? First of all, it is important to note that the "Inviolable House of Worship" refers to the Temple of the Ka'bah, which was originally founded by the prophet Abraham[20] as the first temple in which humans could worship

---

17 Asad, 1984, 996.
18 Q. 17:1-2.
19 Q. 41:12.
20 Q. 2:125.

the one true God.²¹ The Temple of Ka'bah is of great importance of Muslims. "The Remote House of Worship" is the site of the ancient Temple of Solomon and an important site to Muslims, Christians and Jews alike to this day. In this context, we see a reference not just to Islamic theology, but also to the many prophets in the Jewish tradition who came before Muhammad. In referring to both of these ancient temples, the verse is alluding to the fact that Muhammad had not been tasked with introducing a "new" religion but, rather, that Islam represents the development and continuation of the essential message, indicated here by the mention of "symbols" of the one true God that had already been brought to humanity by a long line of prophets through the ages. This is why Jerusalem is such an important site to Muslims to this day, and why early Muslims said their prayers facing the sacred site.²²

Muhammad's extraordinary journey is thoroughly in line with events experienced by other prophets, and can be compared to the revelations received by the prophet Moses. Moses is mentioned in various locations in the Qur'ān, with remarks such as "God spoke His word unto Moses,"²³ and "I have raised thee [Moses] above all people… by virtue of My speaking (unto thee)."²⁴ In general, the various references in the Qur'ān to the religious history of the Jews refer to the fact that they originally introduced the concept of monotheism, the worship of the one true God, providing the ideological and theological foundation on which Christianity and, later, Islam, were built.²⁵

The Reality of the Journey

Most Islamic scholars consider Muhammad's journey to have taken place while the prophet was still in Mecca, a year or two before the young Islamic community migrated to Medina. The Qur'ān itself clearly references the journey,

---

21 Q. 3:96.
22 Busse, 1968, 441.
23 Q. 4:164.
24 Q. 7:144.
25 Asad, 1984, 417-8.

Miracles and the Miraculous Night Journey (Mi'rāj)

while scholars writing many centuries ago have clarified many of the details. For example, Ibn-Ishaq drew on narratives supplied by Muhammad's wife Aisha, and a number of his close companions, to bring together the strands of the account, which covers not just one, but two journeys: one to Jerusalem, and one to heaven.[26] Clearly, the journey itself took place beyond the bounds of ordinary time, because Muhammad is said to have travelled between Mecca and Jerusalem in the course of just one night, and from Jerusalem to heaven.[27] While many of his companions at the time believed him to have travelled in the physical sense of the word, the journey can also be viewed in purely spiritual terms; in other words, Muhammad's spirit may have taken the journey while his body rested in Mecca. The latter view was the one held by Aisha, who insisted that he was transported only in spirit, while his body remained in place.[28] It should be noted that many of Aisha's contemporaries found it very difficult to understand the concept of a spiritual journey, and continued to insist that the journey had been physical.[29] Today, with our more sophisticated understanding of psychology, the serious scholarly consensus is that the journey was indeed a spiritual one, with rich layers of allegorical meaning, rather than a literal journey in the sense in which the term is usually understood. On the other hand, it is also extremely important to draw a clear distinction between the concept of a spiritual journey, when a man's body leaves his soul and journeys to a new destination, and a dream, which is merely a fantasy.[30] As Muhammad's spirit *really* travelled to Jerusalem and heaven, his account of the things he witnessed can be taken just as seriously as his other revelations. Some believe that spiritual travel of this sort is a possibility that might be open to all extremely pious Muslims.

The Qur'ān has various descriptions of Muhammad's encounters with angels. For example:

---

26 Porter, 1974, 64.
27 Busse, 1968, 441.
28 Asad, 1984, 996.
29 Asad, 1984, 997.
30 Asad, 1984, 997.

That (which he conveys to you) is but (divine) inspiration with which he is being inspired, something that a very mighty one has imparted to him; (an angel) endowed with surpassing power, who in time manifested himself in his true shape and nature, appearing in the horizon's loftiest part.[31]

The Qur'ān relates that, in his whole lifetime, Muhammad only twice had a vision of this angelic force shown to him "in its true shape and nature." Elsewhere, he is described as viewing the angelic being "on the clear horizon,"[32] and at a distance of "two bow lengths, or even nearer." Compare this verse: "he truly beheld (the angel – beheld) him on the clear horizon."[33] These accounts are clearly indicative of the descent of a heavenly creature to earth, where he spoke with Muhammad.[34] On the occasion of the second encounter, Muhammad is described as seeing the angel "by the lote-tree of the farthest limit."[35] The species of tree in question has a rich abundance of leaves that provide very welcome shade in the desert country of Arabia. In the Qur'ān, the tree is often used as a symbol of spiritual peace and the ultimate fulfilment of paradise.

Even though Muhammad's experience was an extraordinary, and clearly very profound one, he accepted it, and experienced no distinction between the spiritual, intuitive, and conscious elements of the experience.[36] Muhammad was only able to explain his experience to his followers with symbolic and allegorical language (indeed, the quality of the language itself is further evidence of the essentially spiritual nature of the journey[37]) and there were all too many sceptics eager to use his unusual story to discredit him.[38]

---

31 Q. 53:4-7.
32 Q. 81:23.
33 Q. 81:23.
34 Lange, 2016, 112.
35 Q. 53:13-4.
36 Q. 53:12.
37 Asad, 1984, 996.
38 Q. 53:12.

The Importance of the Night Journey

Muhammad's "night journey" is one of the key events of his spiritual life and of the development of Islam. It has inspired some of the most important artistic expressions to emerge from Islamic culture, in the context of painting and poetry. Aspects of the journey may also have influenced artistic expressions in Western cultures, such as Dante's *Divine Comedy*. The vibrant narrative has also led to the proliferation of largely folkloric traditions around the prophet's journey, including the notion that he journeyed to heaven on the back of a white, winged horse. While entertaining, these accounts have no Qur'ānic verification and should be treated as folktales (described by Lange as "thick layers of legendary narrative"[39]), and no more.

For Muslims, Jerusalem is considered the third most sacred site, precisely because of Muhammad's mystic journey to it.[40] For a number of years after Muhammad's spiritual journey, the nascent Muslim community turned in the direction of Jerusalem to pray, turning towards Mecca after Muhammad received a revelation instructing them to turn towards the "inviolable House of Worship," which is in Mecca.[41] In this way, as in others, the Night Journey left a permanent imprimatur on Islam. Above all, in the context of the current work, it has informed our understanding of heaven and hell considerably.[42]

---

39 Lange, 2016, 112.
40 Nasr, 2015, 694-5.
41 Q. 2:144.
42 Lange, 2016, 115.

CHAPTER 10

Intercession

THE CONCEPT OF intercession is that someone – such as a saint, a prophet (possibly even Muhammad himself) or a martyr – can make a "special case" for someone with God, so that they will be judged more leniently. This is an idea that we find in various religious traditions, above all the Catholic Church. Catholics often pray to characters such as the Virgin Mary or one of their many thousands of saints, with the idea that they will "intercede" with God to encourage Him to view the sins and discrepancies of the person in question with greater favour.

The concept of intercession is an idea that is also widespread in a range of Islamic traditions, particularly at grassroots level,[1] where many believe that intercession takes place after God has decided where the soul in question will be judged, heaven or hell.[2] In order to understand the official Qurʾānic teaching on this matter, however, we need to return to the Qurʾān itself, as well as applying ourselves to understanding the teaching of important Islamic scholars who have explored this important issue. As even the well-meaning sometimes stray away from the Word of God as revealed to Muhammad in the form of the Qurʾān, to embrace ideas that owe much more to wishful thinking than to the truth, it is incumbent on us all to understand what was originally meant, and then to endeavour to live according to God's original teaching, and not the mere accretions of human society.

---

1 Madigan, 2006, 91.
2 Rustomji, 2008, 41.

Repentance

Throughout the Qur'ān, we are frequently reminded of God's mercy and His love for even the least of His Creation. In His wisdom, He has created us humans with both intelligence and free will, and His desire is that we should use these gifts to live in a way that pleases Him, by striving at all times to be virtuous, kind and pious. Yet God knows that we humans are also weak and prone to temptation. For this reason, anyone who sins – and at some point, we all do, to varying degrees – has the opportunity to repent and make amends before it is too late.

There are many discussions of repentance in the Qur'ān, both in terms of the sinners who repent of the bad things they have done, and of how God graciously embraces anyone who truly repents. For example:

> Verily, God's acceptance of repentance relates only to those who do evil out of ignorance and soon afterwards repent; and it is they unto whom God will turn again in His mercy – for God is all-knowing, wise. Whereas repentance shall not be accepted from those who do evil deeds until their dying hour and then say, "Behold, I now repent"; nor from those who die as deniers of the truth; it is these for whom We have readied grievous suffering.[3]

Over the years, most Islamic scholars have maintained that the term "soon afterwards repent" refers to repentance as we near our time to die – the idea, for example, of an older person, knowing that death is approaching and choosing to "fix things" with God before it is too late, or the death of someone who is terminally ill, and waits until the last moment, when his health is failing fast, to start making amends with God.

How are we to interpret the concept of doing evil "in ignorance"? It is easy to understand, for instance, how this term can refer to anyone who sins unintentionally, perhaps because they have not had the opportunity to hear the

---

3 Q. 4:17-8.

teachings of Islam at all, or because they have been badly instructed. However, many scholars have maintained that the term also refers to anyone who carries out evil acts while lacking knowledge of the punishment they will suffer for them, or even that anyone who disobeys God is in a state of ignorance by definition. There are verses in the Qur'ān that show the prophet Joseph as expressing his anxiety that, if he sins, he will become "one of the ignorant,"[4] while a woman who tried to seduce him is described as being in a state of ignorance, even though she was perfectly clear in her intentions from the start.[5]

While God is always loving and merciful, He is also fair, and fairness implies punishing the wicked as well as rewarding the just. Clearly, repentance for dreadful misdeeds carried out at the last moment, when the person in question is about to die, cannot be compared to true, meaningful repentance carried out in the cold light of our everyday existence, when we are called on to change the way we live in a manner that we may find inconvenient. In fact, the Qur'ān states that such acts can actually doom the sinner to an even more severe punishment than if they simply died without repenting, because of the appalling levels of hypocrisy involved.[6]

Intercession in the Qur'ān

As stated above, many of the stories about the Day of Judgement circulated in the Islamic world feature the idea of intercession, which maintains that a third party can intercede with God to remove or lessen punishment.[7] While these stories often have a folkloric aspect that is interesting to explore from an anthropological point of view, it is essential to note that the concept of intercession is certainly dealt with in the Qur'ān, and that its message is clear.

In the early days of Islam, Muhammad preached not just to the nascent Muslim community, but also to the pagans, Jews and Christians who lived

---

4 Q. 12:33.
5 Q. 12:88-9.
6 Idleman Smith and Yazbeck Haddad, 2002, 25.
7 Idleman Smith and Yazbeck Haddad, 2002, 25.

in Arabia at the time. The pagans in particular subscribed to a polytheistic belief system, and were often sure that the many gods they believed in could intercede on behalf of sinners. The Qur'ān rejects this idea without exception.[8] It points out that the "beings" in whom the pagans believed had no power to intercede, while that those who have lived virtuously, spoken the truth, and accepted God's uniqueness would have no need of intercession.[9] Simply stating in words that God is unique and all-powerful is not enough, and such words are pointless unless they come from a personal awareness of the nature of God, Who alone will decide the fate of each individual. As none of His creatures, including His angels, can do anything without His permission, clearly any "intercession" engaged in by angels or other beings can only take place if God has already decided on His judgement in the first place.[10] This teaching speaks directly to those who hope that the angels, the saints, or imaginary gods they worship might be able to "step in" and act as mediators between them and God, and obtain passage to heaven for them, or at least a reduction in their punishment. However, these people have not really thought their beliefs through, to the extent that the Qur'ān actually describes them as similar to those who reject the idea of the afterlife in the first place.[11] Their eventual fate in the afterlife does not depend on the actions of third parties, but is specifically related to their own behaviour, and the way in which they have expressed their understanding of and relationship with God, from start to finish. However, their belief is far too vague to make them realise that the quality of humankind's life in the hereafter does not depend on such outside factors but is causally, and directly, connected with the manner of his life in this world; and so, the Qur'ān declares that their attitude is, for all practical purposes, similar to the attitude of people who reject the idea of a hereafter altogether.

---

8 Q. 34:23.
9 Q. 43:86.
10 Q. 53:26.
11 Asad, 1984, 814, note 20.

Essentially, the Qur'ān states that God alone oversees the relationship between Him and the people whom He has created. As He is possessed of extraordinary powers that mere humans cannot even begin to understand, it is futile to imagine that any lesser being could intercede to change God's mind. This means that none of us can imagine that our sins and misdeeds will be overlooked on the Day of Judgement, when every human being will be made accountable for all of their deeds without the help of an intercessor. This concept of personal responsibility is fully reinforced in many passages of the Qur'an, where it appeals to humankind's better instincts to use reason and intellect so that they may be conscientious of God and His wondrous creations. The Qur'an then implores humankind to behave in a righteous manner in line with God's commandments, and further reminds us that whoever performs good deeds does so for their own good, and those who commit wrongdoing do so for their own loss. The Qur'an then warns humankind that, on the Day of Judgement, each individual must fully account for all of their deeds. The Qur'ān dismisses both the Christian idea of intercession, and the Jewish notion that they, alone of all the tribes and ethnicities placed on this earth by God, would not be punished on the Day of Judgement. Instead, it urges the faithful to warn both the "People of the Book" (Jews and Christians) and anyone who is harbouring doubts about God, to accept life after death and the idea of a final judgement.[12]

Despite the fact that, generally speaking, the Qur'ān rejects intercession, some scholars have interpreted particular passages as indicating that there might, in fact, be some circumstances in which intercession could be considered. Verse Q. 19:87 states, "None will have [power of] intercession except he who had taken from the Most Merciful a covenant." Another verse shows God calling on Muhammad to ask him to forgive living believers:

> Know, then, (O man) that there is no deity save God, and (while there is yet time) ask forgiveness for thy sins, and for (the sins of) all other

---

12 Q. 6:51.

believing men and women: for God knows all your comings and goings as well as your abiding (at rest).[13]

These, and a number of other verses, have given rise to a school of thought in Islam that maintains that intercessions do take place and that they can influence the decisions made by God on the Day of Judgement. However, consider the following:

Verily, your Sustainer is God, who has created the heavens and the earth in six aeons, and is established on the throne of His almightiness, governing all that exists. There is no intercessor whatever, save after His leave (has been granted).[14]

Here, we see that the Qur'ān does not admit that saints or prophets, living or dead, can intercede with God to remove or reduce a sinner's punishment. However, when the Day of Judgement takes place, God will give His prophets the right to "intercede" in a symbolic way on behalf of anyone who has repented and is basically good. This clearly shows that the "intercessions" of the prophets simply indicate that God is pleased with them and is showing them grace, while His will is ascendant above all:

On the Day when all (human) souls and all the angels will stand up in ranks: none will speak but he to whom the Most Gracious will have given leave; and (everyone) will say (only) what is right.[15]

This verse illustrates that nobody will be capable of speaking a mistruth on the Day of Judgement, while also clarifying that the only "intercessions" that take place are those whereby God has already accepted the sinner's sincere repentance anyway. Those who experience a close bond with God, defined

---

13 Q. 47:19.
14 Q. 10:3.
15 Q. 78:38.

as a true understanding of the facts of His unique greatness, can hope to be forgiven, even if they have committed sins, provided they were aware of God's existence and uniqueness, and have truly repented for their misdeeds. This is the only true meaning of "intercession" as it is described in the Qur'ān,[16] which states:

> He knows all that lies open before them and all that is hidden from them, hence, they cannot intercede for any but those whom He has (already) graced with his goodly acceptance, since they themselves stand in reverent awe of Him.[17]

God's Singular Judgement

In general, the Qur'ān is clear in its assertion that intercession will *not* be a feature of the Day of Judgement, when each individual will have to stand before God alone and account for their behaviour during their time on Earth:

> And remain conscious of (the coming of) a Day when no human being shall in the least avail another, nor shall intercession be accepted from any of them, no ransom taken from them, and none shall be succoured.[18]

While the idea of intercession is one that many find very attractive, for obvious reasons, studying the Qur'ān – even on a fairly superficial level – makes it very clear that intercession can only occur with the express permission of God, and then only when He has already decided to forgive anyway, making it purely symbolic in nature. The Qur'ān is very clear in dismissing the false notions of those who claim that they will benefit from intercessions on their behalf, stating:

---

16 Asad, 1984, 468.
17 Q. 21:28.
18 Q. 2:48.

They worship apart from God that which neither harms them nor benefits them. And they say, "These are our intercessors with God." Say "Would you inform God about something in the heavens or on the earth that He does not know? Glory be to Him and exalted is He above the partners they ascribe.[19]

Here, the Qur'ān is referring to the idea, widespread among the pagan Arabs, that their gods and idols would intervene with God to "fix" any issues in their daily lives that were not progressing as they wished. The Qur'ān deals swiftly with this notion. Their idols, after all, were mere objects, made from inert substances such as wood or stone, by ordinary women and men. Clearly, they could not do anything to or for the people who worshipped them. Instead, the Qur'ān asserts, "unto God belongs intercession altogether,"[20] admitting the possibility that God may grant the power of intercession to His prophets on a purely symbolic basis. The Qur'ān also explicitly makes it clear that family members can never intercede with God on each other's behalf.[21] These firm statements against intercession have been described as representing Qur'ānic development towards "a more rigorously conceived monotheism, the notion that God alone decides the otherworldly destiny of humankind, and that not even prophets and angels may intercede on behalf of others."[22]

We can only attribute the abundance of beliefs in intercession in popular Islam to wishful thinking, as these beliefs fly in the face of God's own teachings. Throughout the Qur'ān, we see God as a sole arbiter and judge, who recognises the prophets not as people who are qualified to mediate with Him, but as witnesses and messengers.[23] It is important not to get distracted by discussions of intercession from the core message of the Qur'ān, which is that God is unique and that He alone has the ultimate power to judge us, in all

---

19 Q. 10:18.
20 Q. 39:44.
21 Lange, 2016, 45.
22 Lange, 2016, 48.
23 Rahman, 1989, 31.

His mercy. Note that, in verse Q. 10:18, above, God is urging His people to turn away from their misguided understandings of life after death and their own rights and responsibilities. In the pagan Arabs' befuddled views on the afterlife was a seed of true understanding of the majesty and oneness of God. The Qur'ān urges them to reject their misapprehensions and false idols so as to embrace the reality of a true relationship with the God Who created them and Who loves them.[24] The Qur'ān associates the belief in third parties being able to intercede with God, without His express permission, with a denial of God's omnipotence:

> It is God Who has created the heavens and the earth and all that is between them in six aeons, and is established on the throne of His almightiness. You have none to protect you from God, and none to intercede for you (on Judgement Day); will you not, then, bethink yourselves?[25]

God is our lord and is alone sovereign over the heavens and the earth, and it is unto Him that we will all ultimately return. Clearly, any "intercessions" can only take place with God's permission, even if God has already decided on His Judgement in the first place.[26] This is widely asserted throughout the Qur'ān as, for instance, in the following verse:

> Oh you who believe! Spend (for the welfare of the poor) from what We have provided you before the arrival of a Day on which neither trade shall benefit, nor any friendship, nor any intercession.[27]

---

24 Q. 74:48.
25 Q. 32:4.
26 Q. 39:44.
27 Q. 2:254.

Intercession

Forewarning

The Qur'ān devotes considerable space to warning humanity that each of us is individually responsible for all we think and do. This perspective clearly does not sit well with the idea that third parties have the ability, or indeed the right, to intercede with God. We are taught that, on the Day of Judgement, God will point out to sinners that there are no mitigating factors to their sins, as they had been given ample warning that the day would come, and had been instructed by Him as to how to behave. Thus, whatever judgement God gave them on the last day will be just, and they will have nobody but themselves to blame if they do not like the outcome.[28]

Just as God only admits the possibility of intercession on a purely symbolic basis, on behalf of those whom He has already decided to forgive, it is futile for sinners to attempt to blame others for their own decisions. Ultimately, we can only be "led astray" from the straight path if we ourselves decide to suspend our good judgement and ignore all the teaching we have received from God. The Qur'ān has provided us with all the wisdom we need to know how to conduct ourselves properly, and God also sent earlier prophets to bring His message to the world.[29] Anyone who has had the opportunity to hear His word will have literally no excuse when they find themselves standing before God on the Day of Judgement, are asked to account for all of the decisions they have ever made, and can hide none of their thoughts or deeds, as God knows and sees all.[30]

You may ask, as many have done in the past, why God created women and men in such a way that they are tempted to commit evil acts and engage in wrong-doing. Well, consider this: if we were not capable of doing evil, how could we be considered capable of doing good? The very fact that we are able to make moral choices defines those choices as either immoral or godly,[31] and is a fundamental quality of human beings, who are unique among God's

---

28 Q. 50:28-9.
29 Q. 35:24, 16:36.
30 Q. 53:39; 53:40-1.
31 Q. 91:8.

Creation.³² On the Day of Judgement, we will not be able to blame anyone for our misdeeds or our misapprehensions. The Qur'ān cites the example of those who would be tempted to claim that it was not their fault that they engaged in pagan rites, for the relevant beliefs were passed on to them from their ancestors.³³ Those who attempt to argue in this way, but who actually had been given ample opportunity to listen to the word of God, will be swiftly reminded of this fact,³⁴ and of the fact that God has created each of us with the natural capacity to recognise Him in the world around us, even if we have not received specific Qur'ānic instruction.³⁵

---

32 Asad, 1984, 954.
33 Madigan, 2006, 91.
34 Q. 7:172-3; 4:165; 2:213; 6:48; 7:188.
35 Asad, 1984, 230.

CHAPTER 11

Heaven

GOD HAS PROMISED us all both that we will have ample opportunity during our lives on earth to please Him with the choices we make, and that we will be amply rewarded in the afterlife if our choices are the right ones.

Heaven, which is one of the major themes of the Qur'ān, described or referenced in many verses, both long and short, represents God's promise to His people, that they will be received by Him into His embrace after the Day of Judgement: "Unto Him is your return all together; God's promise is true."[1] The Qur'ān describes that happy moment vividly, stating that "throngs" will be urged joyfully towards the gates of paradise, where its keepers will usher them in, saying, "Peace be upon you," to which they will answer, "All praise is due to God, who has made His promise to us come true, and has bestowed upon us this expanse (of bliss) as our portion, so that we may dwell in paradise as we please."[2] As the virtuous approach heaven, light will be seen emanating from them, and in particular from their right hands.[3] This very public entry to heaven underlines the honour that will be bestowed on the people given the right to dwell in heaven, while the use of the active voice highlights that each human being has agency in the matter of whether or not they will eventually go to heaven. In practical terms, this means that each of us is holding our fate in our own hands. Regardless of our life circumstances and the temptations that we meet along the way, we have all been given the opportunity to go to heaven and spend eternity there with God.

---

1 Q. 10:4.
2 Q. 39:73-4.
3 Q. 57:12.

Heaven is typically described in terms of a beautiful garden in which it is never either too hot or too cold,[4] where the landscape is lush and green,[5] and filled with fruit-bearing trees and plants, and where pure, fresh water flows abundantly.[6] References to heaven as a garden occur throughout over one hundred times.[7] Here, those who lived virtuously on earth, and worshipped God, will spend eternity with Him, praising God[8] and enjoying each other's company forever.[9] It is easy to imagine how evocative these descriptions must have been, to a desert people living in a harsh, arid climate. The term "garden" is typically qualified with words that indicate bliss, pleasure and delight. This is also true of the Bible, which gives broadly similar, but much less detailed, descriptions of heaven.

Although multitudes will enter heaven, the reference to "throngs" refers to them entering in different groups, with those who have pleased God the most entering first, and so on in descending order. Muhammad himself will enter heaven first, followed by groups that are described in poetic terms, as "appearing like the moon on the night when it is full" and "like the brightest star shining in the sky," while God's angels will attend to all their needs. However, everyone who enters heaven will get to experience the overwhelming joy offered to them by God.

The People of Heaven

The Qur'ān describes how, on the Day of Judgement, the people of heaven will be divided from all others, describing them as those who "have attained to what is right," and stating that the best among these will be those who were, "foremost (in faith and good deeds)," because they were "drawn close

---

4 Q. 76:13.
5 Q. 77:41.
6 Q. 16:31.
7 Haleem, 2012, 96.
8 Q. 35:34.
9 Q. 15:47.

unto God." As a reward for the way they conducted themselves during their lives, they will be blessed to spend eternity living in "gardens of bliss."[10] The Qur'ān distinguish between two broad categories of people in heaven. These are known as "those who precede [others in faith or status]" or "Those who are brought near to God" (both humans and angels)[11] and a slightly lower rank, known as companions of the Right Hand" (as mentioned above).[12] The companions of the Right Hand are contrasted with the "companions of the Left Hand," who are in hell.

The Qur'ān points out that the social status we had during our lifetimes is irrelevant to God on the Day of Judgement, and that many who had poor, simple lives but who pleased Him will be elevated to exalted positions in heaven, while many of the wealthy and privileged in life will be condemned to spend eternity in hell. Certainly, whatever riches we have managed to accumulate for our own material well-being during our lives on earth will be utterly irrelevant to Him. Of course, being wealthy per se is not in any way sinful, and those who were materially fortunate during this life, and who lived in accordance with God's law, will be warmly received into heaven.

God is loving and merciful, and many of those who to go heaven to spend eternity with Him have not always conducted blameless lives. We humans are weak and frail in our convictions, and many of us will be tempted into sin at different stages in our lives. The truly important thing is to ensure, through faith and good works, that we can attain righteousness.[13] This extends hope to us all. If we repent our sins, and strive always to do good and love God, then we too can attain the same heavenly state of spiritual fulfilment as the truly virtuous. This is indeed a reason to rejoice and give thanks to God!

The people of heaven are happy, safe, and dwell in peace, away from gossip and all thoughts of death, with food and drink in abundance, and cool

---

10 Q. 56:7-14.
11 Q 56:11; 4:172; Lange, 2016, 43.
12 Q. 90:18.
13 Q. 56:27.

shade to rest in.¹⁴ The Qur'ān uses its characteristically rich language to describe those who will dwell with God in heaven, describing them as "companions pure," using a term that denotes "whiteness" in the symbolic sense of the word, and also as an indicator for beauty – for, in heaven, everything and everyone shall be beautiful.¹⁵ The beauty of those in heaven is often discussed in terms of the beauty of their eyes.¹⁶ This can be explained by noting that our eyes are typically taken to be the most expressive parts of our bodies, and even to reflect our souls. Everyone who is resurrected into heaven will be restored, new and young, even those who died in wizened old age. There, they are described in allegorical terms as living amid the great beauty of the gardens of heaven, wearing luxurious garments, and themselves beings of extraordinary beauty incomparable to anything found on earth.¹⁷ Their wonderful surroundings, and the immense joy that will fill them, can both be understood as representing a sort of rich harvest, the inarguable result of the virtuous way they lived during their time on earth.¹⁸

To add to the description of the incredible riches that the virtuous will experience, we are told that they will wear "green garments" made of silk and brocade, with golden bracelets on their arms.¹⁹ We can read this in allegorical terms. The green colour of their garments must indicate the fact that they are forever young (green being a colour associated with nature and the cyclical "rebirth" of life-giving plants), while the description of gold jewellery and rich fabrics must indicate the perfection of their lives in heaven,²⁰ where they live in endless peace, in no need of any further sustenance – spiritual or physical – than the abundance on offer to them in God's garden.

---

14 Q. 19:62.
15 Lisān Al-Arab, 1997, 183.
16 Q. 52:20.
17 Q. 44:54.
18 Q. 44:51-6.
19 Q. 18:30-1.
20 Asad, 1984, 444, note 41.

Heaven

The people of heaven are described in the Qur'ān as remaining in contact with their families and loved ones in the afterlife, and as having their own private heavens within the enormity of heaven overall.[21] They are described as entering in the company of "their parents, their spouses, and their offspring," and as being greeted and congratulated together by the angels for their perseverance in living well on earth and praising God, despite numerous temptations.[22] The people of heaven are described as living together in bliss, eating and drinking together with either their companions or their children, who will also be in heaven if they have similarly followed God's law during their lifetimes. They are described as talking to one another about their time on earth, before the Day of Judgement and their ascension into heaven, expressing the fear they once had about facing God's anger, how they did their best to live well and how therefore God has been good to them, has admitted them to heaven, and is ensuring that they will not suffer the agonising pains of hell,[23] nor its devastating loneliness.[24] The Qur'ān specifies that they do not engage in "idle chatter"[25] and that their minds are perfectly serene, as they no longer have to worry about hell.[26] Despite being offered all sorts of wonderful wines, they will not make them drunk.[27] We can understand this as an allegorical reference to the elation and joy that the people of heaven will experience – with no fear of it ever coming to an end.

The people of heaven will never hear any "empty talk" or any lies. Instead, all of their social interactions will be part of God's gift to them,[28] in the context of the survival of each person's individual consciousness, even while their bodies have simply ceased to exist at all.

---

21 Haleem, 2012, 97.
22 Q. 13:23-4.
23 Q. 52:17-27.
24 Haleem, 2012, 98.
25 Q. 52:23.
26 Q. 21:103.
27 Q. 56:19; 37:47.
28 Q. 78: 31-6.

Various commentators on the Qur'ān have interpreted references to "splendid companions" (kawā'ib) in heaven as referring to young, beautiful girls who will be available to entertain the male inhabitants. This is partly a misunderstanding passed on the fact that the term for "splendid," which can also be translated as "eminence" or "glory," is sometimes used in everyday speech to mean a young girl whose breasts are growing. One assumes that there is also some wishful thinking at hand; certainly, it is a very male-centred view of paradise. What are we to make of all this? Firstly, it should be underlined that Qur'ānic teaching refers to women and men alike, and both women and men will be admitted into heaven on the basis on how they have lived their lives on earth. There, they will be equally honoured and cherished by God and His angels. In this context, it is ridiculous to imagine that God would set aside female "companions" merely to entertain men, or that He would place women in a subservient position to men to do their bidding and please them, while their own needs are not observed. Moreover, the Qur'ānic descriptions of heaven are in general allegorical, rather than literal, and the references to "companions" should be simply taken to indicate that everyone in heaven will have splendid companions, with no particular reference to gender at all. Rather, each person in heaven will have companions who are perfectly matched to them, with whom they can enjoy a wonderful, and mutually fulfilling, relationship on a spiritual plane.[29] Rahman, however, points out that the undeniable fact of the spiritual delights of heaven does not mean that there will be no physical pleasures, as one simply does not negate the other.[30] The physical sense of happiness and contentment of the inhabitants of heaven should be understood as literal, along with the knowledge that the spiritual experience of joy is most important: "the pleasure of God with them is great and that is the great success."[31]

Many Muslims are of the erroneous view that the attendants in heaven known as "hūr" have specifically been created by God in order to serve the

---
29 Asad, 1984, 924, note 16.
30 Rahman, 1989, 35.
31 Q. 9:72.

needs of the righteous in the afterlife. Tragically, this erroneous thinking drives the twisted, hateful ideology of Muslim fundamentalists hell bent on destruction in the hope that they will be rewarded for their heinous actions by meeting the beautiful creatures known as "hūr." In Western parlance, this belief is frequently referenced as the "72 virgins" that such "martyrs" will receive in heaven. As Asad notes on this issue, a clear examination of the facts proves otherwise:

> The noun hūr – rendered by me as "companions pure," is a plural of both ahwar (masc) and hawrā (fem.), either of which describes "a person distinguished by hawar," which latter term primarily denotes "intense whiteness of the eyeballs and lustrous black of iris." In a more general sense, hawar signifies simply "whiteness" or, as a moral qualification, "purity." Hence, the compound expression hūr ʿīn signifies, approximately, "pure beings" (or more specifically, companion pure"), most beautiful of eye"… As regards the term hūr in its more current feminine connotations, quite a number of the earliest commentators… understood it as signifying no more and no less than "the righteous among the women of human kind."[32]

The Sinners' Plea

The residents of hell are portrayed by the Qur'ān as begging God to let them know if there is any chance that they will ever experience a reprieve from their suffering. They will be reminded that the awful fate that they are suffering is, simply, their own fault, because they consistently denied the truth of God during their lifetimes on earth.[33] But what of an answer to the question? We find one possibility in an authenticated saying of Muhammad's. He described how, on the Day of Judgement, the virtuous will enter heaven and the sinners will go to hell. However, God will order His angels to remove from the fire

---

32 Asad, 1984, 831, note 8.
33 Q. 40:11-2.

anyone whose heart contains at least a little faith (sometimes translated as "good"), even if it is just as small as a mustard seed. The sinners are described as being removed from hell and flung into the River of Life, giving them the chance to live again, renewed and pure once more, in the afterlife. They are not, it goes without saying, given the second chance on earth that they requested. Indeed, this would be impossible, as the world as we know it will have been utterly destroyed by that time.

The Nature of Heaven

Clearly, the afterlife is completely unimaginable to us now. In fact, it will be like nothing that anyone has ever experienced on earth, and we simply have no words to describe it. The Qur'ān rises to the challenge of communicating its reality by using rich language evoking all the luxuries imaginable, on the basis of our lived human experience. For example, consider the following passage:

> They will be (seated) on gold-encrusted thrones of happiness, reclining upon them, facing one another (in love). Immortal youths will wait upon them, with goblets, and ewers, and cups filled with water from unsullied springs, by which their minds will not be clouded and which will not make them drunk, and with fruit of any kind that they may choose, and with the flesh of any fowl that they may desire. And (with them will be their) companion pure, most beautiful of eye, like unto pearls hidden in their shells. A reward for what they did (in life). No empty talk will they hear there, nor any call to sin, but only the tiding of inner soundness and peace.[34]

How should we interpret this passage? The best way is to view the rich language in strictly allegorical terms. In this way, we can understand the fact that,

---

34 Q. 56:15-26.

in heaven, nobody and nothing will get old and die; rather, all will experience eternal youth without a hint of the withering and sickness that accompany advancing years. Whereas every living thing on earth has its natural lifespan, and one day comes to an end (as indeed will the very earth as we know it), in heaven everything remains forever pure and unblemished.[35] The Qur'ān refers to the simple fact that one cannot imagine the joys of paradise, saying: "And no human being can imagine what is kept hidden for them (by way) of a joy of the eyes."[36] In a succinct commentary on the same verse, Muhammad himself is said to have stated, "God says: "I have readied for My righteous servants what no eye has ever seen, and no ear has ever heard, and no heart of man has ever conceived."[37] This hadith has always been regarded by the Companions as the Prophet's own comment on the above verse.

Heaven is described as being neither too hot nor too cold, with abundant shade beneath its beautiful, spreading trees, and a lote tree crowning its summit or upper boundary. These extraordinary descriptions of heaven are clearly intended to be understood in a symbolic way by anyone who listens to or reads the Qur'ān.[38] Drawing on analogies from the physical world, the Qur'ān describes fruit- and flower-laden trees, with the fruit always easy to reach (in fact, it even describes fruit as lowering itself into the reach of the people sitting beneath the trees),[39] and shady gardens with abundant sources of water, among all of which the resurrected live in perfect happiness and youthfulness.[40] The inhabitants of heaven are described as resting on "couches" that are "raised high." To understand this, we need to consider the fact that, in the Arabic of Muhammad's day, the term "couch" was often used to indicate "wife" or "husband." This interpretation is confirmed elsewhere, where the inmates of

---

35 Haleem, 2012, 99.
36 Q. 32:17.
37 Fath al Bārī VIII, 418 f.
38 Asad, 1984, 779.
39 Q. 76:14.
40 Q. 56:28-40.

heaven are described as reclining in the company of their spouses,[41] and as resting on "thrones of happiness" where they shall never experience tiredness, and where they will live in perfect peace, with God having removed whatever lingering imperfections they still contained in their hearts at the time of their deaths.[42] Elsewhere in the Qur'ān, the absolute perfection of these "thrones" or "couches" is underlined by descriptions of them as being encrusted with gold[43] or "raised high."[44] The people of heaven are described as being served with silver plates and goblets of silver so pure that it seems crystalline. They will be given a drink flavoured with ginger, described as bearing the name "Seek Thy Way." Their servers will be beautiful, immortal youths, compared to "scattered pearls."[45] Again, we should read this allegorically, to indicate that heaven is the inevitable result of a life lived well. It should be stressed that descriptions of material rewards and physical delights should not be taken to mean that the inhabitants of heaven will engage in a sort of bacchanalia. Instead, they will receive great spiritual and moral rewards, with descriptions of lavish food and drink, and luxurious surroundings, to be interpreted as allegories for the former and symbols for the great honour that God will bestow upon His people when they come to Him.[46] In heaven, the faces of all of those who get to gaze upon the God who created them are described as "radiant"[47] – and indeed, who can imagine a greater source of joy than the knowledge that God has accepted one into Heaven, to live with Him forever?

Elsewhere, heaven is described as a place through which flow rivers of milk, wine and pure honey, all of which can be freely drunk by the people who live there, while they enjoy the "fruits" of the good way in which they lived their lives, and the forgiveness of God. This blissful state is directly

---

41 Q. 36:56.
42 Q. 15:45-8.
43 Q. 56:15.
44 Q. 88:13.
45 Q. 76:19-20.
46 Haleem, 2012, 101.
47 Q. 75:22-3.

compared to the misery suffered by those who are condemned to hell, where they are given "waters of burning despair" to drink, which will "tear their bowels asunder."[48] The emphasis on the importance of pure, clear water (in heaven) and the absence of it (in hell) is entirely consistent with the fact that the Qur'ān frequently places a focus on water, which is described as an essential building-block in God's Creation, and as having both practical and spiritual cleansing effects.[49]

Heaven is also described in terms of a duality: two gardens, each filled with leafy trees with every sort of fruit, and each containing a flowing fountain. Some scholars believe that the two gardens are relevant in light of the teaching that there are two groups of people in heaven, and that they may be divided between the two gardens accordingly.[50] These gardens are described as being inhabited by "maidens of modest gaze" who have never been touched.[51] How are we to interpret this dual description? Are there two different heavens, which the people of heaven enjoy at the same time? Or is the Qur'ān stating that the joys of heaven will be both spiritual and physical? In general, we should consider the reference to this duality in an allegorical sense, given that discussions of heaven are allegorical in general. In this way, we can see it as a discussion of the intense sensations of joy and well-being that the inhabitants of heaven will experience – joys that are far beyond our current ability to understand. Other dualities emerge elsewhere in the Qur'ān too, such as the reference to "two seas",[52] which many scholars believe to be a reference to the two streams of knowledge and information available to us humans, one through the analysis of the things we see and experience around us, and the other through looking within and exploring our mystic side.[53] The heavenly references to two gardens, said to contain "two kinds of every fruit" may refer,

---

48 Q. 47:15.
49 Haleem, 2012, 103.
50 Lange, 2016, 44.
51 Q. 55:71.
52 Q. 18:60.
53 Asad, 1984, 827.

allegorically, to things that are known and unknown to us now – in other words, to delights that we can imagine on the basis of what we know, and to things that we cannot yet even imagine because we have never experienced anything even remotely comparable. Similarly, the references to the people of heaven lying on couches, or in other luxurious settings, should be taken to mean that they will experience complete restfulness and peace, rather than "luxury" in the banal, earthly sense. A further duality is found in descriptions of heaven as a place in which the virtuous are rewarded with uncountable pleasures and delights, and also protected from the terrors of hell and from negative emotions, such as fear and anxiety.[54]

While the Qur'ān states, explicitly and through the use of rich allegory, that heaven will be beyond anything that we have ever experienced on earth, it also points out that it will have some qualities that will remind us of our time on earth – another example of the duality of heaven.[55] Of course, we cannot yet imagine or understand the points of similarity or difference, as none of us has yet experienced heaven for ourselves. Even the idea of infinity, referenced in the Qur'ān with the phrase, "as vast as the heavens and the earth" (meaning the entire universe created by God),[56] is too much for the ordinary human mind to completely grasp.

Throughout the Qur'ān, we find both explicit and implicit comparisons between heaven and hell. The absolute joy of heaven is compared to the utter horror of hell. We are invited to imagine the most wonderful sensations and sights that we can bring to mind, and the most horrifying and frightening. By invoking what is familiar, we are encouraged to glimpse at least a little of the reality that lies in wait for every human being who has ever existed, and ever will.[57]

For all of us human beings, heaven is both a promise and a blessing. It is a promise, because God has guaranteed a place with Him in the afterlife to

---

54 Haleem, 2012, 99.
55 Q. 2:25.
56 Q. 3:133.
57 Asad, 1984, 991.

everyone who lives as He wishes them to. It is a blessing, because He is loving and merciful, and gives each of us multiple opportunities to redeem ourselves when we sin, to repent for our bad behaviour, and to strive to live as He wishes us to. God will forgive, and admit to heaven, anyone who truly repents, who ceases to engage in sin, and who worships Him as we have been instructed to do.[58] As we are all mere mortals, each of us, even the prophets, will have need of God's forgiveness for the things we have done wrong in our lives. In the creation of heaven, which contains everything – imaginable and unimaginable – that we need for an existence full of endless joy, God is spreading out His bounty before us.[59]

The Qur'ān is written in such a way that descriptions of heaven occur throughout the book, rather than being confined to a particular chapter or sections.[60] This means that observant Muslims, and indeed anyone who reads the Qur'ān regularly, encounters descriptions of heaven every day, which can serve as a cogent reminder that God is always with us, urging us to live the best lives that we can so that, one day, He will take us into His embrace in heaven to be with Him forever.

---

58 Q. 3:133-6.
59 Q. 57:21.
60 Haleem, 2012, 97.

CHAPTER 12

❖ ❖ ❖

Hell

CLEARLY, THE PRIMARY reason for the Day of Judgement is for each human being to receive the fate that they deserve, depending on how they have lived during their brief period on earth. That each of us will receive the reward or punishment we have earned is God's promise to us, and we do well to remember that it is a promise that holds just as true for those who do *not* please Him as it does for those who will spend eternity with Him in heaven.

Qur'ānic descriptions of hell are more full and detailed than its descriptions of heaven,[1] reflecting the central importance of this doctrine to the worshipful observance of Islam, and its role in helping us to make wise choices. At its most simple, we can understand Qur'ānic teaching as confirming that those who have lived in a manner that reflects their virtuous lives and worshipful approach to God will be rewarded by spending eternity in heaven, while those who have not will be condemned to awful punishments in hell, by far the worst of which will be the knowledge that they have missed the blissful experience of returning to God.[2] There is no escaping this simple truth, for, "Verily, hell will lie in wait (those who deny the truth) – a goal for all who are wont to transgress the bounds of what is right."[3]

Imagine, if you can, the most awful psychological and physical suffering experienced by someone who is burned by fire, immersed in loneliness and sorrow, neither dead nor alive. Then imagine all of that magnified a thousand

---

1 Lange, 2016, 46.
2 Q. 10:45; 22:11; 40:78; 7:9, 53; 8:37; 9:69.
3 Q. 78:21-2.

times more, an experience unparalleled by anything in this world. If you can do this, you will understand a fraction of what is implied by the term "hell."[4]

How can we understand this, in light of what we know of God's infinite mercy? Quite simply, throughout the life of each and every one of us, we are offered an almost infinite array of possibilities to do good and please Him. The Qur'ān refers to revelation and the prophets as wonderful examples of God's mercy, as they provide us both with a warning against evil, and God's help in living in such a way that we will receive our eternal reward with Him.[5] In multiple instances, the Qur'ān exhorts us to do good and stay away from evil while, in the world that He created, a world that gives us everything we need, God has provided us with more instances than we can count to see His hand at work and marvel at the greatness of His glorious Creation. The Qur'ān specifically mentions the wealthy, using the rich merchants of Mecca as its example,[6] to highlight the fundamental equality of all human beings when it comes to His determination as to who will go to heaven, and who to hell. It will make no difference how much wealth and comfort we have enjoyed in this life, for we can bring none of it with us in the end, while all of us will be judged according to how we have lived:

> On the Day when that (hoarded wealth) shall be heated in the fire of hell and their foreheads and their sides and their backs branded therewith. These are the treasures which you have laid up for yourselves! Taste, then, (the evil of) your hoarded treasures.[7]

Hell is also described in vivid terms, typically as a place of searing heat, often characterised as fire, but also as hot water,[8] where the guilty live under a

---

[4] Asad, 1984, 991.
[5] Q. 31:2-3; 44:2-6.
[6] Q. 30:7.
[7] Q. 9:35, 21:39.
[8] Q. 55:44.

dark canopy of smoke,[9] and are subjected to terrible punishments by fierce angels who obey God's commands.[10] Those condemned to hell are described as wearing rags made of flames,[11] and as having skin that renews itself after each burning, the better to experience the horrors of it all over again, as the torment of the sinners will be experienced as unceasing for the entire duration of their period in hell.[12]

As dreadful as the physical punishments in hell will be (and the Qur'ān goes into lavish detail on this topic, as we will see), for evil-doers the worst agony of all will be their knowledge of all they have lost through their own wretched foolishness. Hell is discussed above all in terms of this loss; the delights they will now not enjoy, their endless sorrow in accepting that the fault is all their own, and the huge burden of shame they will carry as a result. Just as the ultimate delights in heaven are spiritual, rather than physical, so are the ultimate horrors of hell.

The People of the Fire

Who will go to hell on the Day of Judgement, and what will their experience of it be? The People of the Fire (also known in some contexts as "companions of the left") will include both human beings and jinn,[13] Satan, and Satan's followers.[14] Those people to whom God has not yet sent a messenger do not know how to give thanks and praise, or do not know to whom thanks and praise are due, cannot be blamed for this oversight, as it is clearly not their fault or their responsibility. However, those who deliberately refuse to accept their duty to thank the God who gives them everything they need, and refuse to accept his guidance, are inevitably doomed to punishment in the afterlife,

---

9 Q. 56:43.
10 Q. 66:6.
11 Q. 22:19.
12 Q. 4:56.
13 Q. 11:119.
14 Q. 7:18; 26:95.

while here on earth their behaviour will also lead to their downfall, as no society can expect to live in comfort and ease forever, while also refusing to submit to the God Who has created them![15] Hell is the place to which those who rebel against the truth are sent. It will come upon them like an ambush when they die, because they were oblivious to the truth in this world. The sinners are described as being beaten and struck on their backs and faces by the angels of hell, who will say to them, "Taste suffering through fire, in return for what your own hands have wrought, for never does God do the least wrong to His creatures."[16]

We can understand these descriptions as providing us with an allegorical view of how sinners will suffer in the next world as a direct result of their decision, in this case to deny God's holy truth. The Qur'ān discusses the reality of hell and the experiences of its inhabitants in many instances in its pages, often going into elaborate detail. These verses have been the subject of ample scholarly examination over the years, as they continue to be to this day. Consider the following verse: "For, behold, heavy fetters (await them) with Us, and a blazing fire, and food that chokes, and grievous suffering."[17] Is this just a simple descriptive passage of the conditions that will be experienced by the people of the fire, or can we read some symbolic import into it? In fact, here as in some many elements of the Qur'ān, we find rich symbolic language and layers of metaphor or allegory that we can only attempt to understand by making reference to experiences that we are familiar with. Indeed, it should be borne in mind that all Qur'ānic descriptions of the sinner's suffering in the hereafter are metaphors or allegories relating to situations and conditions that can be understood only by means of comparison with physical phenomena lying within the range of human experience. According to the Islamic scholar Rāzi, this short verse contains rich symbolic significance to be unpicked as follows:

---

15 Asad, 1984, 414, note 138.
16 Q. 8:50-1.
17 Q. 73:12-3.

The "heavy fetters" represent the human soul remaining tied to the physical attachments and pleasure of the flesh that the person experienced during their life on earth. Now that they are in hell and can no longer enjoy these things, the fetters prevent them from transcending their position in hell and finding a new home in heaven with God, alongside those who lived more wisely. In terms of punishment, these shackles will create spiritual "fires", insofar as the soul's strong urges to enjoy the transitory pleasures the body once enjoyed during its time on earth will give rise to a horrible sensation of burning, referred to here as a "blazing fire." In response to this pain, the tormented sinner will try to swallow the "choking agony of deprivation and the pain of separation from the things that he still desires, and will remain forever beyond the possibility of being illuminated by God, together with Him and all of those who are with Him in heaven." This is what is meant by the term "grievous suffering."[18]

The descriptions of hell in the Qur'ān depict the inner state of the soul rather than actual physical locations. We find justification of this view in a verse of the Qur'ān that refers to the resurrected soul as experiencing a "sharp sight"[19], whereby he sees himself with the fate that he has constructed with his own behaviour, "fastened round his neck." According to this interpretation, each of the condemned will find his or her personal hell in the context of the realisation that God gave them every chance to succeed in their life, but that, through their own thoughts and actions, they have disappointed Him. This view is consistent with many other verses that make clear reference to the fire as being essentially spiritual in nature, as the doomed sinner realises, all too late, that they have brought their fate upon themselves. Consider, for example:

Nay, but he shall indeed be abandoned to crushing torment. And what could make thee conceive what that crushing torment will be? A

---

18 Razi, nd. Vol. 30, 181.
19 Q. 50:22.

fire kindled by God, which will rise over the (guilty) hearts, verily, it will close in upon them, in endless columns.[20]

In some cases, sinners are described as enduring punishments that reflect the sins they committed in life.[21] For example, sinners are described as becoming blind, deaf and dumb[22] because of their refusal in life to see, hear and speak the truth of the Qur'ān, choosing to chat idly among themselves, and encourage others to do so, rather than to listen to its holy words.[23] Moreover, the degree of punishment experienced by those in hell depends on the extent of their misdeeds, for God will punish those who have done the worst things more severely than the others.[24]

Fire is a metaphor for hell that is used frequently throughout the Qur'ān, which describes those whose sins condemn them to hell as being "engulfed by an abyss" which is further defined as "a fire hotly burning"[25] and as a "mother," in the sense of something that enfolds or contains, as the fires of hell will certainly do. The Qur'ān describes the condemned being urged towards hell on the Day of Judgement, and entering through its gates while the keepers of hell reproach them, reminding them that God had sent them messengers from Him, warning them of the Day of Judgement and the importance of living as He wishes them to. Sorrowfully, they will answer that all of this is true, but it will be too late for them to escape their punishment, and the keepers will say to them, "Enter the gate of hell, therein to abide."[26] Elsewhere, the Qur'ān affirms that sinners will be gathered together "with satanic forces" and brought to hell on their knees.[27] Satanic forces are often described as being those factors that encourage people to do wrong during their lifetime. In this

---

20 Q. 104:5-8.
21 Rustomji, 2008, 81.
22 Q. 17:97.
23 Q. 41:26.
24 Q. 7:38.
25 Q. 101:8-11.
26 Q. 39:71-2.
27 Q. 19:68.

way, we can understand the "satanic forces" that drive people to hell as being their own sinful natures rather than an external force. In describing sinners as being brought to hell on their knees, the fear and sense of powerlessness that they will experience as they face the fate that they brought on themselves are clearly brought home to us. We are told that, as they approach hell, they will hear "its angry roar and its hiss"[28] (just one of many examples when hell is almost described as though it were a living being with a mind of its own). When they are thrown together into its depths, they will pray to be exterminated in that moment, realising that the punishment that awaits them is far worse, by incredible orders of magnitude, than anything they could have imagined during their time on earth. Of course, the longed-for extermination will not happen. These vivid descriptions – of fear, of constriction, of complete, utter, devastating horror – use experiences and emotions that we are familiar with to evoke some of the sensations that sinners will experience as they confront their doom.[29] The description of sinners as crying out for their own extinction can be compared to the joyous infinity that will greet the virtuous as they enter heaven at the same time. The stark contrast brings home to us just how much the inhabitants of hell are missing.

While the Qur'ān describes the delights of heaven and the horrors of hell in both physical and spiritual terms, it makes it clear that the greatest pleasure and loss come not from physical sensations but from the knowledge of God's presence or absence.[30] Those who have been condemned to hell find that their worst torments are psychological. Not only do they know that they are not with God through their own, and no one else's, fault, but they have lost all honour and bodily integrity and they are forced to dwell in chains and to endure an aeon (sometimes described as an eternity) of being humiliated and reviled.[31] Those who have entered heaven, where they have been reunited with their families and loved ones, will never again experience tiredness, while

---

28 Q. 25:12-4.
29 Asad, 1984, 551, note 9.
30 Q. 9:72.
31 Q. 6:124; 17:18; 25:69; 40:60.

their faces will always be "radiant" because of their great joy in seeing God[32] after a lifetime of service to Him. The humiliation of those in hell, instead, is rendered vividly and in stark contrast to this joyous scene, with descriptions of their regret[33] and their desperate cries to God to release them from their unceasing misery.[34]

Elsewhere, we read of sinners being dragged into the fire on their faces, and being told to experience the touch of hell-fire,[35] and of their faces being "tossed about" in the fire, causing them to exclaim, "Oh, would that we had paid heed unto God, and paid heed unto the Apostle."[36] The face, the part of the body that is the most expressive and individual of all, can be taken to indicate the whole personality of the individual, and as representing the destruction of their individual will as they become completely passive in the face of the torments that they are obliged to suffer. The face is that part of the body that most fully signifies the human person. More than any other part of the body, the face reflects our emotions and feelings, and we are programmed from birth to scan the faces of the others whom we meet, the better to understand them. In Arabic, as in other languages, we can signal our anger with someone whose behaviour has annoyed us by saying, "Never show your face around here again!" while the word "face" also has implications for direction, with the phrase to "set one's face to" indicating the direction in which someone is heading. It also implies someone's dignity, with the loss of dignity seen as "losing face."[37] All of this is posited as being in stark contrast to the righteous, who "surrendered their face" to God.[38] Conversely, the utter helplessness of those who have consistently turned their faces away from God is epitomised in the following verse:

---

32 Q. 75:22-3.
33 Q. 35:37.
34 Q. 26:102.
35 Q. 54:48.
36 Q. 33:66.
37 Haleem, 2012, 110.
38 Q. 3:20.

> And he whom God guides, he alone has found the right way; whereas for those whom He lets go astray thou canst never find anyone to protect them from Him; and [so, when] We shall gather them together on the Day of Resurrection (they will lie) prone upon their faces, blind and dumb and deaf, with hell as their goal, and every time (the fire) abates, We shall increase for them (its) blazing flame. Such will be their requital for having rejected Our messages and having said: "after we will have become bones and dust, shall we, forsooth, be raised from the dead in a new act of Creation." Are they, then, not aware that God, who has created the heavens and the earth, has the power to create them anew in their own likeness.[39]

Here, we see how the Qur'ān asserts the importance of belief in the Day of Judgement and God's ability to raise the dead up. Refusing to believe in these central doctrines is equivalent to refusing to believe that God is all-powerful and all-seeing, and therefore it is a denial of the most fundamental aspects of the Qur'ān as it was revealed to Muhammad. This is a point that is raised in various places in the Qur'ān.[40] On the Day of Judgement they will be utterly humiliated. This humiliation is described in the Qur'ān where it states that, "All who were lost in sin shall by their marks be known, and shall by their forelocks and their feet be seized."[41] In the context of the cultures of ancient Arabia, in which the Qur'ān was revealed to Muhammad, we know that the people of the time discussed one person's subjugation to another by stating, "His forelock is in his hand." The Qur'ān uses this terminology elsewhere, in reference to the all-encompassing power of God, where it says that, "There is no living creature which He does not hold by its forelock."[42]

Clearly, among the people of the fire will be numbered those who engaged in evil acts, and among these, the evil acts that involved the oppression of

---

39 Q. 17:97-9.
40 For example, Q. 17:49, 36:78, 23:35,82, 56:47, 37:16.
41 Q. 55:41.
42 Q. 11:56.

others will be considered the most egregious. Such deeds damage above all the person who engages in them, injuring them spiritually and ultimately condemning them to destruction. In hell, these people are described as "humbling themselves in abasement, looking around with a furtive glance."[43] This clearly implies that every kind of evildoing, and particularly the oppression of others, inevitably results in a spiritual injury to, and ultimately the self-destruction of, its perpetrators and/or their followers. Other references to their abasement, humiliation and suffering are found in references to people being, "Clothed in garments of black pitch, with fire veiling their faces,"[44] and as having their faces thrust into the fire while they are asked if there is any reason why they should be pardoned for the terrible things they did. The same faces are contrasted with the faces of the virtuous which, on the Day of Judgement, will shine with happiness, while those of the condemned will be dark with grief, while they are told that they are bound to suffer for having denied the truth.[45] In the context of the ancient Arabia in which the Qur'ān was revealed, references to faces "blackening" or "darkening" refer to the individual experiencing an overwhelming negative emotion as, for example, when a baby girl was born (because the birth of girls was considered a dishonour at the time, or because of fears that she might be captured by another tribe and grow to like them better to her own) or for other reasons that elicit shame or grief.[46] The Islamic scholar Maulana Muhammad Ali suggests that this may also be a reference to the wealth and happiness of many sinners in this life, who enjoy their wealth and the "sunshine," while the virtuous frequently experience quiet lives with no great luxury, and can be poverty-stricken. These roles are reversed when the Day of Judgement comes to pass,[47] and the virtuous, many of whose lives were characterised by poverty and endless struggle, are brought

---

43 Q. 42:45.
44 Q. 14:50.
45 Q. 3:106-7; 80:38-42.
46 Affi, 2016, 178.
47 Ali, 1934, 1902.

into God's embrace, while the evil-doers, many of whom were wealthy and enjoyed great luxury, are left to suffer.

The Nature of Hell

Although some believe that hell is a punishment that will last forever, major scholars tend to concur that Islamic theology does not permit the idea of eternal damnation, and that in general when the word "eternity" occurs in the Qur'ān it should be read as implying the passage of an unspecified time. According to this view, then, hell is less a place of torment, and more a venue where errant souls can be purified and made anew, with the punishments they suffer a difficult, but necessary, element of their eventual redemption. In this way, we can understand hell clearly within the constraints of our view of God as loving and merciful. Even though it fills Him with sorrow when His people behave in opposition to His holy law, they can eventually be redeemed for even the most appalling of sins. Once redeemed, they are free to develop in faith and knowledge in the context of an infinite life with God.[48] The Qur'ān refers to hell as having "seven gates" through which the sinners will pass on the Day of Judgement.[49] This can be read in reference to the seven degrees of hell, which means the punishment and suffering that the sinners will face, tailored to be consistent with the severity of their sins.

In recognition of the fact that the human mind is not capable of visualising hell, not having yet experienced it, the Qur'ān uses rich metaphorical language to describe it, using seven different names. These are:

- Fire
- Hell
- Blazing fire
- Blazing flame
- Hell-fire

---

48 Iqbal, 1989, 98.
49 Q. 15:44.

- Raging flame
- Crushing torment

As these ways of understanding suffering in hell in the next life are allegories, presumably we can also assume that the references to the "seven gates of hell" are similarly allegorical, and understand them as meaning that there are seven different ways to get to hell. When we consider that in all of the Semitic languages, and especially in the Arabic of Muhammad's day, the word "seven" is also used to signify an indefinite plural number, we can clearly read this as stating that, as there are numerous ways to sin, there are also numerous different ways to get to hell.[50] Given that that Qur'ān makes frequent reference both to the things God wishes us to do, and the opposite, this makes perfect sense.

When we read descriptions of the sinners being cast into hell, we learn that it will make a hideous sound as this takes place: "its breath indrawing as it boils up, well-nigh bursting with fury."[51] Once ensconced in its fiery depths the sinners:

> … will find (themselves) in the midst of scorching winds, and burning despair, and the shadows of black smoke – (shadows) neither cooling nor soothing.[52]

It is interesting to note that the term used to refer to intense heat, hamim, can also imply painful cold. Either way, hell will be a place of intense suffering for all those who are doomed to go there. Bear in mind that, as all of the Qur'ānic references to the afterlife are allegorical by definition, the best way to understand the term is with the concept of "burning despair."[53]

---

50 Razi n.d., Vol. 19, 190.
51 Q. 67:7-11.
52 Q. 56:42-4.
53 Asad, 1984, 182, note 62.

Note, above, that the Qur'ān refers to shadows in hell that will provide no respite from the awful heat, and consider how vibrant this message must have been to the Arabs of Muhammad's day, who lived in a desert climate and knew all too well how welcome shade could be from the burning heat of the sun. Those who have been condemned to hell will never know the blessed relief of shade, as the flaming fire will consume them completely. The only shadow visible will be cast by the smoke that rises from the flames, but rather than providing them with some comfort from their torment, it will contain enormous sparks that will torture them yet further. The Qur'ān compares these sparks to caravans of camels. How are we supposed to interpret this? On the one hand, it refers to the size and colour of the sparks, and the fact that they succeed each other quickly. On the other, it also refers to the sin of pride. Consider the fact that the camel was the mainstay of the economy in ancient Arabia, and that the successful measured their wealth in terms of the number of camels they had. A secondary message here must surely be that our wealth and the things we treasure (today, more typically money and the many luxuries that money can buy) will last just for a moment, in comparison to the eternity of the afterlife, and can even return symbolically to torment us in the afterlife if we do not use them well.[54] Elsewhere in the Qur'ān, shadows are described as offering "no cooling shade" and "of no avail against the flame," which itself is described as creating sparks, "like yellow twisted ropes."[55]

The Qur'ān makes frequent reference to the psychological torment that will greet sinners, alongside the many physical punishments that they will have to endure. God is described as filling them with fear by means of the clouds of fire that they will see both above and below them,[56] and it frequently mentions the role of the fire in instilling fear, describing it as a "great forewarning; a warning to mortal man,"[57] and as causing the sinners to move between physical suffering and the psychological torment caused by their own

---

54 Ali, 1934, 1875-6.
55 Q. 77:30-4.
56 Q. 39:16.
57 Q. 74:35-6.

deep regret that they did not heed the Word of God when there was still time to repent and gain access to eternal life with Him.[58] A particularly eloquent passage reads as follows:

> These two adversaries have become engrossed in contention about their Sustainer. But, as for those who are bent on denying the truth- garments of fire shall be cut out for them (in the life to come); burning despair will be poured over their heads, causing all that is within their bodies, as well as the skins, to melt away. And they shall be held (in this state as if) by iron grips. And every time they try in their anguish to come out of it, they shall be returned thereto and (be told) taste suffering through fire.[59]

The Qur'ān describes specific punishments that are tailored to specific types of sinners. For example, those that believe in false gods, or deny the existence of God, will experience the complete disintegration of their inner and outer personalities, and nobody from either category will ever escape the punishment to which they have condemned themselves. In the following verse, God compares these people to a town that is at peace and prosperous, receiving everything necessary for life, but which refuses to give thanks and praise to Him from whom all blessings flow:

> And God propounds a parable (imagine) a town which was (once) secure and at ease, with its sustenance coming to it abundantly from all quarters, and which thereupon blasphemously refused to show gratitude for God's blessings; and therefore God caused it to taste the all-embracing misery of hunger and fear in result of all (the evil) that its people had so persistently wrought.[60]

---

58 Q. 55:44.
59 Q. 22:19-22.
60 Q. 16:112.

The Ultimate Reward: Eschatology in the Qur'ān

Elsewhere, the Qur'ān reiterates that those who worship objects rather than God, denoted in the text with the word "stones," will certainly experience hellfire,[61] because they have chosen to put their faith in mere objects rather than in the all-knowing God Who has created them.[62]

There are many instances in the Qur'ān where we can see how it presages scientific knowledge uncovered by painstaking research by many centuries. For instance, in describing the horrendous pain that will be experienced by those who are condemned to hell, it makes the following remarks:

> Verily, those who are bent on denying the truth of Our messages, We shall, in time, cause to endure fire, and every time their skins are burnt off, We shall replace them with new skins, so that they may taste suffering. Verily, God is almighty, wise.[63]

Medical research informs us that the skin contains many more nerve endings than our flesh, and that it is therefore far more sensitive. By describing the sinners as experiencing the destruction of their skin, rather than their flesh, the Qur'ān informed of us of the same thing, over fourteen hundred years ago!

The Qur'ān also evokes the natural world in its metaphorical discussions of hell. It asks us to consider which is better, paradise or the Tree of Zaqqūm, which is described as a tree that grows in the middle of hell, with fruit as hideous as the heads of Satan. The sinners are compelled to eat this awful fruit until they are full, and are described as experiencing "burning despair."[64] Scholarly research tells us that the term "zaqqūm" means any deadly food. Note that the Qur'ān characteristically uses rich, multi-faceted language whenever it describes places or things that are beyond current human understanding. Given this, it makes sense to suppose here that the Qur'ān is not actually referring to a literal tree with literal fruit, but instead is using the im-

---

61 Q. 2:24.
62 Abduh, 1999, 164-5.
63 Q. 4:56.
64 Q. 37:62-8.

age as a metaphor to describe how sinners' suffering is the inevitable outcome – the "fruit" – of the many bad decisions that they have made in the course of their miserable lives on earth. Elsewhere, descriptions of the above-mentioned tree show us the reality of hell:

> Verily, the tree of deadly fruit, will be the food of the sinful, like molten lead will it boil in the belly, like the boiling of burning despair [and the word will be spoken] "Seize him, (O forces of hell) and drag him into the midst of the blazing fire, then pour over his head the anguish of burning despair. Taste it – thou who (on earth) has considered thyself o mighty, so noble. This is the very thing which you (deniers of the truth) were wont to call in question."[65]

There are also other references to food and drink in the context of hell. The sinners are described as being given boiling spring water to drink, and as being deprived of all food other than bitter, dry thorns, which give them no sustenance and do not prevent them from experiencing an awful hunger.[66] Again, we can understand this description of food in an allegorical way, indicating the complete hopelessness and abasement that the sinners will experience in hell, when they realise that they are suffering through their own fault alone. In the description of the spring, we find a poignant contrast to the running waters that are often mentioned in descriptions of heaven. Elsewhere, the sinners are described as begging for water that will be like "molten lead" and that will "scald their faces."[67] Their thirst is so overwhelming that they are compared to camels, "desperate with thirst"[68] and cattle "driven to the watering-place of the fire."[69] Again, these descriptions beg comparison with the description of the wonderful drinks available in heaven, with the reference

---

65 Q. 44:43-50.
66 Q. 88:2-7.
67 Q. 18:29.
68 Q. 56:55.
69 Q. 11:98.

to faces being scalded consistent with many references throughout the Qur'ān to punishment being given to people on their "faces," which can be read as symbolic of them as a whole, rather than just a small part of their bodies.[70] The counterpoint of these references to the face is found in descriptions of sinners' backs as being singled out for particular punishment, in reference to their having "turned their backs" on God[71] (or, due to cowardice, in battle[72]).

Whenever they are "caught out" doing something wrong, weak human beings are often all too willing to claim no responsibility for their own decisions and evil acts, but to blame them all on those who were leading them. The Qur'ān makes a specific reference to those who, long before Muhammad was sent the message of Islam, chose to follow the Pharaoh rather than Moses, who was a prophet of God.[73] Like any sinners, they were doomed to hell for their decisions, and no amount of pleading that they were "only following orders" would have saved them. In modern times, the excuse that one was "only following orders" is often known as the "Nuremberg Defence" in reference to the Nuremberg trials that followed the Second World War, when Nazi war criminals attempted to explain their involvement in the extermination of millions of innocent Jews, among others, by stating that they were only following orders. It is safe to say that God will look as kindly on this pathetic attempt to deflect blame as the courts did in those days. The Qur'ān addresses the issue of immoral leadership by stressing that each of us is individually responsible for the things we do, even when we are "only following orders." In these cases, both the leader and the follower are guilty of sin, because we have all been given the gift of free will by God, Who has created us.[74] In other words, when we are given orders that are clearly wrong, we have the liberty to choose not to follow them.

---

70 Q. 4:47; 8:50; 17:97; 27:90; 14:50.
71 Q. 17:46; 70:17.
72 Q. 8:16.
73 Q. 11:96-8.
74 Asad, 1984, 330.

All of those who rejected the truth of God are described as being condemned to hell and made there to drink "the water of the most bitter distress," gulping it down thirstily even though they are hardly able to swallow it. Much as they yearn to die, they never do, and continuous suffering awaits them ahead.[75] The term "sadid," translated here as "water of bitter distress," is also used to describe anything that we find repulsive and revolting, including the pus that flows from infected wounds. We can read it in a metaphoric way as signifying the suffering and frustration that will be experienced in the afterlife by everyone who is committed to hell because of their own bad decisions. There, covered on all sides by the awful reality of the fire,[76] they will be constantly beset by the knowledge that all of the horrors that they are experiencing are their fault alone.[77]

The Keepers of Hell

The keepers of hell, who will open its gates on the Day of Judgement, are described in the Qur'ān as nineteen angels,[78] as "awesome and severe," and as utterly obedient to God, Who has commanded them to carry out this task for Him,[79] showing us that God's dominion over the next life is just as comprehensive as over this one. These keepers are described variously as seizing the damned by the hair and forelocks,[80] as dragging them with hooked iron rods,[81] beating them, and preventing them from escaping the fires of hell. They are implicitly contrasted with the hūr, the attendants in heaven who offer the citizens of heaven food and drink, when they are described as forcing the inhabitants of hell to consume such horrors as boiling

---

75 Q. 14:15-7.
76 Q. 7:41.
77 Q. 29:55.
78 Q. 74:30.
79 Q. 66:6.
80 Q. 55:41; 96:16.
81 Q. 22:21-2.

water, etc.[82] Over the years, most Islamic scholars have interpreted references to these "keepers" relatively literally, as actual angels who guard hell. However, Rāzi has proposed that, instead, we can see them as a reference to the powers that lie within each human being and are an integral part of our capacities – intellectual, emotional, and physical – as human beings; capacities that make us very different to all the other creatures of God's wonderful Creation. These capacities give us the potential to achieve much more than any other living creature, but they also make it possible for us to sin, and to stray from the straight path that God has provided us with, facilitating our downward spiral into hell. Rāzi maintains that these powers can be identified with:

- Our organic functions, defined as the ways in which our physical bodies operate within the environment that we live in, including the ability to have children.
- Our physical senses, defined as sight, hearing, touch, smell, and taste.
- Our intellectual senses, defined as perception, the ability to understand ideas, the ability to commit images to memory, the ability to make sense of new experiences within the framework of what we already know and commit this to memory, the ability to bring our perceptions and understandings together, and the feelings of desire or revulsion, which are rooted in our physical senses.

Together, these capabilities, which are inborn in every human being, give us the ability to think in the abstract, placing us – in this respect at least – above all the other creatures created by God, even the angels. With these abilities, we become able to understand the difference between good and evil, and to make choices accordingly, making full use of the free will that is our precious gift from God. In this way, human beings have the ability to reach a state of heightened spiritual awareness, so in the Qur'ān these abilities are described as

---

82 Q. 56:51-6; 88:5.

angelic. Because we also have the intellectual capacity to use these incredible powers for evil, these powers are also described in diabolic terms, as the "lords of hell." In this way, we can see how the "keepers of hell" can be understood in a metaphoric sense.[83] Whether we understand the idea in a more literal or in a metaphoric way, it is clear that the angels serve, once again, to underline the importance of understanding the awesome reality of God's omniscience and omnipotence.[84]

Without understanding the reasons being the existence of hell, the uninformed might try to find in it proof that God is not loving or merciful, as He is often described as being. In a way, this is understandable, as the vivid images of hell evoked in the Qur'ān certainly evoke shock and horror. Yet, when we look logically at hell, in connection with what we know about God from other elements of the Qur'ān, we can clearly understand that He is not capricious or unkind, and that Creation was brought into existence as part of a divine plan that is entirely consistent with what we know of God's mercy. The distinction between right and wrong – which many Islamic scholars believe to be inborn to a great extent – is continuously shown to us through revelation in the form of God's prophets and sacred books. In this context, the knowledge of hell and its torments serves us less as punishment, and more as a reminder that we must strive every day to live in a way that pleases God, less for His sake than for ours and that of all humanity. Suffering in hell is a fate that we risk only if we break or damage our natural "bond with God."[85]

The Truth about Women and Hell

A minority view within certain segments of the Muslim community maintains that that the majority of the inhabitants of hell will be women. This warped (and, it goes without saying, wholly unsubstantiated) view is derived from a fabricated source, falsely attributed to Muhammad, that describes

---

83 Asad, 1984, 909, notes 15-6.
84 Lange, 2016, 54.
85 Q. 2:27.

women as "ungrateful" to their husbands and untrustworthy in general.[86] This abhorrent opinion, which reflects the unfortunate, misogynistic world view of earlier societies, should be firmly countered whenever it raises its head.

The Qur'ān, which insists on the fundamental equality of men and women, makes it clear that this equality extends to the afterlife, and that neither sex is more likely than the other to be viewed with favour by the Creator. Rather, each individual will stand alone before God to account for his- or herself.[87] On the rare occasions when the Qur'ān specifies the female gender of an individual who has been condemned to hell, it is clear that she suffers this fate because of her actions, and not her sex.[88] One Qur'ānic verse refers to male sinners as being "gathered together with those they have wronged, and their wives."[89] Historically, some commentators interpreted this as stating that women could be punished for their husbands' sins. This fact, and some of the social commentary from the earliest days of Islam, sadly reflects the low social status that women experienced in many societies at the time.

Lamentably, many commentators have drawn incorrect conclusions based on their misinterpretation of the Qur'ānic term for wives, "azwājahum." The verse in question reads: "(And God will thus command) "Assemble all those who were bent on evildoing together with others of their ilk" (azwājahum)."[90] Here, the expression "azwāj" denotes "people resembling one another in their dispositions," "people of the same kind" or "of the same ilk," but not "wives." With this understanding, we can clearly see that the Qur'ān refers to people who behave or act alike in wrongdoing, and is not condemning women because of their gender. To the contrary, the Qur'ān provides us with examples of historical female figures who have been praised for their exemplary lives, or who have been condemned for betraying others:

---

86 Idleman Smith and Yazbeck Haddad, 2002, 162.
87 Idleman Smith and Yazbeck Haddad, 2002, 158. Q. 4:14; 33:73.
88 For example, Q. 66:10.
89 Q. 37:22-3.
90 Q. 37:22.

God has also given examples of believers: Pharaoh's wife, who said, "Lord, build me a house near You in the Garden. Save me from the evildoers," and Mary, daughter of Imran. She guarded her chastity, so We breathed into her from Our spirit. She accepted the truth of her Lord's words and Scriptures; she was truly devout.[91]

And: "Noah's wife and Lot's wife, they were wedded to two of Our righteous servants, and both betrayed them."[92] The story of Lot's wife and her spiritual betrayal of her husband is mentioned in the Qur'ān in several places. As regards Noah's wife, the above is the only explicit reference to her having betrayed her husband.[93] These references clearly show that God will judge women on an equal basis to men, and that even those women or men who are on very close terms with a righteous person, even a prophet of God, must account for their own deeds on the Day of Judgement, and will not gain any special favour from this association. Furthermore, any man or woman who wishes not to be condemned to hell must commit themselves to refusing to associate with anyone who insists on denying the truth, even if they are close family members or friends.[94] Above all, the Qur'ān promises that men and women will treated equally, stating:

> Whereas anyone – be it man or woman – who does good deeds and is a believer withal, shall enter paradise, and shall not be wronged by as much as the groove of a date-stone.[95]

It seems abundantly clear the abhorrent views about women and their place in the afterlife, held in certain sectors during the early Islamic period, really reflect the ignoble desires of the men of the time to exert unwarranted

---

[91] Q. 66:11-2.
[92] Q. 66:10. See also see 7:83 and 11:81 for more information about Lot's wife.
[93] Asad, 1984, 877, note 21.
[94] Q. 11:46.
[95] Q. 4:124.

authority over the women in their lives, and to claim that doing so was part of God's plan. Modern scholarship, however, confirms what the Qur'ān states clearly – that we will all be judged simply on our own merits. Women and men alike are God's creation. Indeed, together they represent the pinnacle of it. Recognising their essential equality is a cornerstone of true recognition of the eternal validity of the Qur'ān. In direct opposition to these unpleasant, erroneous views, we find Qur'ānic references to people finding their own deceased parents – mothers as well as fathers – in heaven when they themselves arrive there, restored to vigorous youth,[96] clearly indicating that the idea that all, or most, women are naturally hell-bound is false.

Will Hell Last Forever?

Although the popular view of the afterlife (influenced in some cases by the views of non-Muslim scholars from Christian cultural backgrounds)[97] is that it is eternal, and that both those in heaven and in hell will experience that state forever, in fact the Qur'ān itself does not promote the idea of an eternal afterlife. Consider, for example, the following verse:

> As for those who (by their deeds) will have brought wretchedness upon themselves, (they shall live) in the fire, where they will have (nothing but) moans and sobs (to relieve their pain). Therein to abide as long as the heavens and the earth endure – unless thy Sustainer wills it otherwise: for, verily, thy Sustainer is a sovereign doer of whatever He wills.[98]

While this verse is certainly unequivocal on the matter of the suffering of the sinners whose actions have doomed them to an afterlife in hell, it does not suggest that they will remain there for "an eternity." Quite the reverse, in fact.

---

96 Idleman Smith and Yazbeck Haddad, 2002, 163.
97 Khalil, 2013, 14.
98 Q. 11:107.

On the one hand, the Qur'ān states clearly, and in many places, that the Day of Judgement will see the end of the world as we know it today. How are we supposed to reconcile this knowledge with the idea of hell lasting, "as long as the heavens and the earth endure"? Firstly, it is important to acknowledge that this term, as well as others (like "as long as the night and day alternate") were commonly used in ancient Arabic to indicate a period of time that cannot be counted. In many translations, this phrase is rendered as stating that the citizens of hell will remain there "forever." This issue has historically been somewhat contentious among scholars of Islam. To some, there appears to be an inconsistency between the Qur'ān, which is the Word of God, and some of the sayings of the companions of Muhammad, who suggested that there would eventually be a reprieve for those in hell, and who had particularly close access to the Qur'ān as it was initially revealed.[99] Some feel that the verse mentioned above, and a number of others, indicate that the sufferings of hell will not be eternal, and that sinners can hope for a reprieve at some point in time – when God wills it. Others, however, maintain that the heaven and earth mentioned indicate a different heaven and a different earth that will come into being after the Day of Judgement,[100] supporting this view by citing another verse, which says, "On the Day when the earth shall be changed into another earth, as shall be the heavens."[101] This verse is generally interpreted as referring to the incredible, devastating changes that will take place on the Day of Judgement; changes so vast that we cannot currently imagine them on the basis of our limited lived experience.

Some of the most important scholars of Islam, including Ibn Taymiyya and Ibn Qayyim, maintain that, while sinners may deserve to remain in hell forever, God is infinitely merciful, and He will cause it to cease to exist one day. Clearly, when hell is no more, the suffering of the people who were once compelled to remain there will be over. They support this point of view by pointing out that, while the Qur'an refers to heaven as "a reward that will

---

99 Khalil, 2013, 15.
100 Rida, 1999, 124.
101 Q. 14:48.

never end"[102] it does not use any similar expression about hell, leaving the door open for the opinion that hell may indeed have an end. We also see various clues that suggest that hell may be finite elsewhere in the Qur'ān. Hell is described as being a "mother," and an "abyss."[103] In ancient Arabic, the term "mother" can be used to indicate anything that enfolds. In the context of descriptions of hell, it must be borne in mind that, as the afterlife is beyond our current understanding, the Qur'ān, of necessity, uses phrases and concepts from everyday life to communicate at least a partial understanding of what it will be like.[104] The Qur'ān also describes hell as an "abode" in which the sinners will be compelled to remain – but it adds "unless God wills it otherwise,"[105] which suggests to many scholars that, whereas heaven will last for an unlimited period of time, sinners will not suffer forever, but only until God has determined that they have done sufficient penance for the misdeeds they engaged in during their lives on earth. It refers to sinners remaining in hell for "a long time"[106]. This is not generally interpreted as suggesting a specific period of time, but as a period of unknown duration that is limited, and certainly not eternal.[107] We are told that sinners will remain in hell "unless thy Sustainer wills it otherwise,"[108] which appears to indicate that they will stay only until God has determined that, in all His mercy, He can now free them from their dreadful punishments. While this phrase is also used to refer to the duration of heaven, the usage there is quite different, as the phrase, "a gift never to be cut off" is appended to it. Although some believe to the contrary, a careful reading of the Qur'ān shows us very clearly that, in true Islamic theology, there is no concept of hell as eternal. Rather, we are taught that it will last

---

102 Q. 41:8, 84:25 and 95:6.
103 Q. 101:8-9.
104 Asad, 1989, 972, notes 2 and 3.
105 Q. 6:128.
106 Q. 78:23.
107 Lisān al-Arab, 1997, Vol.2, 121.
108 Q. 11:107-8 and 6:128.

a particular period of time. This is true even of the small number of instances when the word "eternity" is applied to hell.[109]

One somewhat contentious verse in the Qur'ān refers to people "in the heights," understood as a sort of partition between heaven and hell, being able to look upon both heaven and hell.[110] Some scholars have interpreted this as suggesting that there is a "third place," a sort of purgatory or limbo, where people who were not good enough for heaven nor bad enough for hell will be placed on the Day of Judgement. In most cases, scholars conclude that this "third place" is one of an abundance of signs of God's mercy, as those who are on "the heights" will eventually be admitted into heaven.[111]

---

109 Q. 78:23.
110 Q. 7:46.
111 Idleman Smith and Haddad, 2002, 90-1.

CHAPTER 13

Mutual Wrangling

HERE, WE WILL explore what will happen after all of humanity has been assessed by God, and when each of us has been assigned to our appropriate place in the afterlife. The Qur'ān discusses this issue in a wide range of verses that show the conversations that will be held by the people of heaven, and the accusations and recriminations of the people of the fire. The latter will turn on one another, blaming each other for their dreadful situation, while both groups see for themselves the reality of God's promise to them made true.

Discussions of the People of Heaven

Grateful to God for the great honour He has bestowed upon them, when they look at the sinners in hell the people of heaven will implore God never to place them among those who are serving their punishment for committing evil acts.[1] Those who have been blessed with God's delight because of the virtuous way in which they lived will speak to one another of their past lives, commenting on how they had always feared God's wrath, and always strove to do good. In return for this, God has saved them from suffering the "scorching winds" that torture the inhabitants of hell.[2] The loving sense of comradeship between the inhabitants of heaven shall stand in stark contrast to the relationship between the people of hell, of whom the Qur'ān says, "there shall be no kinship between them."[3] The Qur'ān describes God as removing any linger-

---

1 Q. 7:44-50.
2 Q. 52:25-7.
3 Q: 23:101.

ing unworthy thoughts or feelings from the hearts of those in heaven. While it also describes them as "laughing"[4] at those in hell, this should be understood as their expressions of joy at being so blessed by God, rather than laughing in an unkind or gloating sense at those who are suffering the inevitable result of their own mistakes.[5]

One of the contexts in which conversations in heaven are discussed is that of the prophets. Consider the following verse, which refers to the prophet Jesus:

> And Lo! God said: "O Jesus, son of Mary! Didst thou say unto men, "Worship me and my mother as deities beside God?" (Jesus answered): Limitless art Thou in Thy glory! It would not have been possible for me to say what I had no right to(say)! Had I said this, Thou wouldst indeed have known it! Thou knowest all that is within myself, whereas I know not what is in Thy Self. Verily, it is Thou alone who fully knowest all the things that are beyond the reach of a created being's perception. Nothing did I tell them beyond what Thou didst bid me (to say); "Worship God, my Sustainer as well as your Sustainer. And I bore witness to what they did as long as I dwelt in their midst; but since Thou hast caused me to die, Thou alone hast been their keeper, for Thou art witness unto everything. If Thou cause them to suffer – verily, they are Thy servants, and if Thou forgive them – verily, Thou alone art almighty, truly wise."[6]

It is perfectly clear in this verse that Jesus is being depicted as speaking after his death has taken place (in other words, in heaven, where he will live forever). This clearly implies that Jesus was not divine, as many claim, but rather a mere mortal, resurrected on the Day of Judgement like everybody else, and not provided with special treatment in this area. And, just like anyone else,

---

4 Q. 83:34.
5 Q. 7:43; 15:47.
6 Q. 5:116-8.

Jesus does not know more than God has seen fit to show him. As a prophet, he was made privy to far more than an ordinary man, but as a mortal, by definition he could know only what God has chosen to show him. Jesus also makes it clear that, as one of the prophets of God, he completely repudiates knowledge of many of the things that Christians attribute to him. For example, although Protestants would reject the worship of Mary at the time of the Reformation, this practice was widespread in the early Christian churches (as it still is in the Catholic faith to this day). Jesus's remarks following the Day of Judgement should be read as a warning not just to Christians, but also to Muslims and members of all other faiths not to ascribe divinity to the messengers of God because, regardless of how important they are to the spiritual and moral development of humanity, they are but mortal beings and should never be compared to the one true God.[7] Indeed, comparison of this sort is contrary to everything the Qur'ān teaches, and can even be seen as blasphemous.

Discussions of the People of the Fire

The Qur'ān describes how, after the Day of Judgement, those who have been condemned to hell will fall into long and bitter conversation with one another, blaming everyone but themselves for the dreadful fate that they have been condemned to endure. Their sorrow will be further augmented by hearing God remind them that He had sent them messengers who warned them of the coming Day of Judgement, to which they will reply that they had allowed themselves to be "beguiled" by the ordinary things of this world, and that they are now forced to bear witness against themselves.[8] They are described as having lived together with other evil-doing humans, and with evil "invisible beings." Most scholars have interpreted the reference to "invisible beings" as referring to the jinn, but the term is also used to describe groups or communities of humans or other intelligent beings with qualities in common. In certain contexts, the term can even imply a man's family or close group of

---

7 Rahman, 1989, 114.
8 Q. 6:130.

friends. Therefore, the reference does not necessarily have to mean invisible beings per se, but also the more ordinary men and women who will compose the population of hell. More specifically, it can be read as referring to the human beings who have been misguided, and who listened to words spoken by people other than God's appointed messengers, all of whom were human, as the Qur'ān never once refers to the possibility of apostles coming from within non-human races.[9]

The question of the people of the fire having wilfully refused to listen to the prophets whom God sent them with such good will and grace is a recurring one in discussions of the immediate aftermath of the Day of Judgement. When the good are separated from the bad, and the bad are driven through the gates of hell and into its awful pits of fire, the guardians of hell will ask them, "Have there not come to you apostles from among yourselves, who conveyed to you your Sustainer's messages and warned you of the coming of this your Day (of Judgement)," to which they can only answer, "Yea, indeed."[10] It is possible only to imagine the bigger regret they will experience when they are forced to admit that the only agency they can blame for the dreadful fate that they are suffering is themselves. It will, however, be too late, as they had been offered ample warning during their lifetimes, and were given multiple opportunities to repent and to start living according to what God wanted for them. This, too, they will be forced to admit, as reflected in the following verse:

> (On the Day of Judgement) every human being will be held in pledge for whatever (evil) he has wrought- save only those who shall have attained righteousness: (dwelling) in gardens, they will inquire, of those who were lost in sin: "What has brought you into hell-fire? They will answer: "We were not among those who prayed, and neither did we feed the needy; and we were wont to indulge in sinning together with

---

[9] Asad, 1984, 192, note 1120.
[10] Q. 39:71.

all (the others) who indulged in it, and the Day of Judgement we were wont to call a lie, until certainty came upon us (in death).[11]

The sinners' failure to recognise the messengers or "warners" who were sent to them by God is also made clear in a verse that describes the keepers of hell asking each newly-arrived group of souls what they are doing there, to which they will be forced to reply, "Yea, a warner did indeed come unto us, but we gave him the lie and said: 'Never has God sent down anything (by way of revelation)! You [self-styled warners] are but lost in a great delusion." To this they will add comments about their deep regret that they neither listened to the messengers' warnings nor used their own powers of reason, because if they had they would not be in hell when it was already too late to repent.[12] It is important to point out that the Qur'ān makes it clear that reason inevitably leads human beings to at least some understanding of the existence of God and the logic and planning that underlie Creation. Therefore, even in the absence of a prophet or messenger, it should be clear to any thinking adult, of whatever cultural or religious background, that the world did not simply come into existence by itself, but is part of the plan of a higher power. Historically, the crucial role of the prophets has not been to alert people to the existence of God, but to teach moral distinctions between good and evil.[13]

Clearly, then, the people of the fire will freely admit that they have been brought to hell by their failure to observe the basic tenets of the faith revealed in its clearest form in the Qur'ān: prayer, charity, the avoidance of sin, and the acceptance of Day of Judgement and the afterlife. However, despite the fact that the people of the fire are depicted as accepting their own culpability as a fait accompli, they are also shown as blaming each other for their fate, and attempting to deflect culpability from themselves to others. As each soul enters the fire, it will curse the other damned souls, and all of them will plead with God, stating that they were led astray by others, and that those others should,

---

11 Q. 74:38-47.
12 Q. 67:8-11.
13 Asad, 1984, 880, note 8.

in the very least, be punished with worse suffering. God will not look kindly on this line of argument and will say that each and every one of them deserves to experience a double bout of suffering, even if they refuse to admit it.[14]

Now that they realise how utterly wrong they were, the people of the fire will speak bitterly about their former view that there were deities or other powers that could be considered to be on a par with God. When they are asked where those so-called deities are now, they will be forced to answer, "They have forsaken us – or, rather, what we were wont to invoke aforetime did not exist at all."[15] In other words, they will be forced to admit that they had worshipped false gods that were simply the product of the imagination or of foolish wishful thinking. All the while, they will blame one another for what has become of them, saying, "It is you who have prepared this for us, and how vile a state to abide in" and imploring God to cause those who tempted them to sin to suffer twice as much as they do, with the words:

> How is it that we do not see [here any of the] men whom we were wont to count among the wicked, and whom we made the target of our derision? Or is it that [they are here, and] our eyes have missed them? Such, behold, will in truth be the (confusion and) mutual wrangling of the people of the fire.[16]

The language that the Qur'ān depicts the sinners as using is very telling. We have already explored descriptions of the nature of hell that describe it variously as searingly hot and terribly cold. Asad believes that the context, implying cold and darkness as well as "burning despair," sets the scene for the discussions of sinners, who are depicted above as using language equivalent to a curse. Considering the importance of oath-making and cursing in ancient Arabian culture, this captures a fraction of the pain, grief and ire that they feel moved to express in response to the horrendous situation in which they find

---

14 Q. 7:38-9.
15 Q. 40:73-4.
16 Q. 38:57-64.

themselves. They comment that hell contains none of the men whom they "were wont to count among the wicked" – in other words, the prophets and the other virtuous people whom they repudiated in life, flying in the face of what God wants for them.

Adrift in their misery and woe, the sinners will cast around furiously, seeking to find someone to blame for their current – and eternal – misfortune. The weak-willed will turn to those who led them astray and implore them to relieve them of some of the pain that they are suffering. In response to this, the arrogant, those who had made it their business to lure others away from the path of righteousness, will refuse them and make light of their request, stating that "we are all in it together!" Both groups will implore the keepers of hell to intercede with God on their behalf and ask Him to reduce their burden of suffering. But the keepers will point out that they were sent apostles who brought them the word of God, which they wilfully chose to ignore. It will be too late, now, for anything but prayer, and even prayer will fall on deaf ears after the Day of Judgement, when the opportunity to repent has expired.[17]

One of the tensions reported in the context of conversation between the inhabitants of hell is that between those who were rich during their lifetimes, and those who were not.[18] Bitterly, those who were once poor will accuse those who were rich and influential of using their earthly powers to lead them away from the straight path.[19] This argument will make no difference, however, as we are all equal in the eyes of God, and we are all blessed with the gift of free will.

Over the years, scholars have held diverse views on the matter of the guardians of hell, depicted as angelic forces. In earlier times, the instruction from these angels to the sinners to pray was read as their simple refusal to intercede with God on their behalf. According to Asad, however, we can also read a reference in their words to the fact that many sinners will find themselves in hell because of the ways in which they actually did pray during their lifetimes

---

17 Q. 40:47-50.
18 Rahman, 1989, 115.
19 For example, Q. 34:32; 14:21; 40:47; 50:23.

– not, however, to God, but to the false idols and material values that they allowed to lead them astray. In this context, we can read the angels' remarks as inviting the sinners to pray once again to their false idols, so that they can see if their prayers are answered. This rather grim advice asks a question, and answers it, for there is no god but God and, after the Day of Judgement, not a soul will be in a position to deny it.

The theme of the sinners who were "followers" asking those who led them to relieve them of some of their pain is one that recurs at various points, underlying the fact that each of us must take responsibility for our own actions. With each iteration, we are reminded that, after the Day of Judgement, it will be far too late to hope for clemency, as God will have made His final decision. In this context, the one-time leaders among the sinners are depicted as saying that, "If God would but show us the way (to salvation), we would indeed guide you (towards it). It is (now) all one, as far as we are concerned, whether we grieve impatiently or endure with patience; there is no escape for us!"[20] Once again, there have been varying interpretations of these remarks by Islamic scholars. While some, such as Rāzī and Tabarī, see them as simply meaning that it is now too late to repent, others, such as Zamakhsharī, have interpreted the words as referring to the sinners' lifetimes on earth and to their attempt to deflect the blame for their fate from themselves to God, and to the idea that God had not provided them with sufficient leadership, or leadership of the right sort, and that therefore they cannot be held solely responsible for their actions. Whatever one's view, the simple facts are that it will be too late to repent, that God has provided all of us with more than enough leadership to teach us about the straight path and, ultimately, each of us is fully responsible for our own actions, and answerable only to God for the decisions we take.

The Qur'ān takes an almost comical turn in its descriptions of sinners standing before the God who made them, shrieking insults at one another in a desperate attempt to persuade God that some of them are more culpable than others, and that therefore some are entitled to more lenient treatment in

---

20 Q. 14:21.

hell than others. They will be rebutted with the words, "Why – did we keep you away from guidance after it had come to you? Nay, it was but you who were guilty!"[21] In various descriptions of the sinners in hell, they are described as wearing "shackles" around their necks – a clear metaphor for the fact that they chose to give their lives up to false idols and false gods, for which they will suffer when God makes His final judgement.

The people of the fire are depicted as marvelling at how hell can contain so many sinners. They are shown as asking how it can possibly be that, full as hell is, there is still room for them.[22] The simple fact is that hell has no limits, and there is always room for more. This is firmly brought home to us when hell is shown as being directly questioned, "Art thou sated to the full?" to which the answer comes, "If there are more to come, let them come." Clearly, we are mean to read this symbolically and not as indicating that hell will actually speak. Moreover, the use of expressions that are typically applied to human beings to refer to inanimate objects is one of the interesting features of the Arabic language and is used to great effect throughout the Qur'ān.

The sinners in hell will bemoan the fact that they are condemned to suffer for an indefinite period of time, or perhaps even forever. They are depicted as crying out to God for deliverance, promising that if only they are freed from the pains of hell they will repent and do good works. God will answer, saying that He gave them lifetimes long enough to do good works already, and that He also sent prophets to bring His word to them so that they might be enlightened. Consequently, they, and only they, are responsible for their fate,[23] which will be one of endless humiliations, constant appeals for clemency and special treatment that will fall on deaf ears, bitter regret, and their pitiful hope for access to heaven. Despite all this, the Qur'ān states that if sinners were returned to life, as they ask, they would inevitably return to their sinful ways, as they have already been revealed to be inveterate liars.[24] In their desire to have

---

21 Q. 34:31-3.
22 Q. 50:30.
23 Q. 35:37.
24 Q. 6:28.

a second chance, all they are really expressing is their wish to be released from their pain and suffering, and not a genuine intention to change their ways and live in devout service to God.

The Qur'ān devotes space to discussing the behaviour of false prophets and leaders after the Day of Judgement, and the way in which they will dismiss their followers. The latter will bemoan what has happened, realising all too late that the many hopes they invested in their leaders were futile from the very start. Disowned by the men or idols they once worshipped as gods, they will cry out and say how much they wish they could have a second chance in life, so that they could disown their one-time leaders, as they themselves have been disowned. This, however, will certainly not be possible, as there shall be no escape from the fire.[25] The many social, business and family ties they created in life, without taking care to build a secure foundation of true faith in God, will all be cut and will serve no use in hell.

And what of Satan himself, the ultimate false leader of those who have turned their backs on God? He is depicted in the Qur'ān as turning to the sinners and sneering at their petty foolishness, pointing out that God had made them many promises, all of which turned out to be true, while he lied to and deceived them from the start. Without ever having any true power of his own, Satan simply called to the sinners, and they responded to his lies with enthusiasm. He points out that it would be useless for them to try to blame him for their miserable fate, as their own decisions and behaviour are the only reason why they are enduring it now, and he never said or did anything that would justify the sinners' claim that his power could compare to the awesome divinity of God.[26] Rāzi contends that this verse shows that the true power of Satan lies simply in the desires of human beings, as it is clear that he can only reach human beings when they are open to listening to him because of their own weakness and attraction to evil. Moreover, having no true power of his own, Satan is certainly in no position in hell to offer any help. He rejects the idea that he ever claimed to be the equal of God in any way, even while

---

25 Q. 2:166-7.
26 Q. 14:22.

leading the people astray. This further underlines the fact that it is pointless for the sinners to suggest that they can deflect any of the blame for their own unhappy situation to him.

But while Satan himself does not make any claim to equality with God, the sinner who submits to Satan's blandishments attributes to him thereby, as it were, a share in God's divinity. It must be stressed, in this connection, that the Qur'ānic expression shaytān (generally translated as "Satan") is often used as a metaphor for every human impulse that is intrinsically immoral and, therefore, contrary to man's best – i.e., spiritual – interests.[27] The Qur'ān has made it perfectly clear that, regardless of Satan's empty words, he has no real power and the only true blame for those who commit evil lies within themselves. God is depicted as saying to him, "… verily, thou shalt have no power over My creatures – unless it be such as are (already) lost in grievous error and follow thee (of their own will)."[28]

Discussions Between the People of the Fire and the People of Heaven

Although heaven and hell are certainly separate, and very different, entities, the Qur'ān describes their respective inhabitants as being able to communicate with one another. The people of heaven will call out to those in hell, asking if they have also learned that what God promised to them all is true, to which those in hell will be able to answer only "yes." The sinners will be asked what benefit they gained from their false pride, and their amassing of riches, and they will be able to say little in response. Rather, they will beg the people of heaven to pour water on them, to relieve their suffering, or to share with them some of the food and drink that God has provided to all of those in heaven. To this they will answer, "Verily, God has denied both to those who have denied the truth."[29]

---

27 Asad, 1984, 375-6.
28 Q. 15:39-42.
29 Q. 7:44-50.

Mutual Wrangling

It is interesting to note that, in the context of the description of the people of heaven engaging in discussion with the people of hell, they are described as "discerning" (al-a'rāf'). The Arabic term also indicates the highest, or most easily discerned, element of something, such as the highest part of a wall, or the most obvious feature of a particular animal. Many scholars agree that the salient feature of the people of heaven is that they have nurtured the quality of discernment, made wise choices during their lives and were thus qualified to enter heaven following the Day of Judgement.[30]

The Qur'ān also describes "hypocrites" as pleading from their position in hell with those who were steadfast in their faith and are now in heaven, saying, "Wait for us! Let us have a (ray of) light from your light!" In response, they will be told: "Turn back, and seek a light (of your own)."[31] The hypocrites include those who are unclear in their beliefs and convictions, and deceive even themselves. Reading the "light" in allegorical terms, we can see it as meaning the light of faith that the people of hell nourished throughout their lives, a pale reflection of the divine light of God. We read a similar allegory in the New Testament story of the ten foolish virgins who, when they had let their lamps go out because they did not have enough oil, asked to borrow oil from the wise virgins, who answered that they should go and buy their own.[32]

What are we to make of the Qur'ān discussion of arguments and disputations among the inhabitants of hell, and of conversations held between those in heaven and those in hell? Above all, we should remember that God is loving and merciful, and that He wants more than anything for us to join Him in heaven one day. After all, it was for this purpose we were created in the first place! In this light, we can see the accounts of the bitterness and recriminations among the inhabitants of hell as a timely warning, so that we can do our best to ensure that we are pleasing God and will one day dwell with Him in heaven, where our voices will join in praising and thanking Him for the blessings He has bestowed upon us, for eternity.

---

30 Asad, 1984, 210, note 37.
31 Q. 57:13.
32 Matt. xv -1-13.

CHAPTER 14

Scholars' Views of the Redemption of Humanity

CLEARLY, AS BELIEF in the Day of Judgement and in heaven and hell are fundamental issues to Islam, the issue of the redemption of humanity is an important – indeed, crucial – point of scholarship and debate, and generations of Islamic scholars have dedicated themselves to this topic. In this chapter, we are going to look at the scholarly contributions of several of Islam's most important thinkers, at different periods in history, and establish an essential understanding of their input to this important topic.[1]

As we have seen, Islam is deeply concerned with the issue of salvation in the next life, and the question of whether or not members of other religious traditions can be saved and, if so, under what conditions.[2] Clearly, these two questions are fundamental to any discussion of Islamic eschatology. Islam is different to all other religions, so it is not surprising to find claims that its adherents will be treated differently on the Day of Judgement to other people.

Broadly, Islamic thinking on the issue of redemption and punishment tends to fall into one of two schools of thought, which have been termed, respectively, inclusivist and exclusionary or damnationist. Inclusivist schools of thought generally focus more on God's mercy, and subscribe to the idea that all, or most, people will eventually be taken by Him into heaven (some of them after a period of purification), whereas exclusionary views are more likely to hold that only true Muslims who also live very good lives will one day get to enjoy the delights of heaven and to rejoice in the company of God.

---

1 Except when otherwise indicated, this chapter relies on the scholarship of Mohammad Hassan Khalil. Khalil, 2012, 74-145.
2 Sachedina, 2006, 297.

Scholars' Views of the Redemption of Humanity

Inclusivists generally interpret the Qur'ān as stating that heaven is alone in being eternal, whereas hell will one day cease to exist, just as the earth will cease to exist in its current form on the Day of Judgement. Exclusionists tend to feel that hell will last forever, with its denizens condemned to an eternity of torment. Clearly, these views are essentially incompatible, while subscribing to one or the other would have had great repercussions in the early days of Islam in particular, when there was a great sense of urgency around the important mission of bringing as many new converts to the fledgling faith as possible. In that context, there was considerable motivation to promulgate the view that only believers would be saved. As the faith become more secure, however, it was easier for scholars to admit other possibilities for the adherents of different faiths, and to debate the issues in a more open, inclusive way, while (of course) exploring the Qur'ān itself, so as to determine what God has to say on this essential matter.

Born in northeast Iran in the mid-fifth century, Ghazali devoted his life to the scholarship and exploration of the Qur'ān. As he is one of the most important Islamic scholars of all time, an understanding of his views is absolutely essential to any exploration of eschatology. Ghazali's work is frequently cited in Islamic scholarship to this day.

Ghazali was deeply concerned with the issue of why some people do not accept Islam, even though they have been given every opportunity to embrace it. Of course, there are many people around the world who never have the chance to hear the teachings of Islam, but what of those who do, and yet decide not to heed them? Believing that, deep down, all humans accept the reality of God on the most fundamental of levels, Ghazali wondered why so many opted to simply follow the faith of their parents, rather than exploring the great questions of the world by themselves. Ghazali saw human culture as a sort of corrupting influence that tended to lead people away from their own natural and instinctive belief in God, which he considered an inborn trait. He believed that anyone who did not believe in Muhammad as prophet, and in the messages that he received through revelation, was an unbeliever, and was therefore doomed to spend eternity in hell, whether they were an atheist or claimed to believe in God. This could be the case for anyone raised in a religion that did not believe in Muhammad and his message, and even for Muslims who were Islamic in name only.

Exploring the Qur'ān, Ghazali devised a list of those whom he felt rejected God and His message, which can be divided into two essential categories:

- Atheists, including those who "believe neither in God nor in the Last Day"[3], who consider nature itself as the creator of the universe, and those whose lives are so basic that they are comparable to animals.
- Idolaters, animists and Muslims who have failed to understand the metaphoric elements of the Qur'ān (i.e. who believe things such as the idea that God is actually physically above them in the sky, rather than dwelling in a spiritual realm.)

Conversely, Ghazali believed that those who understand God and His attributes, even if not to the level of understanding achieved by the prophets, and the prophets themselves, were "veiled by light," by which he meant that they were open to God, and understood Him and His intentions for humanity.

Ghazali understood that human beings can never truly know what is in anyone else's mind or heart. Thus, only God really knows whether or not someone believes. The implications of this include the fact that, while Islamic law may recognise certain people or categories of people as believers or unbelievers, the reality of their status is known only to God. Ghazali further argued that "true" unbelief is found when the individual rejects at least one of three basic tenets of Islam: Belief in the one true God, His prophet, and the next life. According to these schema, Jews and Christians cannot be considered believers, despite professing their belief in the one true God, because they do not accept Muhammad as His messenger, while atheists and assorted pagans cannot be considered believers because they do not accept any of the fundamental tenets of Islam at all.

---

3 Q. 4.38.

Scholars' Views of the Redemption of Humanity

What are the implications of Ghazali's view for the concept of redemption? Despite what might seem at a first glance to be a rather damning approach, Ghazali's belief in God's mercy and love led him to believe that God would look benevolently on people who lived far away from centres of Islamic thinking, and whose belief systems had therefore been formed from a place of ignorance. Because of the importance of access to Islamic thinking, he divided non-Muslims into three groups:

- People who have never so much as heard the name "Muhammad."
- People who know about Muhammad and Islam but who have rejected them.
- People who fall between the two groups.

Of these categories, Ghazali takes the dimmest view of the second, as they have been given access to the facts, but have chosen to disregard them, presumably because of their own hubris and arrogance. He compares unbelievers in this category to a person who is told that there is a lion behind him, and that he will be killed if he does not run away, but who refuses to leave until he can see the lion for himself. Such a person will be killed and eaten because of his own stubborn refusal to accept the truth as related by people who are better informed than he is. Those who belong to the other two categories will be in receipt of God's compassion and forgiveness, as will non-Muslims (even some non-monotheists) who sincerely sought the truth throughout their lives, but were never exposed to Islam. Clearly, then, while Ghazali believes that Islam provides us with the clearest path to God, he does not feel that it is the only one. He also believes that God will never punish anyone for factors that were beyond their control.

Ghazali's approach provides us with a vision of the Day of Judgement in which the vast majority of people are accepted into heaven, with the torments of hell being very much the exception, reserved only for those who have gone out of their way to reject God and all His works, despite having been given ample opportunity to embrace Him. This mercy extended also to communities in the past (before the advent of Islam), although Ghazali felt that some would need to be purified in the fires of hell – possibly even just for a very brief period – before being admitted to heaven, where they would spend eternity with God.

Ghazali's generally optimistic view about the fate of Muslims and non-Muslims on the Day of Judgement shifts when it comes to his opinion on what would become of those few who were condemned to hell. He paints a picture of two groups of condemned sinners; those who will remain in hell forever, as there is no hope of their ever reforming, even if they were brought back to life, and sinners who do have a degree of faith, who will be spared from the fires of hell when they have served an appropriate period of punishment.

Ibn Arabi has often been described as the most influential scholarly thinker in Islam, so a brief exploration of his views on the matter of redemption is essential here. Born in 560 in al-Andalus (modern-day Andalucía in southern Spain, a region that was once dominated by Islam), Ibn Arabi had a number of deeply profound spiritual experiences in his youth during which he met Jesus, Moses, and Muhammad. This experience prompted him to move to Mecca, where he began his scholarly work before ultimately settling in Syria. Ibn Arabi's writings explore the teachings of all the twenty-three prophets who are recognised in Islam (including Adam, Jesus, Moses and, of course, Muhammad), and they are frequently cited to this day.

Ibn Arabi's views on salvation rest on his understanding of God's mercy. As God loves all humanity, even the sinners, ultimately every person who has ever lived will be called by Him to heaven and eternal joy. Ibn Arabi maintained that God is manifested in everything; that everything in Creation somehow reflects Him. Among Creation, human beings in particular were created in His likeness, and are therefore special. Ibn Arabi points to the ninety-nine "most beautiful" names of God, as revealed by the Qur'ān, and states that, in order to understand God, it is necessary for His human creations to contemplate each and every one of them. However, the human mind is inherently limited. For this reason, each of us is able to worship only those qualities of God in which we are able to believe within the restraints of our own individual talents and abilities. Because none of us can really understand the totality of God, He accepts this partial form of worship and forgives us our deficits. Continuing with this line of thought, Ibn Arabi maintains that all religions and all manifestations of thought about the nature of the divine represent paths to God. In other words, he believes that adherents of all religious faiths can find their way to God and that all, in their various ways, are seeking the truth. In defence of this view (which is certainly not shared by all scholars of Islam), he cites the Qur'ān, which states that, "Everything is brought back to God,"[4] and "all journeys lead to Him."[5]

Despite this inclusive view, Ibn Arabi clarifies that, while many paths can lead to God, they are not all the same; some are much more direct than others, and offer greater spiritual reward. Some people approach God in a state of "wretchedness" and others in a state of "felicity." The latter state can be reached only by adherence to a knowledge of God arrived at through revelation, with the ideal form of revelation found in the messages received by Muhammad, the final and ultimate of His prophets. Ibn Arabi compares Muhammad's message to sunlight, and other paths to starlight. The implication is clear: Islam offers the straightest, most "well-lit" path to God among all possible routes and is therefore the safest, and most secure, path to God. Moreover, while Islam does not negate the spiritual truths found in other religions, when it comes to God's law, the laws revealed to Muhammad do negate all the laws of religious faiths that came before Islam. Therefore, anyone who becomes familiar with Islam is honour-bound to obey its laws.

On matters of redemption, while Ibn Arabi feels that people from a wide variety of religious backgrounds can one day live in heaven with God, he does state that those who reject God will be punished in hell. Still, his view here is prevalently one of inclusion. God will not punish those to whom He has not sent a messenger, and will punish only those who receive His message and deliberately choose to reject it. Even non-Muslims to whom God's message has not been clearly provided may be judged as Muslim, even if some of their views directly contradict Islamic teaching. According to this view, hell is not a place to which non-Muslims are set for punishment, but to which all of those

---

4 Q. 57:5.
5 Q. 5:18.

who refuse to accept God's truth after it has been revealed to them are sent. In support of this view, Ibn Arabi cites the following verse:

> When your Lord took out the offspring from the loins of the Children of Adam and made them bear witness concerning themselves. He said, "Am I not your Lord?" and they replied, "Yes, we bear witness," So you cannot say on the Day of Resurrection, "We were not aware of this."[6]

Ibn Arabi states that at some point everyone who has ever lived will hear God's message. For many, this may happen after death, even on the Day of Judgement, but before they are sent to heaven or hell. In this way, all non-Muslims who have never had a "compelling" experience of God's message as revealed in the Qur'ān will be given the opportunity, finally, to accept it.

Ibn Arabi considers hell to be eternal, but does not believe that those who are sent there will necessarily be punished "forever." This, he feels, would be inconsistent with what he knows of God's mercy, citing the Qur'ān where it states, "My mercy encompasses all things"[7] and "My servants who have harmed themselves by their own excess, do not despair of God's mercy, God forgives *all* sins."[8] Eventually, then, even those who are condemned to hell will experience a state of bliss – although they will have to live in the eternal fear that their punishment might start again.

While Ibn Arabi is one of the most influential scholars of Islam, his teachings are also divisive, and he has attracted detractors as well as supporters over the many years since his work was first made available. In particular, his view that even those who are sent to hell will one day experience eternal bliss has been seen by some as controversial and problematic, and has been denounced by those who are more damnationist than inclusivist as heretical.

---

6 Q. 7:172.
7 Q. 7:156.
8 Q. 39:53.

Scholars' Views of the Redemption of Humanity

Ibn Taymiyya, who was born in 661 in what is now Syria, experienced great hardship as a boy when he and his family had to flee their home in Harran as a result of the Mongol invasion to live as refugees in Damascus. He would grow up to be one of the most cited, and most controversial, scholars of Islam (he was also a doctor)[9], who never retracted his strongly held view that the best practice of Islam was to observe the faith as it was followed by Muhammad and his closest companions, without any of the "innovations" added by many Muslims in the years following Muhammad's death.[10] A quotation that is often attributed to Ibn Taymiyya states, "The Shaikh of Islam is beloved by us, but the truthful word is even more beloved than he,"[11] while another states, "The truth does not belong to one party exclusively but is divided among all groups."[12] In other words, while Ibn Taymiyya believed that the truth, embodied at its best in the Qur'ān, was fundamental to understanding God and His intentions for us, he did not claim that only Muslims have access to it.

Ibn Taymiyya was fascinated by God's endless mercy, as revealed by his study of the Qur'ān. Because of this divine quality, he believed that, when it came to the Day of Judgement, and the assessment of all the human beings who have ever lived, God would be much more inclined to pardon than to condemn and would not restrict entry to heaven to Muslims only, but would open up the possibility of everlasting life with Him to a large portion of humanity. In terms of salvation, he maintained that God would pardon all of those had never had the chance to hear His word, while everyone would one day have the opportunity to see God in His heaven. In support of this view, he cited the Qur'ān's statement that, "We do not punish until We have sent a messenger,"[13] which clearly indicates God's intention not to condemn anyone who has never had the chance to hear His word. Although Ibn Taymiyya

---

9 Rahman, 1968, 94.
10 Dammen McAuliffe, 2006, 196.
11 Baker, 2003, 235.
12 Rahman, 1968, 134.
13 Q. 17:15.

lived during a time when Islam was spreading rapidly, he knew that there were many societies that had not yet heard the Word of God, and he believed that that their lack of knowledge would not be held against them by a just and benevolent Creator. Instead, he felt that God would send those who never heard the Word of God a messenger on the Last Day who would provide them with the opportunity to hear, listen and embrace God's way.

On the other hand, Ibn Taymiyya believed that God would be less merciful towards those who had had ample opportunity to hear the Word of God, and yet chose to reject it. Within this category, he further believed that the individual's behaviour would temper the way they were treated in the afterlife. For instance, he maintained that Muhammad's uncle Abu Lahab, who did not support him, in particular during his mission to bring the Word of God to the people of Arabia, would be punished more severely than his uncle Abu Talib, who did support him even though he had not embraced the truth of Islam. Both, however, would be punished along with the many others who had heard the Word of God and had chosen to ignore it. Ibn Taymiyya also took a low view of rites that sprang up at grassroots level among some of the Muslim communities of his day, including tomb worship, and the worship of so-called saints,[14] seeing in these behaviours the "innovations" that he did not approve of, as they drifted incrementally further away from the original practice of Islam by Muhammad and his disciples.

While hearing and accepting the Word of God is essential, Ibn Taymiyya believed that an individual's behaviour during his or her time on earth was also essential in determining their treatment in the afterlife. He believed that even those who have never heard the Word of God are capable of distinguishing between moral and immoral acts, and that those who did dreadful things will be punished for them. He cites the Qur'ānic example of the Pharaoh who "exceeded all bounds"[15] before Moses was sent with God's word, and who would be punished for his sins. Conversely, hearing the Word of God and

---

14 Rahman, 1968, 177.
15 Q. 79:17.

paying it lip service was not enough to earn a place in heaven, for which good behaviour during one's lifetime is also necessary.

Ibn Taymiyya rejected the idea that Islam was not meant to supersede Christianity and Judaism, asserting that Islam was the truest form of God's message to humanity, whereas the messages embedded in the Christian and Jewish scriptures had become opaque and corrupted. He pointed to verses in the Qur'ān to support this view, such as, "We have sent you only to bring good news and warning to all the people,"[16] and he isolated each of the major arguments of the Christian faith, so that they could be refuted.[17] He firmly rejected the idea of intercession on behalf of Jews and Christians, although he did believe that intercession could help the cause of sinful Muslims.[18]

Ibn Taymiyya maintained that, while many humans would be condemned to hell in punishment for their failure to heed the Word of God, only heaven is eternal. This idea clearly holds out some hope, even to the most hardened of sinners. According to this view, one day hell will cease to exist, while heaven, like God Himself, will persist forever. In support of this view, Ibn Taymiyya pointed to various passages in the Qur'ān, including the comment that those who have lived righteously will enjoy "a reward that never fails."[19] Eventually, therefore, those who have suffered the torment of hell will be released from it, and will join God in heaven. He pointed to verses in the Qur'ān that described the suffering of the sinners in hell as enduring for "ages" rather than for "ever."[20] Thus, even the most dreadful sinners will one day be released from their punishment and returned to God. God's love is eternal, and His wrath will be felt only on the Day of Judgement. Many Qur'ānic verses can be cited in support of this position, for example, "Know too that God is severe in punishment yet most forgiving and merciful."[21] Even references to

---

16 Q. 34:28.
17 Rapoport and Ahmed, 2010, 256.
18 Rahman, 1989, 31.
19 Q. 41:8.
20 Q. 78:23.
21 Q. 5:98.

hell eventually being "annihilated" do not mean that the citizens of hell will cease to be; after all, the world as we know it will be annihilated on the Day of Judgement, and yet the Qur'ān teaches us that our souls will live forever. Thus, we can see that Ibn Taymiyya's view implies that the punishments of hell are actually an intrinsic element of God's essential mercy, as even the worst sinners can be purified of their sin, whereupon they have earned the right to enter heaven and dwell forever with God. Some even earlier scholars of Islam (including Ibn Jarar al-Tabari and Ibn Ahmad al-Qurtubi) rejected the idea of hell being finite, but Ibn Taymiyya made a convincing case for the idea of hell as having an end, after which God, in all of His abundant mercy, will take all souls into His loving embrace.

Shams al-Din Abu Bakr Ibn Qayyim, also from Damascus, was a student of Ibn Taymiyya, who himself wrote on a wide range of topics, including theology, rhetoric and politics. While Ibn Qayyim shared many of Ibn Taymiyya's views, he also expounded different opinions on a range of topics. He tended to agree with Ibn Taymiyya that God's mercy was extensive, and that this mercy would extend to many people beyond the Muslim fold.

Ibn Qayyim firmly rejected the idea that the sinners sent to hell would be punished only for a brief period of time before being allowed entry to paradise, when they would be replaced by another group. In support of this rejection, he cited a number of verses in the Qur'ān, including the following:

> [The Jews] say, "The Fire will only touch us for a few days." Say to them, "Have you received a promise from God – for God never breaks His promise – or are you saying things about Him of which you have no real knowledge?" Truly those who do evil and are surrounded by their sins will be the inhabitants of the Fire, there to remain.[22]

While the Qur'ān refers to the torments of hell as being "endless," Ibn Qayyim's view is that this means that they are endless within the context of

---

22 Q. 2:80-1.

hell being finite. In other words, the sinners who have been condemned to hell will suffer its punishments ceaselessly until hell ceases to exist at some point in the future. He devised a detailed series of arguments that maintain that heaven is eternal, and for everyone, while hell is finite. Based on Qur'ānic scripture, these arguments can be summarised as follows:

Heaven and hell are both creations of God, but they are fundamentally unalike. God will bring everyone who deserves to live in heaven into it, and only sinners will be condemned to hell. Those who have been admitted to heaven will live there, with God, forever. Those who have been condemned to hell will be compelled to remain there, suffering unceasing torment, and unable to escape, for as long as hell remains in existence. Sinners will be punished in direct response to the extent of their sins. However, while hell should be understood as being temporary, this does not mean that, for the sinners, it will seem as though time is passing quickly. Instead, a single day might feel to them like many thousands of years. Of course, as God is omnipotent, He could certainly condemn someone to everlasting torment should He wish to do so. But His wrath is tempered by mercy, and it is His wish to eventually gather all of His people into His embrace.

Ibn Qayyim urged all sinners to reflect on God's mercy, pointing out that our experiences show us in many different ways that His mercy is far greater than His wrath. He pointed out that God created unbelievers, that He cares for and nourishes them just as lovingly as He cares for and nourishes Muslims, and that, in His mercy, He has sent them messengers to bring them news of the Word of God. Comparing God to a physician, he compares hell to treatments for persistent disease. Sometimes even the kindest doctor will need to resort to cruel, painful treatments, such as cauterising a wound, if it is for the overall benefit of the patient. In this way, the example of hell shows not just God's justice, but also His mercy. Just as every disease is different, and requires a different sort of treatment, which may last varying periods of time, every sinner is different. Some sinners have good in them, and each will spend a period of time in hell that is relative to the number of sins they have committed. Clearly, those who have committed grievous sins will be in hell for a longer period than those who have only engaged in minor sins. Thus, according to this view, the purpose of hell is both to lead to fear among believers, to encourage them to live the right way, and to purify sinners through their exposure to its flames. After a period (which will vary from one individual to the next), each sinner will have been restored to his or her original state of God-given purity, and will be in a position to return to God.

Maulana Muhammad Ali was an important scholar of the Lahore Ahmadiyya Movement, which emerged in the early twentieth century following the schism of the Ahmadiyya Movement into two groups, one which considered the founder, Ahmad, to be a prophet (despite the Qur'ān's insistence that Muhammad was God's final and ultimate messenger), and one that did not. Maulana Muhammad Ali belonged to the second of the two groups.

Like Ibn Qayyim, Ali compares God to a doctor, stating that the punishments He issues can be compared to the operations carried out in hospital which, although painful, save lives. In this context, Ali sees hell as the inevitable result of the evil deeds of the sinners, and a place where they receive the treatments they need in order to become capable of spiritual development. In support of this view, he cites verses in the Qur'ān that refer to the fires of hell as the "sinners' friend"[23] and as their mother.[24] He also points to the fact that the Qur'ān uses a term to refer to the fires of hell that was originally used in the context of purifying gold with fire.

Ali also believes that non-Muslims will also be saved and states that Qur'ānic terms that have often been interpreted as suggesting that they will stay in hell forever should actually be understood as meaning that they will remain in hell for a long time, but not for eternity. His writings refer to God eventually removing from hell every single sinner in whom there is a speck of faith or goodness, even if it is as small as a mustard seed, describing them as growing in goodness from the foundation of this tiny speck.

Ali's teachings have become extremely influential in the Muslim world, in a range of areas, notably in the Nation of Islam movement, which was founded in the United States in the 1930s, and which had an important role

---

23 Q. 57:15.
24 Q. 101:9.

in the genesis of the modern civil rights movement, which sought to obtain equal treatment for Americans of African descent.

Muhammad Rashid Rida was born in 1865 near Tripoli, and benefited from a good education in the sciences and in Qur'ānic scholarship. Rida was concerned by what he felt was the decline in intellectualism in Islam, and found inspiration in the writing of a range of Islamic scholars, including Jamal al-Din al-Afghani and Muhammad Abduh, both of whom worked for the case of the modernisation of Islam, and its integration with what we know about the world from scientific disciplines. Together with Abduh, today Rida is remembered as one of the founders of the Salafi Movement, which spread quite quickly throughout the world of Islam. One of Rida's concerns was around the importance of reading the Qur'ān in the Arabic language, whenever possible.[25] Although he accepted that the Qur'ān would need to be translated into a range of vernacular languages for the purpose of spreading the faith, he was aware that literal translations could be confusing, while attempts to localise the text by translating "the meaning" opened the door to obfuscation.

Rida believed that each individual's responsibility towards God sprang from the extent to which that person had been exposed to God's truth in the form of reason or revelation.[26] In other words, more would be expected of someone who was familiar with the precepts of Islam and thus knew how God wished people to behave, than of someone who had never had the opportunity to learn about Islam at all. Rida accepted that the Qur'ān describes the salvation of non-Muslims who are Christians and Jews, the "People of the Book," which is described in a well-known verse as follows:

> The believers, the Jews, the Christians, and the Sabians—all those who believe in God and the Last Day and do good—will have their rewards with their Lord. No fear them, nor will they grieve.[27]

---

25 Leemhuis, 2006, 156.
26 Sachedina, 2006, 304.
27 Q. 2:62.

Rida pointed out that this verse should be read in its broader context; it comes after a verse that describes those who refuse to listen to God's word as it was sent to them as being struck down by the wrath of God. In this context, one's religious identity as Muslim, Jew or Christian is less important than whether or not one truly believes in God and lives well. Rida explained that the very term "Islam" refers to one's submission to God, and not to a faith identity (which, after all, so many people are born into, rather than choosing). According to this world-view, God's justice will not be meted out according to people's formal religious affiliation.[28] After all, it would not be just at all to grant privilege to one group over all others, merely because of who they are. This view is backed up by verses in the Qur'ān, which make it clear that God has sent His message to earth on more than one occasion:

> We have revealed to you [Muhammad] the scripture in truth, confirming the scriptures that came before it and as a guardian over them: so judge between them what God has sent down. Do not follow their whims, which deviate from the truth that has come to you. We have assigned a law and a path to each of you. If God had so willed, He would have made you one community, but He wanted to test you through that which He has given you, so race to do good: you will all return to God and He will make clear to you the matters about which you differed.[29]

Rida believed that religious pluralism – the existence of a range of religions in the world – was part of God's plan for humanity. In this context, "the external form of religion is relegated to the inward witness of the divine that defies any exclusive and restrictive definition."[30] According to this world-view, God has created everyone with the inborn capacity to understand the difference between right and wrong, regardless of the specific religious tradition

---

28 Sachedina, 2006, 304.
29 Q. 5:48.
30 Sachedina, 2006, 305.

to which they belong. For this reason, all human beings are called upon by Him to find a way to live and work together to make the world a fairer, more peaceful place.³¹

Rida was, however, critical of both Christianity and Judaism. He felt that, while God had sent His word to the Jews and Christians, their scriptures and beliefs had become terribly corrupt (citing as an example the doctrine of the Trinity, which is considered blasphemous in Islam), and that the laws for behaviour commonly followed prior to the arrival of Muhammad were, in fact, not consistent with God's law for this reason, and therefore could not be considered "islamic," in the sense of a simple adherence to the Word of God. Conversely, anyone who does adhere to the Word of God is being "islamic" even if they do not self-identify as Muslim. This view is consistent with Qur'ānic teaching as expounded in the following verse:

> Some of the People of the Book believe in God, in what was sent down to you and in what was sent down to them, humbling themselves before God; they would never sell God's revelation for a small price. These people have their rewards with their Lord; God is swift in reckoning.³²

But what of those who have, unlike Jews, Christians and Muslims, never had the opportunity to hear the word of God at all? In general, Rida's view is that God will spare them the torments of hell, as it is not their fault that they have not had the chance to live according to God's law. Again, this is consistent with the teachings of the Qur'ān, which states: "We do not punish until We have sent a messenger."³³

Rida followed earlier scholars by considering non-believers as belonging to one of three groups:

---

31 Sachedina, 2006, 305.
32 Q. 3:199.
33 Q. 17:15.

- Those who have never heard of the prophet Muhammad and the messages he brought.
- Those who learned about Muhammad and his message, but whose arrogance and negligence prevented them from exploring it.
- Those who were exposed to the message of Islam but who were taught an inaccurate version of it, or to whom it was represented in such a way that even the sincere were not encouraged to explore it.

Rida explained that certain groups of people, such as the indigenous societies of the Americas, belong to the first of the above categories, as they simply did not have the opportunity to hear the Word of God, through absolutely no fault of their own. He also tends to conflate the first and third categories of people, insofar as neither has had the opportunity to hear the true Word of God. When the Day of Judgement comes, all of these people will be given special treatment, as it is not their fault that they never had the chance to hear and obey. However, this does not mean that they will be automatically absolved of all of their sins. Even within the ranks of the "unreached" it is easy to see that some have lived good and virtuous lives to the best of their abilities, while others have committed terrible crimes. Rida states that God will judge the "unreached" according to how they have lived and with respect to the extent to which they understood the true nature of good and evil – an assertion that is based on the assumption that, on some level, all human beings have a natural, instinctive understanding of the fundamentals of good and evil. He also moots the suggestion that, on the Day of Judgement, there may be some sort of a "test" for the unreached that will determine whether they are sent to hell or admitted into heaven.

With respect to Jews and Christians, Rida stated that while their scriptures have become corrupted, they still maintain crucial elements of God's message, and that they cannot therefore be considered analogous to those who have never heard His word at all. In general, Rida believed that God would look mercifully on non-Muslims on the Day of Judgement, but that there would be two exceptions to this rule:

- Those who encountered Islam and were given every reason to investigate it for themselves, but failed to do so.
- Those who investigated Islam and saw for themselves that it is the truth, but whose arrogance or hubris meant that they continued to resist it.

Note that Rida was writing in a time of widespread literacy, when large numbers of people around the world were aware of the Muslim faith. Rida believed that, although many people had heard about Islam, they had never been properly educated about it, and that they remained woefully ignorant as a result of this lack of information. Furthermore, many people in the early twentieth century who had heard of Islam had been taught lies about it. These people, like the rest of the unreached, will be judged mercifully by God. Rida believed that the world would gradually move towards the point whereby more people were in a position to research Islam properly and embrace its truth, whatever their original social or cultural context. As humans have been gifted the capacity to reason, at this point many – if not most – of the people in the world will become Muslims.

Rida also considered hell to be a place of punishment where many sinners would spend a period of time, which could be long or short, before they were admitted to heaven. He cites the fact that the words used in the original text of the Qur'ān which are often translated as indicating "forever" can also denote an extended, but finite, period of time. Rida pointed out that the Qur'ān states that God is so generous that He rewards anyone who does a good deed by many multiples, showing us how bountiful His mercy is. However, Rida did not subscribe to the idea that even the irredeemably wicked would be saved one day, but rather accepted the idea that some people have sinned so badly, and angered God so much, that they will in fact suffer the horrors of hell for eternity. These people, he believed, represented only a very small minority of those who were sent to hell in general, as most people would be released from their torment when they have suffered enough to be considered purified.

The Ultimate Reward: Eschatology in the Qur'ān

Sayyid Qutb, an Egyptian scholar who died by execution in his native land in 1966, was an influential Islamic scholar who took a rather more severe line than Rida. Qutb maintained that what will really matter on the Day of Judgement will be true belief rather than formal religious affiliation. This means that those who self-identify as Muslims, but whose lifestyles and behaviour show that they are not really following the Word of God, will be judged accordingly. Writing in the mid-twentieth century, Qutb was very clear that Islam offers the only way forward, and the only sure way to be admitted into heaven in the afterlife. Thus, people who appear to be living virtuously, and yet do not accept God's message, are demonstrating "false goodness" and will not be admitted into heaven. However, God will be merciful towards those who have not received His "warning." For Qutb, one of the most important messages of the Qur'ān was that it is hugely important for Muslims to spread their faith, offering countless others the opportunity to hear God's message and live in heaven with Him forever.

While other scholars of Islam have often believed that the fire of hell will be temporary for many sinners, Qutb took a more pessimistic view, believing that the Qur'ānic reference to sinners remaining in hell for "ages" meant that their punishment would simply be renewed, over and over again. He felt that sinners had themselves sealed their fate. Quite simply, having turned their back on God, they are no longer His responsibility.

At the time of his writing, Qutb's views were considered controversial. He maintained that the government was not truly Islamic, for if it was it would accept the Qur'ān's message as interpreted by him. Notwithstanding the controversial nature of many of Qutb's claims, he remains influential in some quarters. However, many contemporary Muslims, who have good non-Muslim friends and colleagues are repelled by his idea that, no matter how virtuously they live and how many good deeds they carry out, no non-Muslim can ever be admitted into heaven.

Farid Esack, a contemporary scholar who has also worked together with activists from non-Muslim faiths, firmly rejects the idea of an exclusionist God who will not admit any non-Muslims to heaven. He believes that, while the Qur'ān is frequently critical of "People of the Book", these criticisms should be read as referring to specific groups of individual Jews and Christians who were alive at the time of Muhammad, and that they should not, by any means, be generalised to all non-Muslims. While the Qur'ān can refer to these people as distorting the Word of God, this does not mean that all non-Muslims do so. Esack believes that while many of those who hear the word of God feel drawn to Islam, and become (or remain) Muslims, others are drawn to islam – with a small "i" – and live in a godly way without necessarily becoming Muslims at all. In support of this view, he cites a well-known verse from the Qur'ān:

> We have assigned a law and a path to each of you. If God had so willed, He would have made you one community, but He wanted to test you through that which He has given you, so race to go good: you will all return to God and He will make clear to you the matters about which you differed.[34]

Mahmoud Ayoub, another contemporary scholar, believes that God will be merciful towards all of the People of the Book, and that the only expectation of them with respect to Islam is that they acknowledge Muhammad as a messenger of God, and the Qur'ān as a sacred document that confirms what they have learned about God from their own sacred scriptures. In this view, he has much in common with the work of Fazlur Rahman (who is quoted extensively throughout this book). Rahman maintains that the Qur'ān's message is not just anti-exclusionist, but strongly so, and that it often draws our attention to the fact that good people can be found in all religious communities. Thus, Rahman states, anyone who believes in God and the Day of Judgement, and who lives a good life, will be saved in the end.

What is the contemporary person exploring the issue of redemption to make of the divergence of views on this matter? If we accept that God has created us all as both spiritual and intellectual beings, we can appeal to both the heart and the mind for counsel in this matter. In today's world, many of us

---

34 Q. 5:48.

have the opportunity to live and work alongside others whose religious views and practices may be very different to our own. Anyone with an open mind cannot escape the conclusion that it is possible to find good and bad people in all cultural and religious settings, and that being ostensibly Muslim is no guarantee that one is good. As the Qur'ān has told us that God Himself created people in different communities and placed us on this earth, who are we to judge and blame an entire category of people for the religious tradition in which they have been raised, simply because it is not the same as ours? And how dare we, with our limited human understanding, imagine that we have the ability to tell whom God will admit to heaven, and whom condemn to the torments of hell?

The Qur'ān has been shown, again and again, to be a document that is truly modern, insofar as it contains the answers to the questions of each new generation. Without suggesting that Islam alone is the path to our eternal reward in the afterlife, perhaps it is not too much to suggest that it is one of the most accessible. In the Qur'ān, we find the clearest enunciation of God's will for humanity. As such, it is a gift to us all – Muslim and non-Muslim alike – and a clear guide to how we can live and worship in a way that is truly consistent with God's purpose for us.

CHAPTER 15

❖ ❖ ❖

The Roads to Heaven and Hell

ANY OF US, given the choice, would prefer to spend the afterlife in heaven than in hell. The reality is that we *do* have a choice, and that we can exercise it every day of our lives by deciding to live as God has instructed, to respect others as much as we would like them to respect us, to devote ourselves to honesty and kindness, and to worship Him and know that He is the one true God. Thankfully, the Qur'ān provides us with a clear set of directions that we can follow to stay on the path towards heaven, even as we continue to grapple with our flawed human nature. Here, we will explore the major themes of the Qur'ān in terms of the spiritual and practical guidance it provides to everyone who sincerely wishes to follow God and spend eternity with Him.

The Road to Heaven
TRUE FAITH
Clearly, faith in God is one of the fundamental elements of a life that will lead us to Him after the Day of Judgement. But what is true faith, and how can we identify it? How can we even be sure that we ourselves are true believers? As possessing true faith is essential for anyone who wishes to reach heaven, understanding this is absolutely essential.

The reality is that faith is not necessarily as simple as it seems. The Qur'ān devotes considerable space to discussions of the nature of faith. For example, it points out that "true piety" is not a simple matter of overt religious observance for the sake of show, but rather rests in a deep and abiding belief in God and His angels, God's message as revealed to the prophets, and the Day of Judgement. Faith is seen in actions as well as words. To truly believe, we also need to act on this belief by following God's instructions to humanity, and giving generously to our dependants, the poor and orphans, as well as doing whatever we can to fight against abominations such as slavery, to keep our promises, to support those who are in exile, and to be patient and persevering in difficult times. Without all this, our prayers to God are meaningless, empty words with no substance behind them.[1]

The Qur'ān provides us with a detailed description of a genuinely good, God-fearing person, which we can summarise as follows:

- Their faith is true and sincere.
- They engage in charitable acts to support the less fortunate.
- They are a good citizen who strives to support harmony and order in the society in which they live, wherever it may be.
- Their soul and faith in God remain firm and steady, even in the face of challenges and difficulties.

A person with true faith knows that it is not enough to simply state that they have faith in God or to utter platitudes about belief in God and how important it is. Instead, they spend their lives tirelessly striving and working towards a deep and abiding understanding of Him, in both the challenging and the easier periods of their lives. As their faith grows and develops, their understanding of God and the nature of reality similarly grow and mature. As they become more attuned to a clear understanding of divine reality, they can look around and see God's hand at work in everything. They understand the nature of the Day of Judgement, and live every day in the knowledge that it could come at any time, so it is important to always be ready for it. When they engage in good works such as giving to charity, they do so from a place of genuine love, and never in an attempt to bribe God or as a public display of piety, intended to impress others.[2]

---

1 Q. 2:177.
2 Ali, 1934, 71, notes 178-9.

As it states in many instances throughout the Qur'ān, there is only one God, and believing in other gods, or falsely ascribing divine qualities to human beings, is invariably sinful and wrong. We are urged not to imagine that any entity other than God Himself has divine powers.[3]

The Qur'ān calls on us all to be faithful, with faithfulness defined broadly. Clearly, we should be faithful to God and His intentions for humanity at all times, for it is God from Whom all things come and it is God Who will assess our lives on the Day of Judgement and find us either deserving or wanting. This implies many things: the need to acknowledge that God is the Author and Creator of all things, and that not only do we need to ensure that our own lives are righteous, but that we do not prevent others from following the path of God by leading them astray.[4] It also means that we must understand that the Qur'ān was not composed by Muhammad but was divine inspiration received by him as a series of revelations that have been recorded for us as the Qur'ān. The belief in God as a single, unique deity is a fundamental aspect of Islam. For this reason, adhering to a monotheistic view is a central element of faithfulness to the teachings of Islam. True belief in God implies recognition that He is singular[5] and incomparable with any other being or thing.[6]

Ultimately, only God knows what is in anyone's heart, and He will take everything into consideration on the Day of Judgement, looking with far more mercy on those who are tempted into sin by their mere human weakness than on those who have deliberately, consciously, selected the wrong path above all others,[7] while welcoming the true believers into His loving arms.[8] The Qur'ān is also careful to state that there are many good people among the Jews and

---

3 Q. 7:33.
4 Q. 11:18-9.
5 Q. 42.11.
6 Q. 112:4.
7 Q. 4:98.
8 Q. 33:73.

Christians, and that they will certainly be rewarded for their virtuous and God-fearing lives in the next world.[9]

We show our faith and faithfulness in God in the context of our relationships with other human beings here on earth, too. Above all, we should be faithful to our spouses, protecting both ourselves and them from the perils of marital infidelity. Physical love, the ultimate expression of love between spouses, should be confined within the boundaries of marriage,[10] while marriage must always be freely chosen by both parties to it (or, in rare circumstances, mostly historical, in the context of freely chosen polygamous marriages).

Fidelity, to God and to His holy law, is the only way to heaven.

Avoiding Sin

As we are all flawed human beings, it is all but inevitable that we will sin from time to time. However, God urges us to strive every day to avoid engaging in four major types of sin, which can be summarised as follows:

- Actions that are shameful, such as offences against society. These behaviours may have legal repercussions in the communities or nations that we live in, and they are also sins in the eyes of God.
- Sins of excess and neglect, including a lack of discipline, failing to carry out our duties and being selfish or boastful. These behaviours are sinful even if they are not illegal in the society where we live.
- Worshipping false gods.
- Allowing true faith to become corrupted by superstition.

The Matter of Human Rights

Observing, supporting and actively working for human rights is a key aspect of faith in the Qur'ān. Muhammad received his revelations at a time when slavery was widespread, and there were few support networks for the weak and helpless. The Qur'ān provided instructions intended to gradually lead God's

---

9 Q. 3:113-5.
10 Q. 23:1-10.

people away from the abhorrent practice of slavery. Freeing slaves, referred to colloquially as "liberating the neck," is described as a virtuous act that pleases God and, together with caring for the poor and for orphaned children, as an essential element of faith in God and observance of Islam. References to the freeing of captives can also be understood in a more figurative sense to include those who are "captives" of debt, or of other circumstances that curtail their life choices and, in some circumstances, can even be extended to the idea of the importance of treating kindly anyone in our care – including even animals. Thus, the admonition to free captives applies just as much now as it did in the time of Muhammad, when slavery was lamentably widespread. Thus, we can clearly see that a deep, abiding, and active respect for human rights is a fundamental element of Islam.[11]

Respecting the Religious Freedoms of Others

The Qur'ān makes it very clear that religion is always a matter of personal choice, and that coercion is invariably wrong and sinful. It spells this simple truth out in various ways, including making the plain statement, "There shall be no coercion in matters of faith."[12] In other words, faith in God is *only* valid when the individual in question comes to it on his or her own, and none of us, however faithful we consider ourselves to be, has the right to try to force another human being to bend to our views on religion and faith in God. Moreover, in the context of the Arabic in which the original text was written, the term used, "dīn" bears the implication of "both the contents of and the compliance with a morally binding law"; in other words, it refers to the broadest possible understanding of religion. In this way, we can understand the "religion" referred to here as implying not just one's personal faith in God, but also the religious and moral laws that emanate from adherence to a particular scripture or formalised system of belief. The Qur'ān makes it perfectly clear that anyone who wishes to spend the afterlife in heaven with God needs to respect the religious freedoms of others.

---

11 Affi, 2016, 183-4.
12 Q. 2:256.

Exercising Forgiveness

The willingness to forgive others, and to ourselves ask for forgiveness when we have done wrong, is an essential element of faith. We can show that we truly believe in God by ensuring that we do not allow ourselves to be easily roused to anger, by forgiving those who have offended and hurt us, and by praying earnestly to God for forgiveness when we ourselves have done wrong, as all flawed humans inevitably do.[13] Rather than lashing out and trying to blame others for our own shortcomings, we are willing and able to acknowledge them, and always prepared to do what it takes to amend our own behaviour and bring it closer to God's plan for us. When we examine our hearts, and are forced to admit that we have done wrong, we turn to God and implore His forgiveness, as well as doing whatever we can to right any wrongs that we have perpetrated on others. In our knowledge that God will always forgive someone who is genuinely repentant, we can all find true hope for an everlasting future.

Humility

God has called on each us to be humble, as befits a species that owes absolutely everything to its Creator. If we are sincere in our wish to reach heaven and live there with God forever one day, we all need to work to become, and remain, humble in the face of God's glory. We must not be boastful about what we consider to be our achievements, as all of the good things of this world come from God. We must not imagine ourselves intrinsically better than anyone else, merely because of accidents of birth, or because we are wealthier or more fortunate. After all, we are all equals in the eyes of God.

A Healthy Relationship with Material Success

While the Qur'ān does not teach that there is anything intrinsically wrong with financial or business success, it does make it perfectly clear that true riches are absolutely nothing to do with money or other early trappings of success,

---

13 Q. 3:133-6.

but rather come from God, with the ultimate "richness" found in the glories of everlasting life. Rather than competing with one another to see who can become the wealthiest, it is better if we strive to please God and earn the right to live in heaven with Him forever.[14] We show our devotion to God by giving to charity as generously as we can, and sharing whatever we can with the needy, not just when times are good for us and we have plenty to give, but also when we ourselves are struggling. We understand that, while things may be difficult for us, they are even worse for others. When we manage to rise above our baser instincts, and give to charity even in the midst of personal difficulties, we show a true and abiding faith in God.[15] When we give what we can, quietly and modestly, without showing off to others about what we are doing, or making the recipient of our charity feel bad about their situation, we please God and show that we have a genuine faith in Him and in all of His teachings.[16]

Rather that striving to enrich ourselves, we do better in striving to "fight" every day in the cause of God, by doing whatever we can to live as He wishes us to,[17] instead of allowing worldly concerns to tempt us to belittle God's messages to us.[18] When we do, we will be richly rewarded with the incredible gift of everlasting life with Him in the heaven that He has created for us. This is a promise that is borne out not just in the Qur'ān but also in the other holy books of revelation, the Torah and the Bible.

It is interesting to note that the experience of essentially all the prophets, including Noah, Jesus and Muhammad, has been that the people most open to hearing their all-important message have generally not been the rich and powerful, but the poor, the oppressed, and those in captivity to others. For them, God's message represents a promise that, if His word is followed to the letter, we on earth will enjoy a fair society, while all good deeds will be rewarded in the afterlife. This revolutionary concept is a dramatic challenge

---

14 Q. 3:133-6.
15 Q. 2:274.
16 Q. 2:262-3.
17 Q. 9:111.
18 Q. 45:35.

to the power and authority of the establishment and the wealthy throughout history, right up to the present.[19]

Generosity

Throughout the Qur'ān, God calls on us to share whatever we can, especially with the poor and the needy. We should do so not because we hope to get something in exchange (whether in this life or the next) but because we know that it is the right thing to do. Those who do good, and seek no reward, will nonetheless receive one in the next life![20] Generosity can come in various forms. Most obvious, perhaps, is the giving of alms to the poor. However, generosity also takes the form of providing refuge to those in need of asylum, and not bearing a grudge towards those who have been given things we want for ourselves.[21] As well as providing us with information about the correct way in which to receive those in need of asylum and care, the Qur'ān provides us with tangible examples of this from Muhammad's day. For example, when Muhammad and his followers had to flee his native Mecca, they were graciously received by the early Muslim community of Medina, which took them in as asylum seekers, and shared everything they had with them. In general, anyone who wishes to consider his or herself to be a true Muslim should be prepared to accept those in need and to welcome them. This applies in particular to anyone who is forced to flee their homeland because of faith-based persecution, given that the Qur'ān rules that religious freedom and the lack of religious coercion is an essential human right.

The Road to Hell

The Absence of True Faith

Faith is essential for anyone who wishes to go to heaven, so the absence of faith (in those who have had the opportunity to hear God's revelation) is a

---

19 Asad, 1984, 316.
20 Q. 76:7-12.
21 Q. 59:9.

guarantor of going to hell. However, the matter is more complicated that it may seem. Some people make great public displays of piety, while not necessarily holding a true and sincere faith in God at all. Others maintain that they believe in God, and may even have convinced themselves that they do, but they do not engage in the charitable and other good works that show that their faith is truly genuine, or perhaps they deny key tenets of the faith, such as the belief in God as the creator of all things, or the Day of Judgement. They might ascribe divine or semi-divine powers to saints or other false gods, diluting their statement of faith in the one true God. By doing any of these things, they reveal that they do not possess true faith at all, and they risk spending the afterlife in hell, rather than in heaven with God.

God has called on us all to be true to Him and, by extension, true to the promises we have made, to Him and others, such as the promise to be faithful in the context of marriage. Those who are not consistent in their faith in God, and who betray those whom they are supposed to love and cherish, are inevitably bound to find themselves in hell on the Day of Judgement. Examples of a lack of faithfulness in God include entertaining doubts in the veracity of Muhammad's claim to have received the Qur'ān as a revelation from God, and to believe that anyone other than God is divine. The Qur'ān refers to the fact that many people developed polytheistic views and blasphemous beliefs in a wide range of deities and "invisible beings" to which they attributed qualities and abilities that are God's, and God's alone. The Qur'ān further states that the view that God had "sons and daughters" is closely aligned to these baseless, blasphemous views.[22] In this teaching we can find a reference both to the Christian idea that Jesus was the "son of God," and to the idea, widespread among the Arabs prior to the arrival of Islam, that the angels were in fact the daughters of God, like the female-designated false deities they worshipped.[23] The Qur'ān also references the examples of various other prophets who were sent by God to enlighten His people, and the people who refused to listen – and, in so doing, condemned themselves to hell. For example, Noah was told

---

22 Q. 6:100-1.
23 Rida, 1999, Vol. 7, 533-8; See also the Jews' claim that Ezra is the son of God, Q. 9:30.

by God to inform the people that they should not worship false gods, but many of the powerful and influential people of his day refused to listen, and instead insisted that Noah was just an ordinary man with no insights from God, and indeed that he was lying to them.[24] The revolutionary character of every prophet's mission has always made them distasteful to the upholders of the established order and the privileged classes of the society concerned. As Noah set about preparing for the calamity that he had foretold (which we do not need to discuss in the current context), they continued to make fun of him and his message,[25] stating that they had seen no proof that he was a prophet, and that they saw no reason to cease worshipping their false idols.[26] They suggested that perhaps Noah was simple-minded or insane and that when he instructed them to stop worshipping false gods, this was just the ramblings of a madman.[27] Always with calm and dignity, Noah continued to insist that he worshipped the one true God, and that he would never cease to trust in Him,[28] while also pointing out that he himself had no power to force anyone to believe in anything, and that he was a simple vessel for God's message to humanity, which they refused to listen to at their peril.[29] In the case of Moses, too, he was sent clear messages from God, which he brought to the Pharaoh and the people, all of whom derided them, asking why Moses had not been given the trappings of authority, such as gold jewellery, and why he was not visibly accompanied by the angels he referred to.[30] Like Muhammad, Moses had to deal with critics who wondered why God would send His message to an ordinary man, and not to a wealthy, influential person whom they felt they could respect and listen to.

---

24 Q. 11:25-7.
25 Q. 11:38.
26 Q. 26:105; 26:117.
27 Q. 23:24-5.
28 Ali, 1934, 598, note 1549.
29 Q. 26:105-15.
30 Q. 43:46-7; 51-4.

In another account of the derision that greeted many prophets of days gone by, we are told that the prophet Shu'ayb suffered this considerably. The people of Shu'ayb's day informed him arrogantly that they could not make any sense of what he was saying, while they could clearly see that he was weak and outnumbered. When they told him that they would have stoned him to death were it not for their respect for his family, Shu'ayb calmly asked them if they respected his family more than they respected God Himself.[31]

In relating these stories, the Qur'ān reminds us that, in all their foolishness, people often reject new ideas simply because they conflict with the erroneous, old ideas that they have inherited from their predecessors, and that many are tempted away from true faith to a faith in false gods on the basis of the flimsiest and most absurd of reasons. God warns us in the Qur'ān not to deny His truth, and that if we do we will suffer severely for it in the next life,[32] as God sees all and knows everything that is in our hearts.

Faithfulness to God also implies acknowledging that He is the author of all things, for to claim false attributions clearly indicates a startling lack of faith. The Qur'ān makes it clear that those who do this and, worst of all, attribute to themselves creations or actions of God are "lost in sin" and are certainly not heaven-bound unless they repent and mend their ways.[33] Indeed, the Qur'ān states very explicitly that hell is "the abode for all who deny the truth,"[34] and that while there may be a price to pay on earth for worshipping false gods, the price in the afterlife will be much greater. In the temporal context of the period of revelation, this teaching refers to the accusations facing Muhammad during his life time, that he himself had written the Qur'ān and subsequently falsely attributed it to God. However, the essential message is just as applicable today as it was then.

The Qur'ān discusses the Hypocrites in some detail, describing them as people who say, "We believe in God and the Last Day," while they do not

---

31 Q. 11:91-2.
32 Q. 14:2-3.
33 Q. 10:17; 7: 37; 6:93.
34 Q. 29:68.

The Ultimate Reward: Eschatology in the Qur'ān

believe, and stating that while they attempt to deceive God, ultimately the only one they have really deceived is themselves, and that while they describe others as corrupt and weak-minded, they are really the ones who are spreading corruption on earth, and who are so foolish they cannot or will not see the truth, even though it is in front of them.[35] Again, this element has both temporal and timeless elements. On the one hand, it refers specifically to the historical Hypocrites of Medina, the city to which Muhammad and his followers fled in exile due to the persecution they suffered in Mecca. These Hypocrites claimed to have converted to Islam, but remained secretly unconvinced that the messages being preached by Muhammad were true. On the other hand, it also refers to anyone, at any period in time, who deceives themselves or prevaricates in order not to fulfil their spiritual commitments. The Qur'ān points out that, regardless of the fine words people might use in praise of God, He knows exactly what is in their hearts, and can see straight through their lies and obfuscations. It warns the truly faithful to be wary of hypocrites, who may try to lead them away from faith in the one true God.[36]

With respect to the Hypocrites of Medina, their leader Ibn Ubayy had been the most dominant man in Medina prior to the arrival of Muhammad, and he never forgave the latter for having dislodged him from his perch. While outwardly professing to believe in Islam, Ibn Ubayy tried to persuade the people of Medina to cease supporting Muhammad and the rest of the asylum-seeking Muslims, and thereby to force them to leave. Fortunately, his attempts to hinder the development of Islam failed.[37]

The Qur'ān is explicit and clear about the eventual faith of hypocrites – both the historical Hypocrites of Medina, and the hypocrites that we find in every generation, where it says:

> The hypocrites, both men and women, are all of a kind: they enjoin the doing of what is wrong and forbid the doing of what is right, and

---

35 Q. 2:8-13.
36 Q. 63:1-8.
37 Asad, 1984, 867, note 9.

withhold their hands (from doing good). They are oblivious of God, and so He is oblivious of them. Verily, the hypocrites – it is they, they who are truly iniquitous. God has promised the hypocrites both men and women – as well as the deniers of the truth – the fire of hell, therein to abide: this shall be their allotted portion. For, God has rejected them, and long- lasting suffering awaits them.[38]

The Qur'ān deals firmly with those who ascribe divine qualities to beings or things other than God, and states firmly that they will pay for this when the Day of Judgement comes.[39] We should understand this teaching in a broad sense, as it refers not just to the literal worship of false gods, but also the superstitious beliefs in imaginary beings, the attribution of divine qualities to personages considered to be saints, and even an excessive fondness for material possessions, wealth, power and so forth.[40] It should be noted that these admonitions refer also to Jews and Christians, which share so much with Islam. Over the years, both faiths tended to drift towards practices and beliefs that, at the very least, verge on blasphemy. For example, Christians do not consider their doctrine of the Trinity (the idea of God being embodied in father, son and holy spirit) as detracting from an understanding of the one true God, but the Qur'ān states that this belief is erroneous, along with the widely-held idea that saints have the power to serve as mediators between human beings and God on the Day of Judgement. It also singles out the idea of Jesus as the literal son of God as something that is clearly wrong, given that God is singular and all-powerful,[41] and references similar beliefs that were held by the Jews of ancient Arabia in the time of Muhammad with respect to Ezra, who was a historical character who restored, arranged and edited the Torah after the Jews' period of exile in Babylon.[42]

---

38 Q. 9:67-8.
39 Q. 6:22.
40 Q. 6:23-4.
41 Q. 9:30.
42 Rida, 1999, 292-6.

The Qur'ān addresses Christians directly where it states:

> O followers of the Gospel! Do not overstep the bounds (of truth) in your religious beliefs, and do not say of God anything but the truth. The Christ Jesus, son of Mary, was but God's Apostle – (the fulfilment of) His promise which He had conveyed unto Mary – and a soul created by Him. Believe, then, in God and His apostles, and do not say, (God is) a trinity. Desist (from this assertion) for your own good. God is but One God; utterly remote is He, in His glory, from having a son; unto Him belongs all that is in the heavens and all that is on earth, and none is as worthy of trust as God.[43]

The Qur'ān is also critical of Jews who believe that they are God's "chosen people," thus creating unnecessary division between them and other believers (Christians and Muslims) in the one true God.

At various points in history, people have attempted to downgrade certain of the Qur'ān's teachings about fidelity in the human realm. For example, a verse that refers to "those whom their right hands possess" has sometimes been interpreted as meaning that men can engage in sexual relationships with their female slaves even if they are not married to them. Given the Qur'ān's strong anti-slavery teachings, and its insistence on the essential equality of men and women, both beloved creations of God, this is of course absurd. However, the idea is also explicitly contradicted by specific Qur'ānic teachings.[44] Instead, the reference to "belonging" (mā malakat) refers to both men and women and to the "ownership" we all have over our spouses in marriage, which gives us the right to "possess" one another in the sort of relationship of love and mutual respect that forms the basis of solid family life everywhere in the world.

---

43 Q. 4:171.
44 Q. 4:3, 24, 25 and 24:32.

Engaging in Sin

We are all flawed human beings, but those of us who recognise when we have done, truly repent and make amends have a chance of salvation. However, those who consistently and unrepentantly engage in sin, as defined above, are setting themselves firmly on the path towards hell. It is incumbent on anyone who wishes to avoid hell to strive every day not to sin at all, and to immediately repent and make amends when they do slip from the path of righteousness. It goes without saying that a life steeped in sin is a sure way to get to hell.

Excessive Pride

The Qur'ān cites the example of those, like the Pharaoh of ancient times, who behaved arrogantly, "just as if they thought that they would never have to appear before Us (for judgement)." It is made perfectly clear that such people are destined to hell.[45] While the narrative refers to a specific demographic, in this case Pharaoh and the ancient Egyptians, by logical extension it also applies to everyone who reacts to the teachings of God with arrogance and hubris, despite the teachings of His messengers and the abundant proof of His existence in the world around us. The Qur'ān also points out that these sinful attitudes can also be found even among those who, in theory, follow the teachings of God. It relates the story of a man identified as Qārūn, who considered himself a follower of the prophet Moses. This man enjoyed great material success, and he also allowed himself to think that he was better than others just because he was wealthier. The Qur'ān relates that the true followers of Moses urged him to cease being so arrogant, to stop his involvement in corruption, and instead to adhere to the teachings of God, warning him that just as God gives, so can He take away. Qārūn retorted that he had earned everything he had with no help from anyone, to which the Qur'ān responds that he should have known that God can easily take away everything from the powerful and rich, while warning those who might be tempted to be like him not to become "lost in sin."[46] This story makes it perfectly clear that even the ostensible followers

---

45 Q. 28:39-40.
46 Q. 28:76-8.

of a true prophet of God are not immune to the temptation to become vainglorious and arrogant. In this context of today, we can read it to understand that even the most apparently pious Muslim could be led astray by his own arrogance.

WASTEFULNESS

It is sinful and wrong to waste any aspect of the gifts given to us by God. For example, the Qur'ān refers to those who cry out to God when they are ill, but who carry on as before when they have been cured. This is wasteful in a number of different ways. For one, they have wasted an opportunity to draw near to God and gain a better understanding of Him, and for another they may be wasting "their own selves"[47] if they return to behaviours that compromise their health and impact on their ability to serve God and please Him. In a modern context, we can consider social problems such as the obesity crisis, alcoholism and drug abuse, and so forth. By not caring for the wonderful bodies that they have been gifted by God, people in these situations are being wasteful in the purest sense of all.

The Qur'ān also refers to people who, despite having been presented with God's truth in the form of revelations received by His prophets, continue nonetheless to engage in wasteful and profligate behaviour, described as "excesses on earth."[48] These excesses are clearly various. The Qur'ān recognises that war and conflict can at times be necessary, but also states that violence and killing should be kept to a minimum. After all, what could be more wasteful than the literal "wasting" of human life on the battlefield?

At a time when environmental degradation is doing untold damage to the world and all the species that live in it, we should also remember that the world is a gift from God, and we have been trusted with it as custodians. It is not a resource to be mined and left in poor condition for future generations to deal with. Each of us has the moral imperative to do our bit to take care of the abundance that God has given us.

---

47 Q. 10:12.
48 Q. 5:32.

At its most basic, wastefulness – of our own gifts, of human life, of the environment – represents a profound disrespect for God and the many wonders that He has created. For this reason, all of these behaviours are grave sins that should not even be contemplated.

Materialism

Those who become excessively fond of material wealth, to the extent that they neglect their faith and do not live in a way that pleases God, are likely to find themselves in hell, where they will have ample time to reflect on the absolute futility of having judged their self-worth during their brief lifetimes according to their tally of wealth and possessions.[49] We all stand to be reminded that, on the Day of Judgement, we will have to account for how we have lived our lives, and whatever wealth we enjoyed during our lifetimes will be completely irrelevant.[50] We are taught that this is the doctrine not only of the Qur'ān but of the earlier Revelations, the original Law of Moses and the original Gospel of Jesus. We all need to work hard to ensure that we do not make false idols of our possessions and the experiences that money can buy ("passing delights"), all of which ultimately come from God. The path to hell is well-trodden by those who were tempted to prioritise material wealth during their time on earth!

Religious Coercion

Some people – Muslims as well as adherents of other religions – have insisted in different times and places that it is appropriate to forcibly convert others to their own religious faith. However, nothing could be further from the truth. Within Islam, forced conversions are meaningless, for how can anyone come to a true understanding of God if they are forced to do so? Moreover, any attempt to force, coerce or bribe non-believers to embrace Islam is deeply sinful. The Qur'ān reminds us that, if He wished it, God could have ensured that everyone on earth worshipped Him. As He has not done anything to coerce

---

49 Q. 11:15-6.
50 Q. 6:70.

or force in matters of faith, how dare we imagine that we have the right to do so?[51] Instead, the free will that is the inheritance of every adult, competent person, is a blessed gift that each of us can use to make a wide range of moral choices, including about matters of faith. God invariably respects our human right to free will, and it is incumbent on each of us to do likewise.

The Qur'ān's message about the essential wrongness of coercion in matters of faith is reiterated in various locations. For example, the great prophet Noah is depicted as saying that, although he brought his people clear messages from God, it was not incumbent upon him to force these messages on anyone. As a simple man of God, a human being with no divine attributes of his own, Noah is depicted as stating that he sought no reward other than that he would eventually enjoy in heaven with God, while each human being needs to make up their own mind about what they believe.[52] In general, the Qur'ān repeatedly stresses the importance of never attempting to coerce others in matters of faith, as well as the doctrine that the prophets, while important vessels of God's message to humanity, are also no more than ordinary men.

The Qur'ān also makes it clear to us that no human has the right to judge another person's faith; that is a matter between him or her and God. For example, in Noah's day, some of the unbelievers suggested that his followers were pretending to believe in God and Noah's message because they thought that they would "get something out of it." Noah made it clear that no human being can see what is in someone else's heart, and that when someone makes a proclamation of faith, this should be taken as true, so long as he or she does not clearly act or behave in a way that contradicts it.[53]

Obviously, admonitions against coercing others in matters of faith also apply to those who would attempt to prevent others from following the one true God. The Qur'ān makes specific reference to these people, "bent on denying the truth and on barring others from the path of God" and making it clear that attempting to lead a true believer away from Islam is a dreadful

---

51 Q. 10:99; 6:149.
52 Q. 11:28-30.
53 Asad, 1984, 567.

sin that will certainly condemn them to hell.[54] It references, both directly and obliquely, contemporaries of Muhammad who attempted to lure the early Muslims away from the straight path by telling them that Islam was no more than a corruption of the scriptures revealed to earlier prophets acknowledged by adherents of Judaism and Christianity.[55] God is making it perfectly clear that no one, regardless of what they believe, has the right to try to force anyone into, or away from, the religious path that they are following. For good Muslims, the implications are clear – spiritual leadership should come in the form of education and example, and never coercion in any form. In today's troubled world, non-Muslims and Muslims alike will do well to remember and live according to these basic Islamic precepts.[56]

Listening to the Word of God

Above all, God has asked each of us to listen, and to listen well. Throughout the Qur'ān, it stresses that an open heart and an open mind to hearing God's message to us is essential. Each and every one of us is called to listen to the God Who created us, and who loves us.[57] The Arabic noun used to instruct us thusly is "basīrah," which bears the implication of seeing with the mind, and can be interpreted as meaning the quality of understanding something on the basis of intellectual comprehension. As we have seen before, the Qur'ān essentially argues that anyone who employs rational, reasoned thought can clearly see for his or herself that God's message to humankind, as expounded in His holy messages, is utterly logical. In this way, we can see that belief in God is not "just" a matter of faith (although faith is certainly important) but also a matter of reason and logic. Throughout the Qur'ān, God implores us all to use our powers of reason to truly think about world, our place in it, and the Creator Who has given us all life.[58]

---

54 Q. 47:32; 34.
55 Q. 3:99.
56 Asad, 1984, 57-8, note 249.
57 Q. 12:108.
58 Asad, 1984, 354.

Finding our way to heaven and everlasting life with God is a matter that is both complex and simple. It is complex because we are flawed human beings, and the temptations that surround us are legion. It is simple because, in sending His messages to His apostles on earth, God has provided us with a clear roadmap to follow – and if we do, we will be brought to everlasting life with Him on the Day of Judgement.

CHAPTER 16

❖ ❖ ❖

The Eternity of Afterlife

THE MODERN, SCIENTIFIC view of the universe and all it contains is that all living beings are mortal by their very nature. There is no true scientific formula for immortality. However, rationalist par excellence, Nietzsche, propounded a view of "eternal recurrence," which built on the idea that the energy in the universe is finite, that space is subjective, but that time is objective, a cyclical process that can only be described as "infinite." Perhaps this rare overlap between science and theology, the admission of the possibility of infinity, gives us hope that one day the two will not be seen as in opposition, and allows us to discuss the Qur'ān's teachings in this area in the full light of modern scientific discovery.[1]

Clearly, the concept of going to heaven or to hell is one that is of enormous importance to everyone living now, and indeed anyone who has ever lived at all. It may seem a little surprising to some, under these circumstances, that the Qur'ān leaves ample room for speculation that heaven will not, in fact, be eternal, as the Christians maintain, and certainly not restricted to Jews, whose faith traditionally maintains that non-Jews cannot go to heaven, whereas almost no Jews will ever suffer the pangs of hell – or indeed to any other discrete ethnic or religious group that claims this privilege for itself.

The Nature and Purpose of the Afterlife

At no point is either heaven or hell described in the Qur'ān as a purely "spiritual" place, so we can assume that references to both suffering and pleasure

---

1 Iqbal, 1989, 91.

The Ultimate Reward: Eschatology in the Qur'ān

will be experienced in a bodily way. Although the Qur'ān makes ample use of both allegory and metaphor, with respect to the afterlife, language of this sort is intended to convey a sense of the enormity of the sensations we will experience rather than to suggest that these sensations will be purely spiritual suffering and pleasure. While there may not be a "literal" fire in hell, we will experience the physical, as well as the psychological, impact of fire if we are condemned to the abyss.[2] Of course, the Qur'ān is trying to describe the happiness and punishments as effects, i.e., in terms of the feeling of physical and spiritual pleasure and pain. The vivid portrayals of a blazing hell and a garden are meant to convey these effects as real spiritual-physical feelings, apart from the present psychological effects of these descriptions. There are thus literal psycho-physical effects of the fire, without there being a literal fire.

It is easy to understand the purpose of heaven, which is to reward the virtuous for their charitable and God-fearing lives. The purpose of hell, with its endless torments, is less obvious, at least at first glance. The God we know is loving and merciful, so how can He condemn so many of the most precious examples of His Creation to endure such dreadful agonies? As always, we find the answer to this question in the Qur'ān. Here, the fire is described as the sinners' "only friend"[3] and their "refuge." How are we supposed to interpret this, given what we know of the awful suffering the inhabitants of hell will have to endure? Quite simply, hell offers the otherwise irredeemable sinner a final opportunity to be purified and made ready to be taken into the company of God. The Qur'ān describes how, on the Day of Judgement, our sight will be suddenly made "sharp"[4] and we will be able to see, perfectly clearly, the fate that we have created for ourselves, in the course of our lives on earth.[5]

---

2 Rahman, 1989, 112-3.
3 Q. 57:15.
4 Q. 50:22.
5 Q. 17:13.

There are many visual depictions of hell throughout the Qur'ān[6], and it is described as "God's kindled fire which mounts above the hearts,"[7] a description of sinners' devastating realisation that they failed utterly during their one chance on earth to show God their love for Him. At the same time, heaven should not be imagined as the end of learning and experience, but as a place where those who have been granted access to God's mercy will enjoy "a new glory" with each moment that passes[8] and in which they will continue to grow in joy and knowledge of the God who created them.[9]

The Promise of More

The Qur'ān suggests that those who have been admitted into heaven, in recognition of the virtuous way in which they lived their lives, will remain there "as the heavens and the earth endure."[10] This verse comes with the suggestion that there may, however, be something even greater beyond heaven, a "gift unceasing," or the promise of even greater delights than they are currently experiencing in heaven,[11] or perhaps a new stage of evolution that goes yet further than the new bodies the residents of heaven will have.

The True Nature of Islam

In everyday discourse, both Muslims and non-Muslims often used the word "Islam" without ever pausing to define it. In fact, the very term "Islam" is not even used by the Qur'ān to describe a religious faith per se, and is used instead to refer to submission to God.[12] Throughout history, revelation has

---

6 For example, Q. 37:41-9; 44:41-9.
7 Q. 104:6-7.
8 Q. 55:29.
9 Iqbal, 1989, 98.
10 Q. 11:108.
11 Rāzī, n.d. vol. 18, 63-4.
12 Q. 3:83.

come to us through various different channels, and the Qur'ān recognises a range of prophets before Muhammad, including Abraham, Joseph, and Jesus. In fact, it refers to the followers of these prophets as "Muslims," while the word "islam" can also refer to the submission of all things to God. Therefore, if someone states that only "Muslims" can be saved, or only "islam" is the path to God, whether they know it or not, they are really saying that *anyone* who submits to God is heaven-bound, whatever their official religious affiliation.

Islam has many genuinely revolutionary aspects, but perhaps most revolutionary at all is its ardent rejection of the essential tribalism that marks so many belief systems and faiths. According to the Qur'ān, anyone can get to heaven, provided they recognise God as the one true God, live well and believe in the Day of Judgement. Their gender, race and ethnic and even religious affiliation are irrelevant, provided these criteria are met. In fact, the Qur'ān even posits islam (with a small "i) as, per se, faith in God and complete surrender to Him.[13] We all, humans and other living beings alike, are called to obey God in terms of holding true to the natural laws that He has laid down for us. Traditionally, scholars believe that those who truly submit to God on a conscious level are the angels and the true believers. Those who do not consciously submit to Him, however, are nonetheless obliged to observe the laws of nature, and are thus subject to His will, even if they do not recognise it.

Above all, God is Merciful

God has many qualities and attributes. Above all, however, He is merciful. He loves us, and wants only the best for us and for everything in His wondrous Creation.[14] The Qur'ān underlines this fact by referring to His grace and mercy as "a law,"[15] a term that is never applied to descriptions of any of His other attributes. God's grace and mercy are at the heart of everything He does.[16]

---

13 Q. 3:83.
14 Q. 6:12.
15 Ibid and Q. 6:54.
16 7:156.

The Eternity of Afterlife

Although counter-intuitive, the only logical way to view hell is as a precious gift from our loving Creator. Even the worst sinners amongst us will be given the opportunity to make themselves anew. Hell is just not a place of everlasting torture[17] brought into existence merely to punish the sinners, but an antechamber to heaven where they will be given the opportunity to experience correction[18] until they are ready to be brought into the presence of God Himself. This view, that eventually everyone will be granted the opportunity to spend eternity with God, is (as mentioned in Chapter Fourteen) known as "universalism."[19]

The adherents of many faiths have, over the years, often attempted to claim heaven for themselves. What does the Qur'ān have to say on this matter? First of all, it roundly dismisses the claims by certain Jews and Christians that only they (either Jews or Christians, of course, not both)[20] will be able to go to heaven.[21] It is worth pointing out that some Muslims, too, have made this claim. Like the Jews and Christians who went before them, the Qur'ān states clearly that they are certainly incorrect on this matter:

> Yea, indeed; everyone who surrenders his face unto God, and is a doer of good withal, shall have his reward with his Sustainer; and all such need have no fear, and neither shall they grieve.[22]

In Arabic the "face," the most expressive part of the human body, is used to indicate the person's whole character. In this verse, then, we can see that salvation in heaven is not proposed as a gift that will be given to Muslims alone, but to anyone who accepts God's uniqueness, obeys His will and lives according to His holy law. This teaching is epitomised in the following verse:

---

17 Q. 101:9.
18 Q. 57:15.
19 Khalil, 2013, 13.
20 Q. 2:113; 5:18; 62:6.
21 Q. 2:111.
22 Q. 2:112.

> Verily, those who have attained to faith (in this divine writ), as well as those who follow the Jewish faith, and the Christians, and the Sabians – all who believe in God and the Last Day and do righteous deeds – shall have their reward with their Sustainer; and no fear need they have, and neither shall they grieve.[23]

With respect to the other monotheistic faiths, God promises to confirm to them what is true in their beliefs, and to demonstrate what is not.[24] As well as discussing Jews and Christians, it mentions the Sabians, who were probably a monotheistic group that emerged between the origins of Judaism and the origins of Christianity. They appear to have followed the doctrine of baptism, and are not the same as the gnostic sect with a similar name that co-existed with early Islam.

Consistently, the Qur'ān states that all of the revelation-based faiths are rooted in His divine truth, and that where these do diverge from God's teaching, this is because of the "wishful beliefs" of frail human beings, and the resulting corruption, little by little, of the original teachings.[25]

Of course, there are still many people (and there once were many more) who have never encountered God's truth in the form of revelation at all. They have not had the opportunity to use their God-given free will to accept or reject His holy word. As we discussed in Chapter Eight, these people clearly cannot be judged the same way as those who have had the opportunity to explore God's message for themselves. Never having heard of the Day of Judgement, how can they be blamed for failing to believe in it? Not having been exposed to the Word of God, who would consider it their fault for worshipping graven idols? These people, known collectively as the "unreached," can only be judged according to the way in which they have lived: the good will be rewarded, regardless of the religious views they held (or didn't hold),

---

23 Q. 2:62.
24 Abduh, 1999, 348
25 Asad, 1984, 24, note 94.

and the bad will be punished in accordance with the sins that they have committed.[26] I believe that even those among the unreached who lived sinfully will spend but finite periods in hell, in recognition of the fact that they never had the opportunity to learn about God's intentions for the world.

God's mercy is truly great. The Qur'ān tells that the person who has done a good deed will be given a reward ten times greater in magnitude, while the person who carries out an evil deed will be punished to the same order of magnitude.[27] When we view the reality of the afterlife in the knowledge that God's mercy is the quality that underlies all things, we can see and appreciate that everything – even the agonies of hell – is a representation of His love.

---

26 Q. 28:84; 99:7-8.
27 Q. 6:160.

Index

Abduh, Muhammad, 209
Abraham, 17, 71, 129, 240
Abū Bakr, 44, 83
Abu Hanifa, 2
Abu Lahab, 204
Abu Talib, 204
Adam, 34, 35, 39, 38, 41, 43, 52, 53, 54, 58, 200, 202
agriculture, 10, 27
Ahmad, 208
Ahmadiyya Movement, 208
Aisha, 131
al-a'rāf', 195
al-Afghani, Jamal al-Din, 209
al-Andalus, 200
alcohol, 58
Ali, Maulana Muhammad, 90, 167, 208
Ali, Yusuf, 76
Allah, 1, 3, 85
allegory, xv, 2, 31, 32, 39, 46, 69, 90, 104, 107, 131, 132, 148, 149, 150, 152, 154, 155, 156, 161, 169, 173, 195, 238
angels, 1, 34, 35, 38, 39, 41, 50, 52, 64, 66, 97, 114, 124, 128, 131, 132, 137, 139, 141, 147, 149, 150, 160, 175, 176, 190, 191, 217, 225, 226, 240
anger, xvi, 89, 110, 165, 222
animism, 17, 198

Arabic, 22, 27, 32, 54, 104, 153, 165, 169, 176, 181, 182, 192, 195, 209, 221, 235, 241
Arabs, 4, 20, 49, 60, 88, 89, 141, 142, 170, 225
Aristotle, 30
Ash'arite school, 30
atheists, 197, 198
āyah, 125
Ayoub, Mahmoud, 215
Bā Yazid of Bistām, 30
Babylon, 229
Barzakh, 45
basīrah, 235
Battle of Uhud, 44
beauty, 23, 24, 36, 148
Bible, 146, 223
bin Anas, Malik, 2
bin Hanbal, Ahmad, 2
camels, 68, 111, 170, 173
creation of humanity, 33
Chaldean people, 17
change, 14, 18, 30, 31, 37, 86, 90, 107, 181
charity, xvii, 60, 77, 82, 188, 218, 223
children, 9, 14, 16, 41, 76, 103, 104, 110, 111, 113, 117, 123, 176, 221
Christianity, xiii, 5, 59, 64, 66, 71, 87, 116, 130, 138, 180, 205, 211, 225, 235, 242

Christians, 2, 20, 21, 41, 64, 71, 72, 87, 89, 95, 109, 127, 130, 136, 138, 186, 198, 205, 209, 211, 212, 215, 220, 229, 230, 237, 241, 242
companions of the Left Hand, 147, 160
companions of the Right Hand, 147
covenant, 43, 138
cyclical nature of Creation, 23, 28, 148
cyclical nature of day and night, 26
cyclical nature of life, 8
Dante, 133
decomposition, xiv, 91
diversity, xii, 10, 13, 48, 124
drugs, 58
eternal deity, 3
equality, xiv, xv, xvi, 41, 79, 80, 83, 86, 107, 110, 127, 150, 159, 178, 179, 180, 209, 222, 230
Esack, Farid, 214, 215
eternal plan, 23, 57
eternity, xvii, 39, 75, 79, 80, 82, 104, 105, 115, 117, 145, 146, 147, 158, 164, 168, 170, 180, 183, 195, 197, 200, 208, 213, 217, 241
Eve, 38, 39, 41
evil, xiii, 39, 40, 41, 44, 48, 49, 50, 52, 54, 55, 56, 57, 58, 59, 60, 61, 62, 63, 100, 101, 102, 104, 107, 108, 112, 113, 114, 119, 120, 121, 123, 135, 136, 143, 159, 160, 166, 167, 168, 171, 174, 176, 177, 178, 184, 186, 187, 188, 193, 194, 206, 208, 212, 243
exclusionism, 197
Ezra, 229
faith, xiii, 1, 3, 10, 17, 43, 48, 64, 71, 72, 76, 85, 99, 119, 129, 146, 147, 152, 168, 172, 186, 188, 193, 195, 197, 200, 203, 208, 209, 210, 214, 217, 218, 220, 221, 222, 223, 224, 225, 227, 228, 233, 234, 235, 239, 240
Fall of Man, 38
false deities, 4, 6, 189, 225
false scientific theories, 79
folklore, xiv, xv, 38, 49, 52, 67, 128, 133, 136
forced conversions, 233
forgiveness, 16, 41, 59, 74, 76, 81, 83, 113, 138, 140, 143, 154, 157, 199, 200, 202, 222
free will, xiii, 16, 40, 41, 53, 57, 58, 59, 61, 62, 100, 112, 135, 174, 176, 190, 234, 242
Gabriel, 128
gambling, 58
Garden of Eden, 38, 39
gender equality, 37, 41, 81, 127, 150, 178, 240
generosity, 60, 77, 213, 218, 223, 224
Ghazali, 197, 198, 199, 200
guardians of hell, 187, 190
hadith, 50, 66, 153
hamim, 169

Index

hatred, xvi, 58, 151
heaven as a garden, 102, 128, 146, 148, 153, 155, 238
heavens, 9, 17, 18, 20, 22, 27, 29, 31, 32, 69, 85, 86, 99, 107, 139, 141, 142, 149, 155, 156, 166, 180, 181, 230, 239
heresy, 2, 202
hope, xi, xiv, xvi, xvii, 47, 54, 78, 137, 140, 147, 151, 181, 205, 222, 224, 237
humility, xii, xv, 24, 27, 63, 94, 222
hūr, 275
hydrogen gas, 27
Hypocrites of Medina, 228
Iblis, 34, 52, 53, 54, 55, 56, 57 See Satan
Ibn Ahmad al-Qurtubi, 206
Ibn Arabi, 200, 201, 202
Ibn Jarar al-Tabari, 206
Ibn Qayyim, 181, 206, 207, 208
Ibn Taymiyya, 104, 181, 203, 204, 205, 206
Ibn Ubayy, 228
Ibn-Ishaq, 131
idolatry, 4, 60, 141, 142, 191, 192, 193, 198, 226, 233, 242
inclusivism, 197
inequality, xiv, 86, 107
infanticide, 110
infinity, 12, 21, 28, 30, 31, 52, 156, 164, 168, 237

intercession, xv, 134, 136, 137, 139, 140, 141, 142, 143, 205
Iraqi, 31
irrationality, 6, 7, 58, 79
ishārāt as-sā'ah, 68
Isra, 129
Israfil, 85
Jannat, 40
jawāhir, 30
Jerusalem, 128, 129, 130, 131, 133
Jesus, 5, 43, 44, 62, 67, 68, 71, 72, 116, 127, 185, 186, 200, 223, 225, 229, 230, 233, 240
Jews, 2, 20, 21, 38, 41, 71 72, 95, 109, 127, 130, 136, 138, 174, 198, 205, 206, 209, 211, 212, 215, 219, 229, 230, 237, 241, 242
jinn, 49, 50, 51, 52, 160, 186
Joseph, 136, 240
Judaism, xiii, 10, 59, 71, 205, 211, 235, 242
Ka'bah, 129, 130
Khaybar, 73
legislative material, 16
Lot's wife, 179
love, xi, xii, xvi, xvii, 8, 16, 37, 38, 48, 76, 79, 108, 110, 135, 142, 147, 149, 152, 164, 199, 200, 205, 218, 220, 225, 230, 235, 239, 240, 243
mā malakat, 230
martyrs, 134, 151
Mary, daughter of Imran, 179
materialism, 82, 233

Materialists, 2
Mecca, 65, 82, 95, 99, 129, 130, 131, 133, 159, 200, 224, 228
Medina, 65, 130, 224, 228
mercy
  of God, xii, xvi, xvii, 5, 9, 20, 58, 60, 95, 113, 117, 135, 142, 159, 177, 182, 183, 196, 199, 200, 202, 203, 206, 207, 213, 219, 239, 240, 243
metaphor, 2, 10, 11, 14, 23, 49, 86, 104, 119, 122, 161, 163, 168, 172, 173, 175, 177, 192, 194, 198, 238
Mi'rāj, 124, 129
miracles, xiii, 8, 43, 92, 124, 125, 126, 127, 128
misogyny, 178
Mithras, 116
monotheism, xiii, 1, 130, 141, 219, 242
moon, 17, 23, 25, 28, 69, 146
mortality, xi, 44, 45,
Moses, 51, 62, 71, 129, 130, 174, 200, 204, 226, 231, 233
Mu'tazilite doctors, 2
Muhammad, xiv, xv, 1, 4, 5, 6, 13, 16, 23, 27, 38, 44, 48, 49, 50, 59, 62, 65, 66, 67, 68, 71, 72, 73, 77, 78, 81, 83, 88, 89, 90, 94, 96, 101, 103, 104, 108, 111, 124, 125, 126, 127, 128, 129, 130, 131, 132, 133, 134, 136, 138, 146, 151, 153, 166, 167, 169, 170, 174, 177, 181, 197, 198, 199, 200, 201, 203, 204, 208, 211, 212, 215, 219, 221, 220, 223, 224, 225, 226, 227, 228, 229, 235, 240

nafs, 34
Nation of Islam, 208
natural disasters, 25
Nazis, 79, 174
New Testament, 72, 195
Nietzsche, 257
Noah, 223, 225, 226, 234
Noah's wife, 179
Nuremberg trials, 174
Old Testament, 21
omnipotence, 1, 3, 13, 48, 55, 142, 177, 207
original sin, 42, 116
pagans, 2, 4, 88, 89, 136, 137, 142, 144, 198
Pharaoh, 174, 204, 226, 231
Pharaoh's wife, 179
planets, 7, 24, 27
polytheists, 4, 10, 115, 137, 225
patriarchy, 81, 110
prayer, 129, 130, 188, 190, 191, 218
pride, 76, 77, 94, 114, 170, 194, 231
prophets, xiv, xv, xvii, 5, 6, 13, 17, 27, 31, 41, 44, 55, 62, 64, 65, 67, 71, 83, 96, 98, 101,102,103, 107, 109, 121, 122, 124, 125, 127, 128, 129, 130, 139, 141, 143, 157, 159, 177, 185, 186, 187, 188, 190, 192, 193, 198, 200, 201, 217, 223, 225, 227, 232, 234, 235, 240

Index

Protestants, 186
Qārūn, 231
Qutb, Sayyid, 214
racism, 79
Rahman, Fazlur, 112, 113, 123, 150, 215
rationality, xiii, 18, 24, 37, 89, 104, 113, 235, 237
Rāzi, Fakhruddin, 26, 161, 176, 191, 193
redemption, 17, 116, 168, 196, 199, 200, 201, 215
Reformation, 186
revelation, xi, xiv, 5, 13, 18, 20, 23, 64, 65, 67, 70, 71, 72, 73, 79, 81, 97, 99, 108, 109, 111, 127, 130, 131, 133, 159, 177, 197, 200, 201, 209, 219, 220, 223, 224, 225, 227, 232, 233, 239, 242
Rida, Muhammad Rashid, 209, 210, 211, 212, 213
Roman Catholic Church, 116
Rūmi, 47
Sabians, 109, 209, 242
sadid, 175
saints, 134, 137, 139, 204, 225, 229
Salafi Movement, 209
Satan, xiii, 38, 39, 48, 52, 53, 54, 55, 56, 57, 58, 59, 60, 61, 62, 63, 112, 160, 163, 172, 193, 194

science, xiv, 3, 10, 11, 23, 27, 31, 36, 46, 47, 70, 79, 89, 91, 92, 209, 237
scrolls, 100, 102
Second World War, 174
seven degrees of hell, 168
shackles, 162, 192
Shafi'i, 2
Shāh Walī Allāh, 90
Shu'ayb, 227
sky, 7, 17, 22, 23, 26, 32, 69, 146, 198
slavery, 218, 220, 221, 230
stars, 17, 24, 25, 27, 68, 69
sun, 7, 17, 23, 24, 28, 67, 68, 69, 170
superstition, 17, 58, 220
Syria, 200, 203
Tabarī, 191
Temple of Solomon, 130
Theory of Evolution, 46
Torah, 38, 51, 223, 229
Tree of Zaqqūm, 172
Trinity, 211, 229, 230
Ubayy, 65, 228
ummah, 105
uniqueness of God, xii, xiii, 3, 4, 5, 6, 9, 10, 11, 24, 118, 137, 140, 141, 142, 219, 229, 241
Virgin Mary, 134, 186, 230
water, 7, 23, 24, 69, 70, 99
Zamakhsharī, 191
Zoroastrians, 64

Bibliography and Further Reading

Abduh, Muhammad, *Risālat al-Tawhīd,* Dār al-Shurūq, 1994.

Abduh, Muhammad Tafsīr al-Manār, *Dār al-Kutub al-Ilmiyah,* vol.5, Beirut, Lebanon, 1999.

Abou El Fadl, Khaled, *Speaking in God's Name: Islamic Law, Authority and Women,* Oneworld, 2001.

Abu-Hamdiyyah, Muhammad. The Qur'ān; an Introduction, Routledge, 2000.

Abul Quasem, Muhammad, *Salvation of the Soul and Islamic Devotions,* Kegan Paul, 1983.

Affi Ali, Ahmed, *Laqbaynta iyo sharaxa, juska 28d oo Quraanka,* Zaytūn, 2003.

Affi, Ahmed, *The Modern Qur'ān: Lessons for Today,* Ahmed Affi Ali, 2016.

Affi, Ahmed and Affi, Hassan, *Contemporary Interpretation of Islamic Law,* Matador, 2014.

Al-Ashqar, Umar, *al-Janna wa-l-nār*; Dār al-Salām, 2005.

Alexander, Samuel, *Space, Time, and Deity,* The Gifford Lectures at Glasgow, 1920.

Al-Ghazālī Abū Hāmid b. Muhammad, *Al-Munqidh min al-Dalāl,* trans. Claud Field, London, 1909.

Al-Hibri, Azizah, *Women and Islam,* Bergamon Press, 1982.

Ali, Abdullah Yusuf, *The Holy Qur'ān English Translation*, King Fahad Holy Qur'an Printing Complex, 1934.

Al-Qaradawi, Yusuf, *Allah lam yakhluq al-insān li-yu'addibahu wa-lan takhlud al-nufūs al-nār,* Al-Ahrāmal-Arabi, 2002.

Al-Qurtubi, M.b.A, *al-Jāmi' li Ahkām al-Qur'ān,* Dār al-Kutub al-Ilmiya, 1988.

Al-Shātibī, Abū Ishāq Ibrāhīm b. Mūsā, *Al-Muwāfiqāt fi Usūl al-Ahkām,* 4 vols., Cairo, 1341 A.H.

Al-Sibā'i, Mustafa Husnī: *al-Sunnah wa Makānatahā fi'l Tashri' al-Islāmi,* 3rd edn, Beirūt, 1982.

Al-Suyūti, Jalāl al-Dīn, *al Durr sl-Manthūr fi al-Tafsīr bi'l Ma'thūr,* Beirut: Dār al-Fikr', 1993.

Arberry, AJ, *Revelation and reason in Islam,* George Allen and Unwin, 1957.

Asad, Muhammed, *The Message of the Qur'an,* Dār Al-Andalus, 1984.

Asad, Muhammed, *This Law of Ours,* Dār al-Andalus, 1987.

Ashmawi, Muhammad Sa'id, *Sharīa: The Codification of Islamic Law,* Oxford University Press, 1998.

Asqalani, Ibn Hajar, *Fath al-Bari,* Beirut: Dār al-Fikri li al-Tiba'a wa al-Nashr wa a-Tawzī, 1990.

Atiyeh, George N, *Al-Kindi: The Philosopher of the Arabs,* Islamic Research Institute, 1966.

Bibliography and Further Reading

Ayoub, Mahmoud, *Nearest in Amity: Christians in the Qur'ān and Contemporary Exegetical Traditions*, Taylor and Francis, 1997.

Badawi, Muhammad Zaki, *The Reformers of Egypt: A Critique of al-Afghani, Abduh and Ridha*, Croom Helm, 1978.

Baker, Raymond William, *Islam Without Fear*, Harvard University Press, 2003.

Bālī, Wahīd 'Abd al-Salām, *Wasf al-Janna wa-l-nār min sahīh al-akhbār*, Dār al-Kutub al-Ilmiyya, 1987.

Baljon, JMS, *Modern Muslim Koran Interpretation*, Brill, 1961.

Barlas, Asma, "Women's Readings of the Qur'ān," *The Cambridge Guide to the Qur'ān*, edited by Jane Dammen McAuliffe, Cambridge University Press, 2006.

Bergson, Henri, *Creative Evolution,* King Fahad Holy Qur'an Printing Complex, 1911.

Bodman, Whitney, "The Poetics of Iblis: Narrative Theology in the Qur'an," (review), *Harvard Theological Studies*, 62, Harvard University Press, 2011.

Boullata, Issa J., *Literary Structures of Religious Meaning in the Qu'rān*, Routledge, 2000.

Bucaile, Maurice, *The Bible, The Qur'an and Science,* CreateSpace Independent Publishing Platform, 2003.

Buck, Christopher, "Discovering." *The Blackwell Companion to the Qur'ān*, edited by Andrew Rippin, Blackwell Publishing, 2006.

Busse, Heribert, "The Sanctity of Jerusalem in Islam," *Judaism* 17.4, 1968.

Chittick, William C, "The Islamic Concept of Human Perfection," in Ryce-Menuhin, Jung and the Monotheisms, 1994.

Chittick, William C, *"Imaginal Worlds: Ibn Arabi and the Problem of Religious Diversity."* State University of New York Press, 1994.

Chittick, William C, "The Ambiguity of the Qur'anic Command" in Khalil, Mohammad Hassan, *Between Heaven and Hell: Islam, Salvation, and the fate of others,* Oxford University Press, 2012.

Colby, Frederick S, *Narrating Muhammad's Night Journey: Tracing the Development of the Ibn Abbas Ascension Discourse*, SUNY Press, 2008.

Cragg, Kenneth, *The Mind of the Qur'ān*, George Allen & Unwin, 1973.

Dammen McAuliffe, Jane, "The Tasks and Traditions of Interpretation," in Dammen McAuliffe, Jane. *The Cambridge Companion to the Qur'ān*, Cambridge University Press, 2006.

Eddington, Arthur Stanley, *The Nature of the Physical World*, Gifford Lectures, London, 1928.

Engineer, Asghar Ali, "Islam and Pluralismn," In Knitter, P, *The Myth of Religious Superiority: A Multifaith Exploration*, Orbis, 2005.

Esposito, John, *Islam: The Straight Path*, Oxford University Press, 1998.

Esposito, John L., *What Everyone Needs to Know about Islam*, Oxford University Press, 2002.

Fakhry, Majid, *A History of Islamic Philosophy*, Columbia University Press, New York, 3rd ed., 2004.

Bibliography and Further Reading

Fakhry, Majid. *Fanā al-nār 'ind Ibn Taymiyya wa-Ibn al-Qayyim*, Fatwa 64739, July 16, 2005.

Ghazali, Abu Hamid, *Ihya Ulum-id-Din*, trans. Fazul-ul-Karim, Islamic Publications Bureau, n.d.

Haleem, Muhammad Abdel, *Understanding the Qur'an, Themes and Style*, I.B. Tauris, London, 2012.

Hallaq, Wael B, *A History of Islamic Legal Theories: An Introduction to Sunni usul al Fiqh*, Cambridge University Press, 1997.

Hamza, Feras, *To Hell and Back: The Making of Temporary Hellfire in Early Muslim Exegesis*, Brill, forthcoming.

Hitu, Muhammad Hasan, *al-Wajīz fī Usūl al-Tashrī'*, 2nd ed., Mu'assasah al-Risālah, 1984.

Ibn al-Arabi, Mhyi al-Dīn. *Fusūs al-hikam*. Ed. A. Afīfī, Dār al-Kutub al-Arabi, 1946.

Ibn al-Muthanna, Abu Ubayda Ma'mar, *Majāz al-Qur'ān*, ed. F. Sezgin, 2 vols, Cairo, 1962.

Ibn Hazm, Abu Muhammad Ali, *al-Ihkām fī Usūl al-Ahkām*, ed. Ahmed Muhammad Shākir, 4 vols, Dār al-Afāq al-Jadīda, 1980.

Ibn Hishām, *Al-Sīra al-NabawĀya li-Ibn Hishām*, T.A.-R. Sa'd, ed., Dār al-Jīl, n.d.

Ibn Kathīr; *Tafsir Ibn Kathir*, Dār al-Fikri, 1980.

Ibn Qayyim al-Jawziya, *al-Tibyā fī Aqsām al-Qur'ān* (ed. M.H., al-Faqī), Dār al-Ma'rifa, n.d.

Ibn Rushd, Abū al-Walīd Muhammad, *Bidāyat al-Mujtahid wa-Nihāyat al-Muqtasid,* Beirut, Dār al-Fikr; n.d.

Ibn Rushd, *Fasl al-Maqāl,* Markaz Dirasat al-Wihda al-Arabia, 1999.

Ibn Sa'd, *al-Tabaqāt al-Kubra,* Beirut; Dār Sādir, 1960.

Ibn Taymiyya, Taqiyy al-Din, *al-Tafsir al-Kabir,* ed. Abd al-Rahman Umayra, Dar al-Kutub al-Ilmiya, n.d.

Idleman Smith, Jane and Yazbeck Haddad, Yvonne, *The Islamic Understanding of Death and Resurrection,* Oxford University Press, 2002.

Iqbal, Muhammad, *The Reconstruction of Religious Thought in Islam,* Iqbal Academy Pakistan, 1989.

Isack, Farid, *Qur'ān, Liberation and Pluralism,* Oneworld Publication, 2001.

Izutsu, Toshihiko, *Ethico-Religious Concepts in the Qur'ān,* McGill University Press, 1966.

Kamali, Muhammad Hashim, *Principles of Islamic Jurisprudence,* Pelanduk Publications, 1995.

Khalil, Mohammad Hassan, *Islam and the Fate of Others; the Salvation Question,* Oxford University Press, 2012.

Khalil, Mohammad Hassan, *Between Heaven and Hell: Islam, Salvation, and the Fate of Others,* Oxford University Press, 2013.

Khan, Muhammad Zafrullah, *Islam, its Meaning for Modern Man,* Harper and Row, 1962.

Khorchide, Mouhanad and Hartmann, Sarah, *Islam is Mercy: Essential Features of a Modern Religion*, Verlag Herder GmbH, 2014.

Lane, W.E., *Arabic-English Lexicon* I, London,1892.

Lange, Christian, *Paradise and Hell in Islamic Traditions*, Cambridge University Press, 2016.

Lapidus, Ira M. *A History of Islamic Societies*, Cambridge University Press, 1988.

Legenhausen, Muhammad, *Islam and Religious Pluralism*, Al-Hoda, 1999.

Leemhuis, Fred, "From Palm Leaves to the Internet," in Dammen McAuliffe, Jane, *The Cambridge Companion to the Qur'ān*, Cambridge University Press, 2006.

Lisān al-Arab, Dār Sāder, Beirut, Lebanon, 1997.

Mackie, JL, "Evil and Omnipotence," in Nigel Warburton, *Philosophy: Basic Readings,* Routledge, London, 1999. 40-51.

Maimonides, Moses, *The Guide of the Perplexed*, trans. by Shlomo Pines, with introductory essay by Leo Strauss, University of Chicago Pres, 1963.

Madigan, Daniel A, "Themes and Topics," in Dammen McAuliffe, Jane, *The Cambridge Companion to the Qur'ān*, Cambridge University Press, 2006.

Mahmassani, Sobhi, *Falsafat al-Tashri' Fi al-Islam*: *The Philosophy of Jurisprudence in Islam,* trans. Farhat J. Ziadeh, E.J. Brill, 1961.

Mahmūd, Mustafā. *Al-Rūh wa'l Jasad*, Beirut, 1974.

Mawdudi, Abul A'la, *Towards Understanding the Qur'ān*, trans. Zafar Ishaq Ansari, The Islamic Foundation, 1995.

McAuliffe, Jane, *Qur'ānic Christians: An Analysis of Classical and Modern Exegesis*, Cambridge University Press, 1991.

Mernissi, Fatima, *The Veil and the Male Elite*, New York; Addison-Wesley Publishing Company, 1991.

Nasr, Seyyed Hossein, *The Heart of Islam: Enduring Values for Humanity*, Harper-Collins, 2004.

Nasr, Seyyed Hossein, *The Study Qur'ān*, Harper Collins, 2015.

Neuwirth, Angelika, "Structural, Linguistic, and Literary Features," in Dammen McAuliffe, Jane, *The Cambridge Companion to the Qur'ān*, Cambridge University Press, 2006.

O'Shaughnessy, Thomas, *Muhammad's Thoughts on Death*, E.J. Brill, 1969.

Porter, JR, "Muhammad's Journey to Heaven," *Numen*, Vol. 21, Fasc. 1, 1974.

Qattān, Mannā', *al-Mabāhith fī ulūm al-Qur'ān*, Mu'assasat al Risālah, 1994.

Rahman, Fazlur, *Islam*, Anchor Books, 1968.

Rahman, Fazlur, *The Philosophy of Sadra*, State University of New York Press, 1975.

Rahman, Fazlur, *Islam and Modernity*, University of Chicago, 1982.

Rahman, Fazlur, *Major Themes of the Qur'ān*, The University of Chicago Press, 1989.

Bibliography and Further Reading

Rahman, Fazlur, *Major Themes of the Qur'an*, 2nd edition, Bibliotheca Islamica, 1994.

Ramadan, Tariq, *In the Footsteps of the Prophet; Lessons from the life of Muhammad*, Oxford University Press, 2007.

Ramadan, Tariq, *Radical Reform: Islamic Ethics and Liberation*, Oxford University Press, 2009.

Ramadan, Tariq. *The Quest for Meaning: Developing a Philosophy of Pluralism*, Allen Lane, 2010.

Rapoport, Yossef and Ahmed, Shahab, *Ibn Taymiyya and his Times, Studies in Islamic Philosophy*, General Editor: S Nomanul Haq, Volume IV, Oxford University Press, 2010.

Rāzī, at-Tafsīr al-Kabīr, Dar Ihya al-Turāth al-Arabi, vol.30, n. d.

Ridā, Rashid, Tafsir Manār IV, Dar al-Kutub al-Ilmiyah, 1999.

Robinson, Neal, *Discovering the Qur'ān: A Contemporary Approach to a veiled Text*. SCM Press, 1996.

Robson, James. *Is the Moslem Hell Eternal?* The Moslem World, 1938.

Rustomji, Nerina, *The Garden and the Fire; Heaven and Hell in Islamic Culture*, Columbia University Press, 2008.

Rubin, Uri, "Prophets and Prophethood," in Rippin, Andrew, The Blackwell Companion to the Qur'ān, Blackwell Publishing, 2006.

Sachedina, Abdulaziz, *The Islamic Roots of Democratic Pluralism*, Oxford University Press, 2001.

Sachedina, Abdulaziz, "The Qur'ān and Other Religions," in Dammen McAuliffe, Jane, *The Cambridge Companion to the Qur'ān*, Cambridge University Press, 2006.

Saeed, Abdullah, *Interpreting the Qur'ān: Towards a Contemporary Approach*, Routledge, 2006.

Saeed, Abdullah, "Contextualising," in Rippin, Andrew, *The Blackwell Companion to the Qur'ān*, Blackwell Publishing, 2006.

Saeed, Abdullah, *The Qur'an: An Introduction*, Routledge, 2008.

Saeed, Abdullah and Saeed, Hassan, *Freedom of Religion, Apostasy and Islam*, Ashgate Publishing, 2004.

Schimmel, Annemarie, *Mystical Dimensions of Islam*, University of North Carolina Press, 1975.

Shah-Kazemi, Reza. *The Other in the Light of the One: The Universality of the Qur'ān and Interfaith Dialogue*, Islamic Text Society, 2006.

Shaltoūt, Muhammad, *al-Islam 'aqīda wa-Shar'ia*, Dār al-Shurūq, 1990.

Shihāb al-Dīn Suhrawardī Maqtūl, *Kitāb Hikmat al-Ishrāq*, ed. Henri Corbin, Tehran University Press, 1952.

Sonn, Tamara, "Introducing," in Rippin, Andrew, *The Blackwell Companion to the Qur'ān*, Blackwell Publishing, 2006.

Swinburn, Richard, "Why God Allows Evil," in Warburton, Nigel, *Philosophy: Basic Readings*, Routledge, 1999, 52-63.

Tabari, Abu Jafri Muhammad b. Jarir, *al-Jami' al Bayan 'an Ta'wil al-Qur'ān*, Dār al-Fikri, 1988.

Taji-Farouki, Suha, *Modern Muslim Intellectuals and the Qur'ān*, Oxford University Press, 2004.

Thiering, Barbara, *Jesus the Man*, Doubleday, 1992.

Tottoli, Roberto, Narrative Literature, in Rippin, Andrew, *The Blackwell Companion to the Qur'ān*, Blackwell Publishing, 2006.

Wadūd –Muhsin, Amina, *Qur'ān and Women: Rereading the Sacred Text from a Women's Perspective*, Oxford University Press, 1999.

Walī Allāh, Shāh: *Hujat Allāh al-Bālighah*, vol.1, Cairo, 1961.

Watt, W. Montgomery, *Free Will and Predestination in Early Islam*, Luzac and Co. 1948.

Watt, W. Montgomery, *The Faith and Practice of al-Ghazali*, George Allen and Unwin, 1953.

Watt, W. Montgomery, *The Formative Period of Islamic Thought*, Oneworld, 1998.

Watt, W. Montgomery, *Islamic Philosophy and Theology*, Aldine Transaction, 2008.

Winter T, *The Last Trump Card: Islam and the Supersession of Other Faiths*, Studies in Interreligious Dialogue, 1999.

Yazicioglu, Isra, *Understanding the Qur'ānic Miracle Stories in the Modern Age*, The Pennsylvania State University Press, 2013.

Younis, M. Abdel Moneim, *The Religious Significance of Mi'raj*, Majallat al-Azhar, 1967.

Zebiri, Kate. "Argumentation," in Rippin, Andrew, *The Blackwell Companion to the Qur'ān*, Blackwell Publishing, 2006.

Zurqānī, Muhammad Abd al-Azīm, *Manāhil al-'irfān fī ulūm al-Qur'ān*, 3 vols. Dār al-Kutub al-Ilmiyyah, 1988.

www.ingramcontent.com/pod-product-compliance
Lightning Source LLC
LaVergne TN
LVHW051545070426
835507LV00021B/2411